QuarkXPress® 6
KillerTips

The hottest collection of cool tips and hidden secrets for QuarkXPress

Eda Warren

Killer Tips series developed
by Scott Kelby

QUARKXPRESS 6 KILLER TIPS

PUBLISHER
Stephanie Wall

EXECUTIVE EDITOR
Steve Weiss

PRODUCTION MANAGER
Gina Kanouse

ACQUISITIONS EDITOR
Elise Walter

SENIOR DEVELOPMENT EDITOR
Jennifer Eberhardt

PROJECT EDITOR
Jake McFarland

COPY EDITOR
Linda Laflamme

INDEXER
Lisa Stumpf

PROOFREADER
Beth Trudell

COMPOSITION
Wil Cruz

MANUFACTURING COORDINATOR
Dan Uhrig

COVER DESIGN AND CREATIVE CONCEPTS
Felix Nelson

MARKETING
Scott Cowlin
Tammy Detrich
Hannah Oldham Latham

PUBLICITY
Susan Nixon

www.newriders.com
www.go-training.com

International Standard Book Number: 0-7357-1303-0

Library of Congress Catalog Card Number: 2002101876

Printed in the United States of America

First printing: August 2003

07 06 05 04 03   7 6 5 4 3 2 1

Interpretation of the printing code: The rightmost double-digit number is the year of the book's printing; the rightmost single-digit number is the number of the book's printing. For example, the printing code 03-1 shows that the first printing of the book occurred in 2003.

Trademarks

Warning and Disclaimer

For Eddie, the love of my life.

For Mom and Dad, thank you from the bottom of my heart
for all the many riches you have given me. And the wonder is,
the older I get, the more I discover just how many jewels there are.

ACKNOWLEDGMENTS

First, I want to thank Scott Kelby, who came up with this incredible Killer Tips book/concept/series that was an idea just waiting to be born. Of course, tips have been around since IBM-day one, but making a book *just about tips*—now *that* was brilliant! His *Photoshop Killer Tips* and *Mac OSX Killer Tips* have provided me with superb models for writing my contribution to this series. But even more important to me personally, Scott, as the Series Editor, gave me the opportunity to write this book! Of course I had to prove myself, but he was the one to finally say, "Thumbs up, Eda." Thanks so much, Scott. It has been a privilege to be part of this awesome series.

Thank goodness that I've been in the computer-design community of Chicago since day one because that means I know a *lot* of people. And believe me I got a lot of help from many people to whom I am most grateful. First, I would like to thank the many Quark students I have taught over the years who have taught me in more ways than one. Through the process of teaching Quark, beyond using Quark, I have gotten some of my best revelations. The questions and problems that students have asked have often led me to new insights and new solutions. I hope this book will be especially helpful for them.

Second, I want to thank two people who come from deep production backgrounds, who provided invaluable tip ideas for the book. Toby Zallman, a very longtime friend and colleague, is someone who, through years in a typesetting house or two, developed a keen level of skill and art with type. She translated that right into her Quark practice, where her typesetting is perfection. She was one of the earliest Quark users and to this day spends most of her time with Quark. Thank you so much Toby for all your insightful ideas and support.

Clint Funk is another longtime colleague whom I first met in the early '90s when he presented to the Chicago Mac-user graphics SIG that I ran for many, many years. Even then, he was an incredible Photoshop expert and has traveled widely as a prepress and printing expert. I've been talking to Clint on email regularly. It's hard for me to catalog all the ways Clint has helped me. He's given me a bunch of tip ideas, sold me on using SnapZ for screen shots (thank goodness I finally listened!), tested PPDs for me, clarified some color issues, and gave his advice on a whole host of questions I kept feeding him. I can't thank you enough, Clint!

I am most indebted to the incredibly talented and devoted staff at New Riders Publishing, with whom I have worked so closely: Stephanie Wall, Publisher; Elise Walter and Deb Hittel-Shoaf, Acquisitions Editors; Jennifer Eberhardt, Development Editor; and my first contact, Executive Editor Steve Weiss. All these people have so impressed me with their patience, their willingness to pitch in at any time to make the process easier and trouble-free, and their incredibly hard work. They've even listened to my long rambling discourses on the phone and never interrupted me. They are one hell of a crew and I am so grateful that I managed to land in such a fabulous publishing group. One of my luckiest breaks. Thank you all from the bottom of my heart!

Many, many thanks to my expert and forthcoming tech editors Kim Scott and Simon Gurney. Their comments and insights kept me on track, while offering me ample positive feedback as well. You guys were my fall-back. Thanks so very much, Kim and Simon.

Finally, many other people need a mention. Dave Doty, another wonderful longtime colleague and designer, who inspired me with all the creative ideas in his journal, *ThePage*, published in Chicago for many years in the early days. Joe Grossman, a graphics author, designer, and colleague who also wrote for *ThePage*, provided some terrific tips, which he gave years ago at the graphics SIG, and also offered valuable suggestions related to writing a book. Rose Rosetree, a dear friend who has written many books, also helped me in the early stages of writing this book. Michael Thompson is an excellent literary lawyer who taught me a lot about contracts. Richard Bresden, a designer colleague, has always been an inspiration to me. Eric Wagner of Infocomm, Chicago's longest running service-bureau and prepress shop, cleared up some points for me on hi-res output and prepress. Thanks to my friends at CUBE, new music ensemble, who let me freely use my design work for them in this book. Chuck Boysen of Dynamic Graphics generously gave me the Contemporary People CD to use for stock photos. And thanks to Larabie Fonts for the use of the more funky fonts I got from larabiefonts.com. To all these wonderful people, many thanks!

Last but not least, I got some really wonderful help from the people at Quark, Inc.—Glen Turpin, Communications Manager, made sure I got the support I needed from engineers and developers. Most notably David Allen, who opened my eyes to Quark CMS in a big way! Special thanks to Ernie Jones, who in the last weeks answered every nerdy question that I threw his way, sent me new builds, and all with a fast turnaround that made such a difference. Thank you so much!

Thank you one and all who have helped me make this book become a reality.

. . . .

New Riders Publishing and the author gratefully acknowledge Ray Larabie of Larabie Fonts for allowing us to showcase his unique work in this book. The following typefaces were used:

Coolvetica

(Counterscraps)

Cuomotype

HOME SWEET HOME

Kicking Limos

Kleptocracy

PLANET BENSON 2

Sandoval

Shifty Chica

Still Time

Vipnagorgialla

WILD SEWERAGE

For more information, please visit www.larabiefonts.com and www.typodermic.com.

ABOUT THE AUTHOR

Eda Warren is President of Desktop Publishing Services Inc., a graphic design and training firm in Chicago. Eda has been developing and delivering desktop graphics training since the advent of desktop publishing technology in 1985 with the beta version of PageMaker 1.0. She is an Authorized QuarkXPress Trainer and has trained hundreds of users over the last 10 years. She is also an Adobe Certified Training Provider (ACTP)—only one of a small handful of companies who are Adobe-certified *as trainers* in the state of Illinois. Besides QuarkXPress, she offers training in Adobe InDesign, Photoshop, Illustrator, GoLive, and PageMaker (Mac and Windows).

As a graphic designer of 25 years, she has also been regularly teaching graphic design to desktop publishers for Dynamic Graphics Training (DGT) in this country and abroad for 14 years. She has also taught multimedia design at the Illinois Institute of Art, Chicago, and has worked on numerous web-based projects in Academic Technologies at Northwestern University in Evanston, IL.

Eda's writing and design work have been published in regional and national magazines, books, and brochures. She has written a long tips chapter in four editions of what was a best-selling Bantam book, *Using Aldus PageMaker*. She has published many articles on desktop design in *ThePage*, *Publish*, and *Aldus* magazines. Her educational background includes two Master of Fine Arts degrees, most recently in 1995 at University of Illinois, Chicago (UIC) in Electronic Visualization. Eda lives in Chicago.

Please contact Eda at edawarren@ameritech.net or www.go-training.com.

ABOUT THE TECHNICAL REVIEWERS

These reviewers contributed their considerable hands-on expertise to the entire development process for *QuarkXPress 6 Killer Tips*. As the book was being written, these dedicated professionals reviewed all the material for technical content, organization, and flow. Their feedback was critical to ensuring that *QuarkXPress 6 Killer Tips* fits our readers' need for the highest quality technical information.

Simon Gurney has been based in London, England for the past ten years, working in print, web, and new media design. He also works as a design lecturer, running professional design courses on Quark, Macromedia, and Adobe products, among others. Happily working between Mac and PC, Simon been dedicated to Quark since version 3.1, before which time Pagemaker was the weapon of choice. You can find out more about Simon at http://www.simongurney.co.uk/.

Kim Scott is a freelance book designer and compositor based in Los Angeles, CA. She received a BFA in graphic design from the Herron School of Art in Indianapolis, IN, and has been working in publishing for nearly 10 years. A QuarkXPress geek since 1991, Kim has been involved in the design and production of hundreds of computer books, including Jakob Nielsen's *Designing Web Usability* and *Web Redesign: Workflow That Works*. Kim shares her living space with three adult male green iguanas, and even went so far as to name her web site after one of them: http://www.bumpy.com.

TABLE OF CONTENTS

CHAPTER 1
Get Under the Hood

Setup Tips ... 3

Customize Quark's Look and Feel for All New Files ... 4

Scroll 'n' Go ... 4

Save a Life—Back Up Your Preferences File ... 5

More Insurance—Auto Save ... 6

Take Out Insurance—Back Up Files Two Ways ... 6

Get the Print Box the Way You Want—Print Styles ... 7

Serial Number? Environment Dialog Has It and More ... 7

Print Layout Preferences—for *All* New Docs
  or *Just* This One? ... 8

It's Greek to Me—Get the Real Thing Instead ... 8

Trade in Nasty Numbers—.167", .3125", or .625"—
  for Picas ... 9

Delete Bogus Colors for All Time ... 9

Get Your Favorite Settings Built into Every New File ... 10

Speed to Your Tool Preferences ... 10

Get the Right Runaround Every Time—Automatically ... 11

Set Picture Box Background Color to None ... 11

Get Commands Where You Are—Context Menu ... 12

Remembering Keyboard Shortcuts ... 13

Launching Quark Faster by Removing PPDs ... 14

Shortening Your Time in the Print Box ... 14

Pick Your XTensions as You Launch Quark ... 15

XTension Sets for Different Clients and Projects ... 15

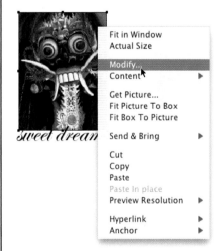

TABLE OF CONTENTS

CHAPTER 2
The Green Flag Drops
Master Pages & Templates Tips 17

Get a Grid 18
Strategic Margins—Using White Space 19
Gutters Keeping You Drained? 20
With the Automatic Text Box, You Get Linking Heaven 20
Changing Print Layout Settings 21
Changing Margins and Columns—Settings Dimmed? 21
Automatic Page Numbers Instantly Aligned 22
Centering Page Numbers Easily 22
Draw Fewer Text Boxes Faster—Do It on
Master Pages 23
Running Headers and Footers That Match
Page Content 23
Locking Master Items—a Good Idea,
But Not Foolproof 24
Master Page Picture Boxes—Runaround or Not? 24
Just About Done, then *Changing* a
Master Item <Groan> 25
Keep or Delete Changes—Now Your Head Is Spinning 25
Don't *Re*-invent the Wheel—Use Duplicate Master 26
One Too Many Multiple Masters 26
Adding Pages? Apply Masters Two Ways 27
Quark's Template Versus the *Real* Thing 28
Don't *Re*-invent the Wheel #2—
Append Setup Options 29
"What, We Need That Logo *Again*?" Get a Library 29

TABLE OF CONTENTS

CHAPTER 3
Don't Forget Your Map
Quark Interface Tips — 31

Zoom In or Out to a Specified Percent—No Mousing — 32

Zooming with Bigger or Smaller Steps — 32

Fastest Zoom — 33

Get Back the Zoom Tool Shortcut That Quark 5 Stole
(Mac Only) — 33

Toggle Between 100% and 200% View — 34

Go to Fit in Window? You're Zapped to Another Page!
%#@+$!! — 35

Grabber Hand Is the Best Scrolling Tip Ever — 35

Watch the Action on the Fly with Live Scroll — 36

See Both Pages of the Spread — 36

Fast Lane Changes—er, Page Changes — 37

Going Between a Layout Page and Master Pages — 37

Undo—Undo—Undo—Undo… — 38

Get Picture with the Item Tool? — 38

Temporary Access to the Item Tool Any Time — 39

Content Tool Is Not Just for Content — 39

Tools Without the Toolbox — 40

Faster Access to "Fly-Out" Tools — 40

Keep a Tool Forever! — 41

See the Page Without the Mess — 41

Strategic Guides on Masters Ensure
Exact Positioning — 42

Snap-to-Guides Is for 99% of the Time, But… — 42

Position a Guide Numerically with X and Y — 43

Delete All Horizontal or Vertical Guides in
One Fell Swoop — 43

Limit Guide Clutter—Set a View Threshold — 44

Plowing through the Guide Manager Maze — 45

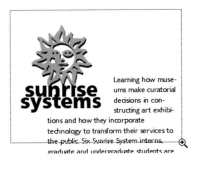

sunrise systems

Learning how museums make curatorial decisions in constructing art exhibitions and how they incorporate technology to transform their services to the public. Six Sunrise System interns, graduate and undergraduate students are

TABLE OF CONTENTS

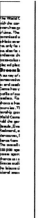

CHAPTER 4

Parts Is Parts

Lines & Boxes Tips | 47

When You Want a Straight Line, Do It Right | 48

Resize Lines at the Same Angle | 48

Five Ways to Change a Line "Width" or Weight | 49

Match a Line Length to a Box Width | 49

Get Identically Styled Lines Every Time | 50

You Look Dashing! | 50

Designer Frames | 51

Drawing More Than One | 51

Perfect Squares and Circles | 52

No "X" on That Nice, Colored Picture Box | 52

Try on a New Shape! | 53

Make a Wacky or Sublime Picture Box | 53

Draw a Heart-Shaped or Scalloped Curve | 54

Bezier Drawing Shortcuts | 54

Bezier Editing Shortcuts | 55

Flip Horizontal and Flip Vertical | 55

Moving a Shape or Editing Points? | 56

For Complex Shapes, Merge | 57

CHAPTER 5

Fine Tuning

Selection & Transformation Tips | 59

Selecting a Buried Item | 60

Deselect All Items | 60

Nudge an Item One Point in Any Direction | 61

Hidden Commands—Bring Forward and
   Send Backward (Mac Only) | 61

Constrain a Move Without Deselecting   62

Keep 'em Together   62

Size Items Together   63

Moving and Sizing Items Within a Group   63

Zoom Around the Measurement Palette   64

Measurements Palette *Calculates* Moving and Sizing   64

Aligning by X and Y   65

When Rules Need to Top Align to Other Items   65

Locate an Item from the Bottom of the Page   66

Size a Box *and Its Contents* Proportionally   66

Size Type or Pictures Incrementally   67

Transforming Boxes   68

Rotate an Item Freely or in Fixed Increments   69

Experience the Real Thing, Not the Box   69

Delete an Item with the Content Tool   70

Don't Accidentally Delete a Locked Item   70

Comic Relief—Delete with Martians or Meltdown   71

CHAPTER 6

Enjoy the Scenery

Picture Tips   73

Did You Know You Can Import a PDF?   74

Got a Two-Color Job and Four-Color Images?   74

Drag and Drop Pictures from Your Desktop
(Windows Only)   75

Fit to Box and Box It Up   76

Cropping—Up Close and Personal   76

Get the Picture Centered   77

Eyeball It   77

Need the Picture Bigger, But Not the Box?   78

Thou Shalt Know Thy Bits and Pieces   78

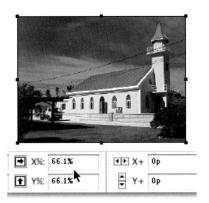

TABLE OF CONTENTS

Ultimate System for Avoiding Bad Resolution | 79
Fuzzy Type in Your Photoshop Image? | 79
Graphics as Fun-House Mirrors | 80
Accessing Image Editing Commands (Mac Only) | 80
Negative and Positive Together | 81
Faux Duotones #1 | 81
Faux Duotones #2 | 82
Turn a Boring Image into a Graphic | 82
Skew a Graphic or Image Within a Box | 83
Making a Clipping Path | 83
Short Tips for Clipping Paths | 84
Full-Resolution Preview for Images | 85
Full-Resolution Preview on the Fly | 85
Lower Than Low—Keep That File Size Down | 86
Quark, Servant of Mine, Alert Me to Picture Changes | 86
Update That Picture and Retain Cropping and Sizing | 87

CHAPTER 7
Gas Keeps You Goin'

Import Text & Word Processing Tips | 89

When Getting Text, Link Fewer Boxes | 90
Save Endless Time When You've Got Lots of Links | 90
Worry-Free Linking and Unlinking | 91
You're Linking and You're Out of Pages | 91
Don't Let Your Body Copy Go Wandering | 92
To Unlink or Not Unlink? | 92
Highlighting All the Text That's There? Don't Drag | 93
Don't Deselect the Text to See What You Did | 93
Selecting a Word, Line, or Paragraph and More | 94
Easy Text Edits Over Pictures—Opaque Text
   Box Editing | 95

Drag and Drop Text—Always and Sometimes 95

Moving the Insertion Point Using Arrow Keys 96

Deleting Characters—Six Shortcuts 96

Typing Dumb Quotes—Inch and Foot Marks 97

Getting a Quick Zapf Dingbat (Mac Only) 98

Proofing Text? Skip the Pictures 98

Make Spell-Checking Go Faster and Do More 98

Spell Checking from the Keyboard 99

Skipping Portions of Your Document When
You Search? 99

Making Text Look Like Typesetting Without
Anyone Noticing 100

Replace Unsightly Underlines with Italic 100

Clean Up Text That's Pasted into an Email 101

Remove Strange Characters in Your Text 102

You Just Did Change All, Then Realized
Your Mistake :-(102

Replace Editorial Style Tags with Style Sheets 103

Change All Those 11pt Hobo Subheads
to 10pt Brush 104

Make Snazzy Bullets Without Groaning 105

Be Thorough—Search Text on Master Pages 106

Search for Special Characters 106

Wild Card Searches for Numbered Lists 107

CHAPTER 8
Your Own Bumper Stickers
Screamin' Type Tips 109

Get the Font You Want When You Type in a New Box 110

Avoiding Long Lines for Fonts 110

Use "True" Fonts, Not Bold and Italic Type Styles 111

TABLE OF CONTENTS

Getting a Good Point Size	111
Find the Perfect Size—Visually	112
Quick Type Styles	113
Superscript or Superior—Which Is Which?	114
Fast Track to Track and Kern to Tighten Headlines	114
Track Body Copy to Fix Short Lines	115
Track a Font for All Time with Tracking Edit	115
Tweak Bad Letter Pairs with Kerning Table Edit	116
Remove Manual Kerning	116
Adjust Type Vertically with Baseline Shift	117
Increase Drama with Reverse Type	117
Small Caps with a Twist	118
Track Type for a Wide-Open-Sky Look	118
Hanging Punctuation—Large Quote or Bullet	119
Type in a Box with a New Angle	119
Perfecting the Drop Cap—Part I	120
Perfecting the Drop Cap—Part II	120
Perfecting the Drop Cap—Part III	121
Fancy Type with Two Colors Using Text to Box	122
Type with Gradients	122
Type on a Path	122
Wrap Text Inside a Shaped Box	123
"Grunge Type"—Vertically Overlapping Type	123
Strange Type Effects	124
The *Real* Shadow Text	124
Automatic Ligatures with Character Preference (Mac Only)	125
Fancy Pricing and Fractions	125
Soft Returns—More Readable Headlines	126
Long and Short Dashes (Em and En)	127
Special Word Spaces	128

Leading—Not Auto Leading 129

Paragraph Spacing, the "Hidden" Attribute 130

Paragraph Spacing and Indents—Specify in Points 130

Reset Quark's Default *Global* Word Spacing of 110% 131

Trying to Set Tabs and Nothing's Working? 131

Tabs—Line 'em Up Equally 132

Aligning Numbers When Some Are in Parentheses 132

Bullet Copy—Code Name: "Hanging Indents" 133

Designer Charts—No Leaders, Paragraph Rules 133

Fake a Right-Aligned Tab 134

Indenting Without Dialog Boxes 134

Continuous Apply in Tab (or Any) Dialog Box 135

No-Hyphens Setting for Heads, Subheads, Captions 135

Hyphens—Getting Too Many or Not Enough? 136

Automate Hyphenation with Styles 137

On–the–Spot Fixes—Discretionary Hyphens 138

Hyphenation Exceptions—Where to Hyphenate 139

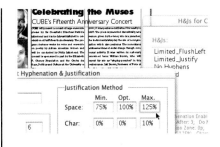

CHAPTER 9
Power, Power, Power

Style Sheets Tips 141

Go Home Early—Ha Ha—Style Sheets Forever! 142

Character Styles for Polishing 142

Applying Styles—Look Ma, Two Hands Are
    Better Than One 143

Applying Styles—When They Don't Work 143

Modifying Styles—Quick Changes to Style Sheets 144

Based-on Styles—Watch Them Cascade 145

Squeaky-Clean! Styles "Take" and Fonts Are True 145

Compare Two Style Sheets 146

Recycle Your Styles 146

TABLE OF CONTENTS

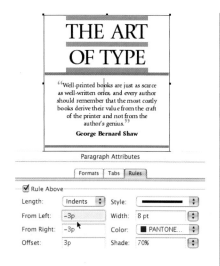

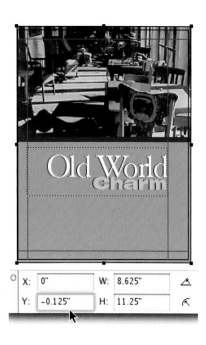

If You Know What's Good for Ya, Include Style Sheets 147

Format Text on the Fly as It's Importing 147

When Your Client's Styles Get into Yours 148

Style as You Type with Next Style 148

Headlines with Style 149

Indenting—Two Styles: One with, One Without 149

Paragraph Spacing—Bliss with Styles, Agony Without 150

Tabs—Once and for All 150

Styles for Widow and Orphan Control 151

Paragraph Rules with Styles Are a Snap 151

Subheads Reversed Out of a Bar—
Paragraph Rule Style 152

Paragraph Rules Hang Out 153

CHAPTER 10
Livin' la Vida Layout
Can't-Live-Without Layout Tips 155

Layout Spaces for Different Versions and Page Sizes 156

Title Bar Blues—Project 1: Layout 1: Huh? 156

Synchronize Text (or Not) in Different Layouts 157

Fitting the Text to the Layout 158

Controlling the Layout with Special Characters 159

With Subheads, Aligning Body Copy Takes Tricks 159

Baseline Grid—Text Alignment Across the Page 160

Vertically Justifying Text 161

Rearrange Your Pages in Thumbnails View 161

Two Ways to Remove Pages 162

Text Recomposing when Opening
Someone Else's File? 162

Text Recomposing while Opening an
Older Quark Doc? 163

Bleeds—Going Over the Edge   163

Spread Guides Make Alignments Easy   164

Align Items from Their Centers   164

Spacing Items—All Things Being Equal   165

Step and Repeat *and* Super Step and Repeat   165

Identical Boxes That Perfectly Fit a Given Space   166

Don't Always Want Your Text at the Top of a Box?   166

Multiple Pictures with Exact Positioning   167

With Colored Boxes, Try Unequal Text Insets   168

Going All the Way…Around   168

Boss Says, "Keep Those Pictures Locked to the Text!"   169

Run, Run, Runaround, I Get Around—Irregularity   170

Doesn't Look Like a Runaround Unless…   170

Type Masks Image—Text to Box   171

Getting Text into a Table   171

Formatting the Text of an Entire Table   172

Insert Rows and Columns Using Existing Formatting   172

If You HATE Math, But Need More Rows and Columns   173

Combining Text and Pictures in a Table   173

Gridless and See-Through Tables   174

Miscellaneous, But Crucial, Table Tips   174

Snazz Up That Table with Color   175

Layer Palette Tricks   175

Turn Off Those Layer Markers   176

Select Items on Layer   176

The Layered Look—Versioning   177

Speed Performance—Hide Pictures Globally   178

Text Boxes with Versions   179

Printing Layers   179

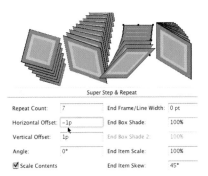

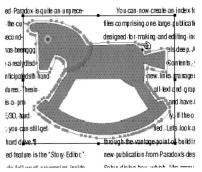

TABLE OF CONTENTS

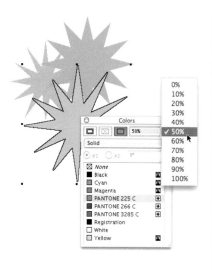

CHAPTER 11
Time for a Paint Job
Killer Color Tips   181

Fast-Track to Colors Dialog Box   182

Tinting a Box Background   183

Be a Dare-Devil—Mix Two Spot Colors   183

Don't Keep Choosing the Same Tint   184

Budget Says No to a Spot Color in Your CMYK Job?   184

"Rich Black" Adds, Well, Richness   185

Spot Varnish Perks Up Those Pictures—Big Time   185

Try On a Color Before You Apply It   186

Apply Color to Type and Paragraph Rules
     Automatically   186

Need to Change That Color You've
     Generously Applied?   187

Registration Color Is Not Black!   187

Optical Effects with Blends in Box Backgrounds   188

Put Blends into Lines   188

No Work-Arounds Needed for Imported PMS Colors   189

Spot-Color EPS Going into CMYK Quark Job   189

Color Management in Quark   190

Print Separations to Check Color Breaks   191

CHAPTER 12
Detailing Makes the Difference
Printing & Preflight Tips   193

Don't Keep Choosing Those Same Print Box Settings   194

Got a Big Page to Print?—Tiling!   194

Turning on Registration Marks   195

Want to Check Bleeds, See Registration Marks?   195

Doing a Comp and Want Spreads?   196

Better Results with Black-and-White Printers 196

Gotta Change Those Spot Colors to CMYK? 197

Prevent Type Recomposing at Hi-Res Output
(Win Only) 197

PDF Is the Way to Go for Hi-Res Output 198

Making a PDF from Windows 198

Save Page as EPS Saves the Day 199

What's Worth Trapping in Quark, and What's Not 199

Speed Printing—Turn Off Trapping 200

Collect for Output—Let Quark Package It for You 200

"Batteries Not Included"—Picture and Font Usage 201

Generate a Complete Report About
Your Layout *Anytime* 201

Use Layers to Communicate with Your Printer 202

Faster Output, Less Hassle (and Less Money?) 202

On a Mac with a Windows Client? (Mac Only) 203

Master CheckList #1—Get Ready (Final File Cleanup) 204

Master CheckList #2—Go (Pack It All Up) 206

CHAPTER 13
The Winner's Circle
Way Cool Design Tips

Way Cool Design Tips 209

Use Margins to Clarify Your Content 210

Indicating Fold Lines for the Printer 211

The "Three-Fold" Brochure 212

Roll-Fold Brochure—More Than Three Panels per Side 213

Artwork Spanning Front and Back Covers 213

Gate-Fold Brochure 214

Short Panel Cover or Reply-Tear-Off Panel 215

Great-Looking Pages with Lots of Columns 216

The Flush-Bottom Layout 217

TABLE OF CONTENTS

Get Consistent Vertical Spacing Between Items	218
Pull-Quotes Are Eye Candy	219
Newsletters Look Great with Vertical Rules	219
Jump Lines—Auto-Update Continued On and From	220
Decks for Magazines—Give the Reader a Peek	221
Break Up a Large Document into Multiple Files	222
If You're Doing Multiple Files, You Need This Tip	222
Great Layout for Text-Heavy Docs	223
Paragraph Rules—Clarifying What's Important	223
Anchored Headlines Stay with Body	224
Table of Contents Using Lists	225
"10-Up" Layout	226
Crop Marks for Business Card Art	227
INDEX	228

As the reader of this book, you are the most important critic and commentator. We value your opinion and want to know what we're doing right, what we could do better, what areas you'd like to see us publish in, and any other words of wisdom you're willing to pass our way.

As an editor for New Riders Publishing, I welcome your comments. You can fax, email, or write me directly to let me know what you did or didn't like about this book—as well as what we can do to make our books stronger. When you write, please be sure to include this book's title, ISBN, and author, as well as your name and phone or fax number. I will carefully review your comments and share them with the author and editors who worked on the book.

Please note that I cannot help you with technical problems related to the topic of this book, and that due to the high volume of email I receive, I might not be able to reply to every message.

Fax: 317-581-4663

Email: elise.walter@newriders.com

Mail: Elise Walter
          Acquisitions Editor
          New Riders Publishing
          800 E. 96th Street
          Suite 200
          Indianapolis, IN 46240 USA

INTRODUCTION

Why you need this book

It's true. Not too many people buy Quark books because Quark isn't that hard to figure out—at least not from the outset. Sure, you've got the Item and the Content tools and you've got a whole lot of boxes going on, but after all, it seems doable. And it is…. *But,* being an accomplished-to-expert user in Quark is quite another matter. And that's because you're not just learning or perfecting how to use a piece of software. Not hardly. You're trying to master the field of graphic design and layout that sits between the lines of your Quark software. That's where *how you use* Quark separates the proverbial men from the boys. There's a whole lot more going on.

And that's why I wrote this book. Knowing where the Leading tool is on the Measurements palette or even knowing the keyboard shortcut for leading is one thing. But knowing how to set leading for subheads so that your body copy lines up by the baseline across the page and spread is another thing. When your copy is running long, how many Quark ways can you pull out of your hat to make it fit, gracefully? Or, knowing how to use multiple master pages to make your facing pages both have the same set of unequal margins (perfect for product catalogs and other layouts) is not something you'll easily or ever find in another Quark book. These are just a very few of the more than 300 exciting and useful tips you'll find here.

This book is the one you're going to want to buy *and read,* because it goes where no previous Quark books have gone—into the realm of the unknown and unknowable. Okay, okay, I'm going off the deep end. *But,* on every page, this book has all those great kernels of wisdom that you have to hunt for in any other Quark books and, in many cases, you will not find. Instead of flipping through the book, looking for those little boxes of juicy tidbits—*the tips*—every page in this book is filled with *just tips!* Right out front. Amazing!

Is this book for you?

Yes, unquestionably, whether you have been using Quark for years or you're a newer user—because this book brings together years of collective wisdom about using Quark. As a digital designer (since 1985) and longtime pre-digital designer, authorized Quark trainer, and graphic design instructor, I've used Quark over many years. My colleagues, Toby Zallman and Clint Funk, who contributed some invaluable tip suggestions, are longtime users and designers from the pre-desktop publishing era of "analog" graphic design.

Even though the book is called *QuarkXPress 6 Killer Tips*, it's not just about the "6" part. It's about everything you ever wanted to know, and more, about using Quark. The only Quark users who should *not* buy this book are those who are using Quark exclusively to do web design. There is absolutely nothing in this book about the web capabilities of Quark. It's not that I don't like doing web work, but when it came right down to it, there simply wasn't enough room to include Chapter 14, "Quark for the Web," and believe me, I didn't want to end on a Chapter 13! Other than that, any print designer or production person should learn a lot from these well-seasoned tips.

What's the best way to read this book?

Because this is a tips book and not what I call an A-to-Z book, you can read these tips in any order you like. Each one is self-sufficient and is written to stand alone, without reference to other tips. (Well, okay, there are a couple here and there that say you should read the tip above, but, as my Mom says, "They're the exceptions that prove the rule.")

The tips are organized into common sense groups—chapters that more or less follow the layout process, so it's easy to find all the tips on one topic in one place. Occasionally, a closely related tip had to go in another area, where it was needed more, so you'll find a "see also" given, with the tip name and chapter number. And of course, I know you'll want to use the excellent index that New Riders Publishing put together—thank goodness I didn't have to do that!

Is this just for Mac? Is this just for Windows?

Okay, it's for everyone! I have both, so no problem. Every time you see a keyboard shortcut, *both* Mac and Windows keys are included. But to make it easier to glide right through those shortcuts, I decided not to say /Mac and /Win. Too many words. After all, when it's Mac, it's Cmd-Option-Shift; and when it's Windows, it's Ctrl-Alt-Shift. So they're easy to spot without all those platform labels. Occasionally, on a Mac, you do use the Control key, but then the word is spelled out, every letter, because most Mac users don't even know they have a Control key! Windows users are old-timers with Ctrl keys so they can have the no-vowels version, and that's how you tell those Mac and Win keys apart.

More on those keyboard shortcuts

One last note—my apologies to those fast-track Quark users who only want keyboard shortcuts and don't want to know the command name and menu. Well, first of all, there are quite a few commands (I stopped counting at 25) that don't have keyboard equivalents. Some people just don't like using shortcuts anyway. Of course in Quark, you really have to, because so many things are too hard or impossible to do without shortcuts. However, my tips are not usually just a keyboard shortcut, particularly if they're already on the menu. They go deeper. So to make everyone happy, along with the shortcut, I usually give the menu and command name, like this:

Item> Content> Picture

Notice, the word "menu" is avoided. Again, too many words.

Contact me with your tips

I'm sure to upgrade this book for future versions of Quark. So while you're reading this book or not reading the book, I'm sure you'll remember some of those cool things you did to get through your worst deadlines and even your best ones. Let me know what works for you! I'll be happy to credit you in the tip.

May your Quark days (daze?) be smart, easy, fun, and fruitful, and may these tips help multiply your paycheck by many zeros!

FOREWORD

QuarkXPress 6 Killer Tips
Edited by Scott Kelby

As Editor for the Killer Tips series, I'm delighted to introduce you to Eda Warren, a really talented author who is going to take you to a whole new level of speed, efficiency, and productivity with QuarkXPress 6. But first, a little background on this book and what makes it different from every other QuarkXPress book out there.

The idea for this type of book came to me one day when I was at the bookstore, browsing in the computer section, when I thought to myself, "Man, these authors must be making a ton of money!" No wait, that wasn't what I was thinking (it's close, mind you, but not exactly). Actually, I was standing there flipping though the different books on Adobe Photoshop (I'm a Photoshop guy at heart). Basically what I would do is look for pages that had a tip on them. They're usually pretty easy to find, because these "rich book authors" usually separate their tips from the regular text of the book. Most of the time, they'll put a box around the tips, or add a tint behind them, maybe a "tips" icon—something to make them stand out and get the readers' attention.

Anyway, that's what I would do—find a tip, read it, and then start flipping until I found another tip. The good news—the tips were usually pretty cool. You have to figure,that if an author has some really slick trick, maybe a hidden keyboard shortcut or cool workaround, they probably wouldn't bury it in blocks of boring copy. No way! They'd find some way to get your attention (with those boxes, tints, a little icon, or simply the word "Tip!") So, that's the cool news—if it said tip, it was usually worth checking out. The bad news—there's never enough tips. Sometimes they'd have five or six tips in a chapter, but other times just one or two. But no matter now many they had, I always got to the last chapter and thought, "Man, I wish there had been more tips."

Standing right there in the bookstore, I thought to myself "I wish there were a book with nothing but tips. Hundreds of tips, cover-to-cover, and nothing else. Now *that's* a book I would go crazy for. I kept looking and looking, but the book I wanted just wasn't available. That's when I got the idea to write one myself. The next day I called my editor to pitch him with the idea. I told him it would be a book that would be wall-to-wall cool tips, hidden shortcuts, and inside tricks designed to make Photoshop users faster, more productive, and best of all, to make using Photoshop even more fun. Well, he loved the idea. OK, that's stretching it a bit. He *liked the* idea, but most importantly, he "green-lighted it" (that's

Hollywood talk. I'm not quite sure what it means), and soon I had created my first all-tips book, *Photoshop 6 Killer Tips* (along with my co-author and good friend, *Photoshop User* magazine Creative Director Felix Nelson).

As it turned out, *Photoshop 6 Killer Tips* was an instant hit (luckily for me and my chance-taking editor), and we followed it up with (are you ready for this?) *Photoshop 7 Killer Tips*, which was an even bigger hit. These books really struck a chord with readers, and I like to think it was because Felix and I were so deeply committed to creating something special—a book where every page included yet another tip that would make you nod your head, smile, and think "ahhh, so that's how they do it." However, it pretty much came down to this—people just love cool tips. That's why now there's also a *Dreamweaver MX Killer Tips*, a *Mac OS X Killer Tips*, a *Windows XP Killer Tips*, and a host of others now in development.

So how did we wind up here, with *QuarkXPress 6 Killer Tips*? Actually, QuarkXPress is an ideal program to have its own Killer Tips books for two main reasons: (1) The product is mature (it's already up to version 6) and has lots of depth, which is an absolute requirement to have enough really killer tips to create an entire book, and (2) if there was ever a product where being an absolute speed demon when using it puts money right in your pocket, it's QuarkXPress. It's a page layout app, a production tool (if you will), and the more productive and efficient you are, the more valuable you'll be. Perhaps best of all, knowing all the cool shortcuts, the inside tips, and the absolute fastest ways to do everything is just flat out fun (and I'm not even talking about all the bragging and showing off to friends and co-workers. OK, I am, but that's not the point).

But finding the right software package is only one piece of the puzzle. Finding the right author—someone who totally "gets" the Killer Tips concept, is a talented and experienced writer, and, most importantly, is an absolute expert in QuarkXPress. That's Eda Warren, and that's why she's the author of this book. Eda totally "gets" it—she probably knows QuarkXPress tips that Quark itself doesn't even know, and she shares them all in this book.

Eda has really captured the spirit and flavor of what a "Killer Tips" book is all about, and I can tell you this—you're gonna love it! I can't wait for you to "get into it" so I'll step aside and let her take the wheel, because you're about to get faster, more efficient, and have more fun using QuarkXPress 6 than you ever thought possible.

All my best,

Scott Kelby, Series Editor

Get Under the Hood

SETUP TIPS

When a job hits your desktop, are you crashing out of the starting gate, no stopping until you're done? Of course!

Get Under the Hood

setup tips

But what about those few minutes of downtime you get now and then, when a little prep work can save you many minutes down the line? You're likely to make fewer mistakes without the scrambling. You're less likely to be in a panic because everything's in place, your tools are behaving, and your work space is performing like a well-tuned engine. In that downtime, you can tweak Quark with settings that suit your style and your kind of jobs. And once you do, those settings are working for you every time you start a new project. Just think—whether it's colors, styles, hyphenation settings, line styles, box properties, or something else—you don't have to keep choosing those settings again and again. What a relief! Working smart means you're ready to fly, coming in first, and with greater chances that you're delivering one great product.

   CUSTOMIZE QUARK'S LOOK AND FEEL FOR ALL NEW FILES

When you've got a few minutes to spare, clean up your Quark workspace so your next deadlines are easier. Quark's Application preferences are the secret. Improve the scroll bars. Prevent disaster with file corruption. Get insurance with automatic saving and backup. Customize the Print box so it looks like yours. All these are choices in Application preferences, covered in the next five tips. It doesn't matter whether you have a Quark layout open or not—your choices affect how Quark looks and acts from now on—but only on your machine. These settings don't travel with the file. Zip to the Preferences dialog by pressing Cmd-Option-Shift-Y or Ctrl-Alt-Shift-Y (QuarkXPress> Preferences/Mac or Edit> Preferences/Win).

   SCROLL 'N' GO

When you're zoomed in to one place and need to get to some other spot on the same page or spread, don't touch those scroll bars—at least not without enabling Live Scroll. In the Interactive settings of Application preferences (Cmd-Option-Shift-Y or Ctrl-Alt-Shift-Y), turn on the Live Scroll option so that you can see where you're going as you drag. Otherwise, it's hit or miss getting to the right spot. Be sure Speed Scroll is on, which grays out pictures and blends while you scroll, redrawing them only when you release the mouse. Then change the Scrolling slider all the way to Fast so that you can drag less to go farther. Do this when no files are open to make it true for all files you create from now on.

SAVE A LIFE—BACK UP YOUR PREFERENCES FILE

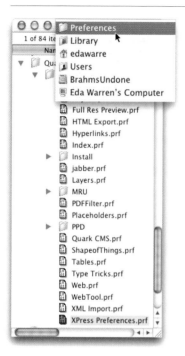

Backing up your preferences file can be a life saver. This file stores not only all your Application and Default Print Layout preferences, but also such custom default settings as colors, style sheets, hyphenation and justification (H&Js), hyphenation exceptions, kerning and tracking tables, and print styles. Also, when you're trouble-shooting corrupted files or having problems launching Quark, the preferences file is often the culprit. Back up your Preferences file regularly by locating the XPress Preferences.prf file in the Preferences folder. On Mac OS X, it's in your boot drive> Users> (username)> Library> Preferences> Quark> QuarkXPress 6.0. Windows users will most likely find the Quark application folder inside Program Files, at the top level of the C: drive (in Win XP, it's boot drive> Program Files> Quark> QuarkXPress 6.0> Preferences). Back it up with Cmd-D or Copy and Paste, and move the duplicate file out of the application folder.

MORE INSURANCE—AUTO SAVE

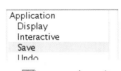

Project1.a$v

In the Save panel of Application preferences, turn on Auto Save. Although the best tip for saving is Cmd-S or Ctrl-S, the Auto Save feature lets you recover from a crash! *And* it doesn't save over your original working file—thank heavens! Instead, there's a temporary file of the same name with an extension .s$v tacked on the end of the filename. It's gone when you close your project. But after a Quark or system crash, open the file and click OK to a warning dialog, which directs you to File> Revert to restore to last auto-saved version. Another cool benefit— if Auto Save is on, at any time you can retrieve the last auto-saved version by pressing Option or Alt with File> Revert to Saved, which affects *all* layouts in your file. In Save preferences, tell Quark how often you want an auto-save. The default of 5 minutes is probably more often than needed, especially with large files.

 ## TAKE OUT INSURANCE—BACK UP FILES TWO WAYS

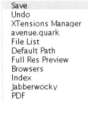

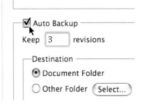

Maybe it's too hard to remember backups, so check Quark's Auto Backup feature in the Save panel of Application preferences. Choose the number of backups you want and the folder to save to. The default location is the same folder as your project. Each time you save, Quark creates one backup, up to the number you specify. Because each back-up is as large as your original file, you might want to only have two or three backups. Each backup file has the original filename, followed by a number—safetyNet.qxp has the backups SafetyNet #1.qxp, SafetyNet #2.qxp, etc. You'll never have more files than the number you specify, but the numbers increment each time you save your original file. Instead of SafetyNet #1 to SafetyNet #3, those same backups might eventually be SafetyNet #25 to SafetyNet #27. If your file starts to get flakey, turn off Auto Backup so the backups don't get corrupted.

GET THE PRINT BOX THE WAY YOU WANT—PRINT STYLES

Your Print box settings are saved with each file and layout. They are remembered even after switching files or printers within one Quark session and after re-launching. But print styles really make it easier. As your file goes from design through production, you need different sets of print options. When designing, how about a style to print spreads using composite CMYK? When proofing text, you might use a style that turns down your picture output to Low Resolution or Rough for faster printing. Then, when finishing, grab a third style for color separations. Don't choose settings over and over. All you have to do is choose Edit> Print Styles, set up a style or two, and those styles are available in the Print dialog for every project you open from now on, even if you had a file open to start with.

 SERIAL NUMBER? ENVIRONMENT DIALOG HAS IT AND MORE

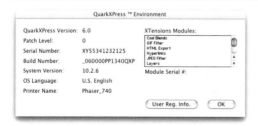

Here's a slick little trick that you can use to impress your friends and colleagues. Bring up Quark's Environment dialog, which is buried in a shortcut (Option-About QuarkXPress, QuarkXPress menu, or Cmd-Option-Control-E for Mac; Ctrl-About QuarkXPress, Help menu for Win). It tells you everything you want to know about the "environment" that Quark is running in—Quark version number, serial number, operating system version number, and more, plus a list of the XTensions that are installed. So, if you ever need to know, don't hesitate to look in Quark's back closet!

PRINT LAYOUT PREFERENCES—FOR *ALL* NEW DOCS OR *JUST* THIS ONE?

Application
Display
Interactive
Save
Undo
XTensions Manager
avenue.quark
File List
Default Path
Full Res Preview
Browsers
Index
Jabberwocky
PDF
Placeholders
Fraction/Price
Project
XML Import
Default Print Layout
General
Measurements
Paragraph
Character
Tools
Trapping
Quark CMS
Layers
Default Web Layout
General
Measurements
Paragraph
Character

Unlike Application preferences, which customize Quark as your work space, Print Layout preferences (formerly called Document preferences) are saved with the Quark file. Whether you set up a measurement system, put guides in front or back, or change how layers, trapping, and tools work, these settings can be kept intact when your layout is opened on another computer. You can also set up different preferences for each layout in your file. But even better—customize Quark at a global level by setting Default Print Layout preferences when no files are open. Press Cmd-Option-Shift-Y or Ctrl-Alt-Shift-Y to quickly open preferences. Once you're done and you click OK, your changes to Default Print Layout preferences are true for all files you create from now on—but not for *existing* files. In short, when a file is open, it's just a tweak. But when no files are open, changes are sweeping.

IT'S GREEK TO ME—GET THE REAL THING INSTEAD

When you go to Fit in Window view, don't you just hate those greeking bars that Quark uses in your layout to indicate lines of small text? (Of course, if you've got a giant monitor, you won't have this problem.) You can turn them off so that Quark simulates actual text. It's not exactly readable in Fit in Window view, but at least your layout looks like a real page seen at a distance. In the current layout, press Cmd-Option-Shift-Y or Ctrl-Alt-Shift-Y, then click General under Default Print Layout. Uncheck the Greek Text Below option on the right, and click OK. Now, in a reduced view, your layout looks onscreen like the real thing. To automatically turn Greeking off for all new projects, close all Quark projects, and then turn off Greeking. What a relief!

TRADE IN NASTY NUMBERS—.167", .3125", OR .625"—FOR PICAS

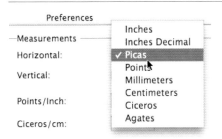

Picas work better than inches for designing a typical page. Inches become decimal numbers—hard to visualize and unrelated to typesetting. And, you're prompted to specify indents and paragraph spacing in inches! But in conventional typesetting, an indent typically equals the *point* size of the type. Paragraph spacing is equal to, or an interval of, the leading value, again in points.

You can temporarily override inches with points or picas, but when you apply that number, points convert to inches, and you're back to decimals. Have fun changing it later! With no files open, go to Preferences. Under Default Print Layout preferences, click Measurements, then set the Horizontal and Vertical measure to Picas. The large tick marks in the rulers are still an inch apart, but now they mark six picas. One caveat with picas—use the form "4p" to set margins and columns, because just "4" becomes 4pts—that's Quark logic!

- 6 picas = 1"
- 12pts = 1 pica
- In a Quark dialog box, entering points and picas:
  To say 14 points, type p14 or 14 pt, 14pt, or 14
  To say 4 picas, type 4p
  To say 4-and-1/2 picas, type 4p6 (four picas and six points)

DELETE BOGUS COLORS FOR ALL TIME

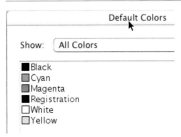

When you're doing print layouts, clean up your color palette so that colors you shouldn't use aren't cluttering up the list—or worse, getting applied accidentally. At Quark's desktop, with no files open, press Shift-F12 (Edit> Colors). There are three colors in the default set that you'll want to delete: Red, Green, and Blue—defined in the RGB color model and inappropriate in a color palette used for print. Click on Blue, then use Cmd-click or Ctrl-click to add the other two colors to the selection. Click the Delete button, and now your color list is shorter and sweeter. Should you ever want Red-Green-Blue back again, you can easily create them. Each color is 100% red, green, or blue in the RGB Model, with 0% for the other two values. You can also restore those colors by deleting your preferences file, although that might be too drastic.

See also "Save a Life—Back Up Your Preferences File" (this chapter).

 GET YOUR FAVORITE SETTINGS BUILT INTO EVERY NEW FILE

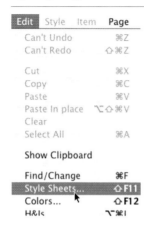

Applying a color, style sheet, H&J setting, or line style to text or items in your layout usually takes two steps. First, make a setting using commands in the Edit menu—Style Sheets, Colors, H&Js, Lists, and Dashes & Stripes. Second, apply those settings from a palette or another dialog. For example, set up colors by pressing Shift-F12 (Edit> Colors). But use the Colors palette or the Character dialog to apply color. With all this back and forth, wouldn't it be great to have all that setup work done so when you're on deadline, you only need to apply those settings? If the answer is yes, simply choose these commands *when no files are open in Quark*. The settings will then be in effect for all new files. Instead of making these choices over and over, do the setup work *once* and enjoy it in every new layout you make.

 SPEED TO YOUR TOOL PREFERENCES

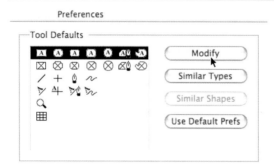

Setting Tool preferences ahead of time is another wonderful way to make your Quark life go easier and faster. Do this when no files are open so that your choices affect how all creation tools work forever more. For instance, set defaults for box frame width, corner radius, type-on-a-path, tables, and more. Or you can tweak the default settings for just the specific layout you're working on. To quickly get to the Tools preferences, just double-click any tool in the toolbox that creates an item—all the box and line tools, plus the table and starburst tools. You can set preferences for multiple related tools simultaneously. Use the Similar Types and Similar Shapes buttons. Or Shift-click to select a range of tool icons or Cmd- or Ctrl-click to select non-adjacent tools. Because the starburst tool is a Quark XTension, it has a separate Preferences dialog.

GET THE RIGHT RUNAROUND EVERY TIME—AUTOMATICALLY

| Box | Picture | Frame | Runaround |

Type: Item

Top: 12 pt

Left: 12 pt

Bottom: 12 pt

Right: 12

Quark's default 1pt box runaround for all new files is somewhat useless. It keeps text from disappearing under pictures, but it's never enough for prime time. Typical runarounds range from 9 to 12 pts. By setting the runaround when no Quark files are open, your runaround works for all new files. Double-click the Picture Box tool in the toolbox to open preferences with Tools highlighted and the picture box icon selected on the right. Click the Modify button and then the Runaround tab at the top of the Modify dialog. Quickly enter the same runaround in points for all four sides of a box by pressing Tab to highlight the first runaround text field and enter a number; then repeat Tab and the number three more times to complete all four runarounds. Close the Modify dialog with Return or Enter. Now repeat for the rectangular text box. Note, you can't set runaround for multiple tools at once.

SET PICTURE BOX BACKGROUND COLOR TO NONE

Modify

| Box | Picture | Frame | Runa |

Box

Color: ☑ None ■ Black ☐ Cyan ■ Magenta ■ Registration ✓☐ White ☐ Yellow

Shade: 100%

You'll no longer see a white background when you put a text box over a picture, colored box, or line. In Quark 6, the default text box background color is None. Picture boxes, however, still have white backgrounds—not good if want to overlap cutout images and irregular-shaped graphics. Even with simple rectangular images, you don't want an unintentional edge of white space to show when you overlap that picture on another color. Set all picture box backgrounds to None ahead of time. With no files open, double-click a Picture Box tool in the toolbox to open Tools preferences with the Picture Box tool icon already selected. Click the Similar Types button to select all the Picture Box tools. You can Shift-click to select a range of box icons, or Cmd- or Ctrl-click to select non-consecutively. Click Modify, then click the Box or Group tab and choose None for Box Color.

   GET COMMANDS WHERE YOU ARE—CONTEXT MENU

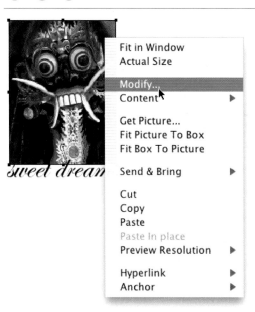

Ever need a command but don't remember the shortcut? Not crazy about keyboard shortcuts? The context menu makes commands available to you on the fly, in a popup menu on your page. Exactly which commands pop up depends on the tool and elements selected (or not). In short, the commands are customized. For instance, if you have a text box selected with the Content tool, the popup menu includes Get Text, Save Text, Send & Bring commands, Modify, and more. With a picture box selected with the Item tool, you get Get Picture, Fit Box to Picture, Cut, Copy, and Paste, plus more. Even when you click a blank spot on the page or pasteboard, you get another set.

Use the context menu also on lines, rulers, text paths, tables, and some palettes—*wherever* your mouse happens to be. Press Control for Mac or right-click for Windows.

- **Mac:** Press the Control key.
- **Windows:** Click the right mouse button.

See also (Mac only) "Get Back the Zoom Tool Shortcut that Quark 5 Stole" (Chapter 3).

 REMEMBERING KEYBOARD SHORTCUTS

Ways to remember those darn keys…

Cmd or Ctrl. Aside from the standard keyboard shortcuts listed on the menus (such as Cmd-S or Ctrl-S to Save), and some that are Quark-specific (such as Cmd-M or Ctrl-M for Modify), the only time the Cmd or Ctrl key is used solo is to allow you temporary access to the Item tool when another tool is selected. That's really handy when you've got the Content tool, which you probably use most. This is one of the most important tips in Quark.

Shift. Aside from helping out in the key combinations, Shift has two reasons to live— constraining and multiple-item selecting. To move an item on one axis only (left-right or up-down), press Shift as you drag. But if the item is already selected, press your mouse button down first, *then* add Shift to avoid deselecting the item.

Option or Alt. Think of this as the "clean up" key. All those oddball things that use *just one key*, aside from the above mentioned, are always Option or Alt. What gives you the Grabber Hand? What turns the Zoom-in tool to a Zoom-out tool? What changes Find Next to Find First? The Option or Alt key does all this—and more!

Combos. There are a lot of combo shortcuts that use all three power keys—Cmd-Option-Shift or Control-Alt-Shift. It's hard to remember such a mouthful. So turn that jumble of syllables into something fun and memorable, like "lean on the keyboard." Scale a picture box and its image? Lean on the keyboard and drag. Fit the image to the box? Lean on the keyboard plus F. It sticks!

See also "Fast Track to Track and Kern to Tighten Headlines" (Chapter 8) and "Keep a Tool Forever" (Chapter 3).

LAUNCHING QUARK FASTER BY REMOVING PPDS

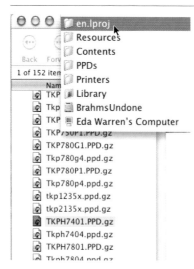

Does it take longer than it should for Quark to launch? Having lots of PPD files in your system is making it worse. PPDs are Postscript Printer Description files that let you customize your Print box settings based on the particular features of your printer. Although your printer PPD was installed in the operating system when you installed the printer, there may be many more PPD files that came with the system or were installed with other programs. To speed up Quark's launch time, move all the PPD files for printers you don't own or use to another folder. Do it now and get it over with. Reboot your computer so Quark can take advantage of your slimmed-down list.

- **Mac OS X:** Find PPDs in your OS X boot drive> Library> Printers> PPDs> Contents> Resources> en.1proj.

- **Windows:** Find PPDs in C:\WINDOWS\SYSTEM32\spool\ drivers\w32x86. There are two folders: 2 and 3. You can put your PPDs into either folder and Quark will find them.

  ## SHORTENING YOUR TIME IN THE PRINT BOX

When you go to the Setup tab of the Print box to select from the Printer Description popup, do you have a long list to wade through? Again, get rid of unnecessary PPDs. (*See above tip.*) Removing the PPD files from your system folder will solve this problem, but there's another way to shorten your printer list. From Quark's Utilities menu, select the PPD Manager, where you'll see a long list of printers. Each has a PPD in your system. Uncheck every printer you're not using so that your PPD list in the Print box only shows printers you're using. In the PPD Manager, you can click Update to have the changes take effect immediately. Otherwise, your changes will be updated the next time you start up Quark. This method doesn't reduce Quark's launch time, but it does make Printing easier—from now on.

PICK YOUR XTENSIONS AS YOU LAUNCH QUARK

Enable	Name	Status
☑	Custom Bleeds	Active
☑	Dejavu	Active
☑	EPS Preview	Active
☑	Full Resolution Preview	Active
☑	Guide Manager	Active
☐	HTML Text Import	Active
☐	ImageMap	Active
☐	Index	Active
☑	Item Sequence	Active

When you install Quark, numerous XTensions are placed into the XTension folder inside the Quark application folder. When you launch the program, they're all turned on by default. XTensions are great, but you don't need to have them all open all the time. Each one uses RAM and causes Quark to take more time to launch. But you can turn XTensions on and off on the fly, as Quark launches. When you see Quark's splash screen come up, just press the Space Bar and don't release it until the XTensions Manager displays. Then uncheck to deselect any XTension you want turned off. Once Quark is already open and you change your mind, you can go to XTensions Manager (Utilities menu) but you'll have to quit and restart Quark for the XTension to be activated.

Suggestions for XTensions to turn off:

- Not using Quark for web work? Turn off ImageMap and PNG filter.

- Not using XML? Turn off avenue.quark, Item Sequence.

- Turn off these features if you're not using them:
  Index, Kern-Track Editor, OPI (swapping in hi-res images at output) and Quark CMS (color management).

XTENSION SETS FOR DIFFERENT CLIENTS AND PROJECTS

Enable	Name
☑	Kern-Track Editor
☑	MS-Word 6-2000 Filter
☑	OPI
☑	PDF Filter
☐	PNG Filter
☑	Quark CMS
☑	RTF Filter
☑	Scissors
☑	Script

XTensions—they're great when you need them, and when you don't, put them away. But instead of just turning them off and on repeatedly, create sets of XTensions to use for different clients and projects. For instance, when you're doing full-color jobs for a high-end workflow, you can turn on OPI, Quark CMS, text and picture filters, Custom Bleeds, Guide Manager, Kern-Track Editor, and Type Tricks. By opening the XTensions Manager when you're launching Quark (*see previous tip*), you can create an XTensions set that will take effect immediately. Just check all the XTensions you want turned on in the Enable column. Click the Save As button at the top of the Manager, and type in a name for that set. The new set is already in place

in the Set popup, where your other sets are found. If you're on your way to opening Quark, your new XTensions set goes right into effect.

The Green Flag Drops

MASTER PAGES & TEMPLATES

This chapter continues the themes of time-saving setups and working systematically. Being more systematic with a layout lets you spend more time

The Green Flag Drops

master pages & templates tips

creating and less time producing. For instance, find out the best and only good use for the Auto Text box. How about tips on getting the most from master pages, an indispensable tool for multi-page layouts? My favorite is instantly aligning identical headers or footers for facing pages with virtually no dialog boxes. That's a technique that can be used in many other situations. Or, once a layout is underway, how do you change the basic print layout settings you started with, such as page size, orientation, margins, and column guides? Finally, take a few minutes to set up powerful and fully developed templates that let you rip through production of one or more layouts. Create libraries to hold all those things you keep using, such as logos. Pretty soon you're on your way to being a sassy Quarker.

GET A GRID

How many columns should you use? Based on a standard page, the two most common grid choices are two and three columns. Two columns get the job done fast. It's easier to lay out text and pictures because there are fewer decisions—just size pictures and text boxes to the width of one or two columns. But the downside is that it can be a bit boring. Pictures often end up larger than they should be, especially head shots. Using three or more columns makes a more interesting layout because there are more choices for sizing items and, consequently, more size contrast—always desirable. A picture can be the width of one, two, or three columns. That also means more items on the page, more decisions, and more work. But, when marketing is the goal, a page with many columns is often the answer. It's more engaging for the reader and so more gets read!

STRATEGIC MARGINS—USING WHITE SPACE

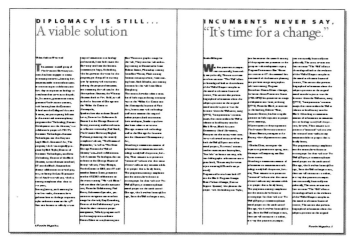

Do you use equal margins? They give a formal and static look. But you can give the page a more dynamic look with *unequal* margins. Build in more white space with a wide margin (more than 8p or 1.33") paired with a smaller one (4p or .66"). Another idea—if you have a facing-pages layout where each spread contains one idea with a single heading, you can pull the pages of the spread together by using a large outside margin and a narrow inside margin. But when there's a single topic *per page*, use margins that emphasize the individual page over the spread—a "modular" layout of unequal margins. In other words, give both pages of the spread the same combination, such as wide left, narrow right. Or try emphasizing the horizontal movement across the spread, using big equal margins on the top and bottom and small equal margins on the left and right. Reverse that for vertical movement.

See also "Use Margins to Clarify Your Content" (Chapter 13).

GUTTERS KEEPING YOU DRAINED?

┌─ Column Guides ─────────────┐
│ Columns: 2 │
│ Gutter Width: 1p6 │
└──────────────────────────────┘

┌─ Column Guides ─────────────┐
│ Columns: 3 │
│ Gutter Width: 1p │
└──────────────────────────────┘

Sometimes it's just nice to know what the graphic standards are. Not that you have to go there, but at least you know where you're departing and you've got a point of reference. Setting the gutter width in the New Project dialog (Cmd-N or Ctrl-N) for the space between the columns typically calls for one of two numbers. When you've got three or more columns, the gutter width is typically 1p (or .167"). This number gives you just enough space to cleanly separate columns, but not so much that your eye gets stuck in the gutter. With two columns on your page, you've got a longer line length and your gutter width can be more generous— 1p6 or .25". And, if you're adding vertical rules between columns, it's likely you'll want to add another 6pts—1p6 for three or more columns, and 2p for two columns.

  WITH THE AUTOMATIC TEXT BOX, YOU GET LINKING HEAVEN

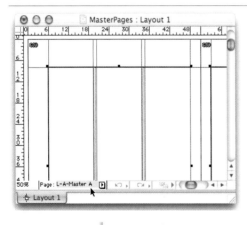

☑ Facing Pages
☑ Automatic Text Box

The Auto Text Box is a great solution for layouts where text runs sequentially, column after column, page after page, throughout the layout. Pictures can be anywhere, but the text never quits—or not until every word is in sight. In File> New> Project (Cmd-N or Ctrl-N), click the Automatic Text Box option. No need to draw text boxes. There's one ready and waiting on page one with the columns you specified. When you Get Text, pages are automatically added to accommodate all the text in the file. (Auto Page Insertion must be *on,* and it is by default, in Default Print Layout preferences). Linking Heaven means *no* linking!

P.S. If you want to import another text file at the top of a new page, but can't get the insertion point to go there, see also "Controlling the Layout with Special Characters" (Chapter 10).

CHANGING PRINT LAYOUT SETTINGS

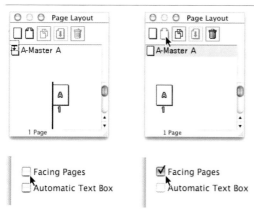

To change page size, orientation, or Facing Pages format, first go to a document page, then choose Layout> Layout Properties. Document settings used to apply to the entire file, but now they're only layout properties and can be different for each layout in your file. With multiple layouts for different but related projects, changing Layout Properties settings affects only the active layout. Second, when changing between facing pages and single-sided layouts, there are additional, although easier, steps with master pages. Switching from single-sided to facing pages? Your original A-Master A page icon in the Page Layout palette is still single-sided. To complete the conversion, drag down the blank facing pages icon at the top of the palette into the masters area and onto the A-Master A page icon. Switching to single-sided? Use the blank single-sided icon instead. If you've set up items on the master, copy them first, then paste them onto the converted master.

See also "Layout Spaces," (Chapter 10).

   CHANGING MARGINS AND COLUMNS—SETTINGS DIMMED?

The Layout Properties dialog looks a lot like the New dialog, but how come you can change the page size, orientation, and facing pages, but can't change the margin and column guides? The answer is, Who Knows? But in fact, when you want to make changes to those guides, they're not in the same place as they were when you started. Check out the Master Guides command in the Page menu. Okay, but wait, it's dimmed! So here's the tip—to get that command, you've got to go to a master page *first*. Gee, Quark sure can be sneaky sometimes! Warning: You may have to manually adjust the positions and even the size of your existing text boxes to fit the new margin and column setup—unless you've used the Auto Text box or set up the equivalent text linking on the master pages. Note that margin and column guide settings can vary from one layout to another in the same file, or "project."

AUTOMATIC PAGE NUMBERS INSTANTLY ALIGNED

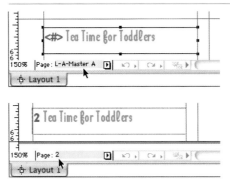

On the left master page, make a small text box the width of the column, in the bottom or top margin. With the Content tool, type Cmd-3 or Ctrl-3. The <#> sign that appears becomes the page number on a layout page. Duplicate the selected box for the right page with Cmd-Option-D or Ctrl-Alt-D (Item> Step and Repeat). Change Horizontal and Vertical Offsets to zero, then click OK. Move the duplicate box across the spread so it stays aligned to the original. Press and hold Cmd or Ctrl to temporarily access the Item tool, while you press the mouse down on the duplicate box. Then add Shift, the constraining key, and drag the box across the spread. When you're there, let go—mouse first, *then* Shift and Cmd or Ctrl. Now change the paragraph alignment from left- to right-aligned with the Content tool using Cmd-Shift-R or Ctrl-Shift-R.

CENTERING PAGE NUMBERS EASILY

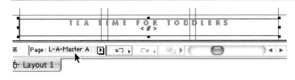

Sometimes page numbers need to be centered on the page in the top or bottom margin, rather than placed in the corners, aligned to the outside margin guides. Even if your margins are unequal, getting the page numbers exactly centered is easy when you realize that "centered" means with respect to the *live area,* the area defined by the margin guides. On the master page, draw a text box for the page number going from the left to the right margin guide, in the top or bottom margin. With the Content tool, enter the page number marker by typing Cmd-3 or Ctrl-3 to see the <#> sign, which becomes the page number. Last, press Cmd-Shift-C or Ctrl-Shift-C to center-align the text to the box, visually centering it on the page.

DRAW FEWER TEXT BOXES FASTER—DO IT ON MASTER PAGES

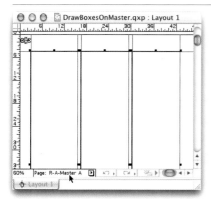

Got a multi-page document? Save time by drawing text boxes on the master pages, instead of doing it over and over on layout pages. On the master pages, draw one text box for each column—a great layout method because you can size each box a little shorter or longer, on the spot, to make a nice *rag-bottom* (uneven columns) or to avoid a widow or orphan. So here's a tip within a tip—no more repeat trips to the toolbox after every box you draw! Instead, get continuous use of that or any tool by pressing Option or Alt when you click to select that tool in the toolbox. And with the resulting ready-made boxes on all your pages, you're ready to roll. You want a box wider or shorter? Just resize it to fit the layout. Need more boxes? Just select an empty box and duplicate it with Item> Duplicate (Cmd-D or Ctrl-D).

RUNNING HEADERS AND FOOTERS THAT MATCH PAGE CONTENT

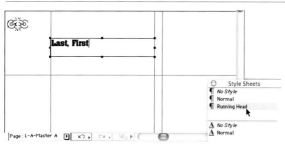

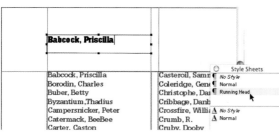

Some documents with listings are set up like a phone book. In the margin of each page, there's a unique running head that matches the top or bottom listing on that page. On the master page, put a text box for the running header or footer where it will appear on layout pages. Type in placeholder text and style it the way you want the header to look. With a facing-pages layout, duplicate the text box using Step and Repeat, then Shift-drag across the spread to the equivalent position on the facing master. Next, use the placeholder text to set up a Running Head paragraph style sheet for those attributes. At the final stage of production, for each page in turn, copy the top or bottom listing for the page and paste into the highlighted placeholder text. Apply the style and on to the next….

See also "Automatic Page Numbers Instantly Aligned" (this chapter).

LOCKING MASTER ITEMS—A GOOD IDEA, BUT NOT FOOLPROOF

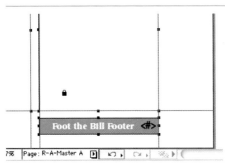

Master pages are great for footers, auto-page numbers, logos or other repeating items, borders, and vertical rules that you want to appear on most or all pages of your layout. Master items should usually stay put on document pages. (Watch out when you use Select All with the Item tool—whatever you do next, your master page items are also selected!) You can head off problems by locking master items. Select all the boxes and lines, then press F6 (Item> Lock). This protects the master items *on your layout pages* from getting accidentally moved or sized. Big *but*—it's no protection against other kinds of changes. In fact, a locked item and its contents can be edited or entirely deleted! To move or size a master item on a layout page, just unlock it with F6. Don't worry; all the other instances of that master item are still locked.

   MASTER PAGE PICTURE BOXES—RUNAROUND OR NOT?

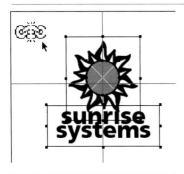

When you want a picture in the same place, same size on multiple pages, put it on the master page. If you want text on the layout pages to wrap around it, set a runaround for it *on the master*. Use Cmd-T or Ctrl-T to open Item> Runaround for the selected item. But on the layout pages, you'll notice the text isn't wrapping because the logo isn't on top. Select the logo, press F5 (Item> Bring to Front), and watch the waters part! For a different effect, use a picture as a watermark, screened back with the type on top. No change to the runaround is necessary because as a master item, it's automatically behind other page items and won't cause a runaround. But be sure it's stacked *behind* any master page text boxes. Overlapping text boxes are transparent by default so your watermark is fully visible.

JUST ABOUT DONE, THEN *CHANGING* A MASTER ITEM <GROAN>

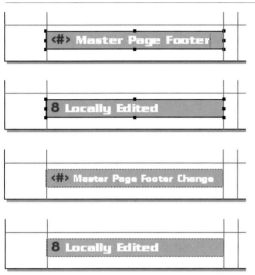

On the master page, you change the footer text; recolor, size, or move an item; change margins or columns; add or delete items; then go to a layout page based on this master, and everything you did on the master is up-to-date…with one exception, and that is "locally edited" master items. For example, if you make changes to the text or picture *contents* of a master item on a layout page, that locally edited content won't update if you later change that item's content on the master page. Likewise, if you locally edit any *item* attribute of a master item on a layout page, such as moving, sizing, or re-coloring it, that item won't update if you later change an item attribute for that element on the master page. So the tip is, watch out when you locally change a master item—it may get left out in the cold tomorrow!

  KEEP OR DELETE CHANGES—NOW YOUR HEAD IS SPINNING

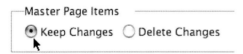

When you reapply a master to a page in the Page Layout palette (dragging down a master page icon onto a page layout icon), what happens is controlled by the General Print Layout preference for Master Page Items— Keep Changes or Delete Changes. With Keep Changes, the default, Quark retains changes you've made to a master item that's been locally edited on a layout page. *But,* now there's a copy of the original master item underneath, or, if you've moved it, at the same spot on that page that it appears on the master. You'll probably see the two boxes with overlapped text because in Quark 6, text boxes don't have white box backgrounds anymore. Obviously, you have to delete one of those boxes. Because Delete Changes has fewer advantages, keep the default setting. *And* when you reapply the same or a new master to a page, immediately check master items on that page for visible duplicates.

DON'T *RE*-INVENT THE WHEEL—USE DUPLICATE MASTER

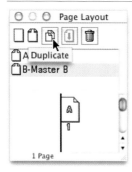

On master pages, you've got some page footers in the outside corners and some vertical rules. The page number marker and footer text use different fonts and styling. Now you'll need another set of masters to handle a layout option. You could easily create a new master in the Page Layout palette—just drag a blank single or facing pages icon from the top left of the palette down into the master pages area. But don't fall for that! You'll have to redo all that work to make the new masters consistent with the first set. Instead, select the A-Master A page icon in the master pages area of the palette and then click the Duplicate button (looks like two overlapped page icons). Go to the new master pages by double-clicking the new page icon and make whatever changes you need. The rest is already in place!

ONE TOO MANY MULTIPLE MASTERS

Having a lot of master pages strains the mind with names like A-Master A and B-Master B. So, when you have more than a couple, rename your master pages. Click once (Mac) or double-click (Win) on the master page icon name near the top of the Page Layout palette. Then type a useful name with a matching prefix, such as I-Intro or S-Sidebar. The prefix on a layout page icon tells you which master has been applied. But sometimes you can avoid making yet another master—if you can make a simple change on the layout page that gets the same result. For example, you don't want the header box to appear on a section opener, as it does on the basic master. If that's the only change, just delete that header box each time you layout a section opener. Admittedly there's room for error here, so carefully proof your hardcopy for these corrections.

ADDING PAGES? APPLY MASTERS TWO WAYS

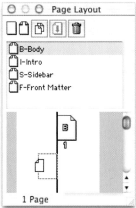

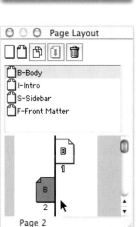

Using the Page Layout palette, you can add pages by dragging the master page icon of your choice down into the layout page icon area. But it's tricky. In a facing pages document, if you see a down-pointing arrow cursor, you'll get a single new page there instead of a spread. Or with a page-icon cursor, you'll have three pages side by side and no shuffling down of pages. If you want to maintain your two-page spreads, look for the little right-pointing arrow cursor immediately to the left of the page icon before which you want to insert pages, prior to releasing the mouse. With a single-sided document, the down-pointing cursor is fine for inserting. The right-pointing arrow cursor gives you two single-sided pages side by side. With all these variables, it's easier to use Page> Insert (no shortcut). Enter the number of pages, where you want them, and what master you'll base them on. Easy.

QUARK'S TEMPLATE VERSUS THE *REAL* THING

Making a Quark "template" takes a second. But go the extra mile to make a template powerful—you'll be paid back plenty in time and consistency. Use it to produce multiple files for a long document (product catalog) or multiple editions of the same file (newsletter). Make any file a template by simply selecting Project Template (*.qpt) from the Type popup menu in the Save or Save As dialog. Template files open as untitled documents, so they don't get overwritten with the stuff of your layout. But go further. Set all print layout preferences, layout defaults, master pages, and especially style sheets. From the Edit menu, set up default colors, H&Js, Dashes & Stripes, and Lists. Add the right number of pages. Finally, include all standing items, such as a newsletter nameplate on page 1. Although it's time-consuming now, in the end you'll produce a better quality product easier and faster.

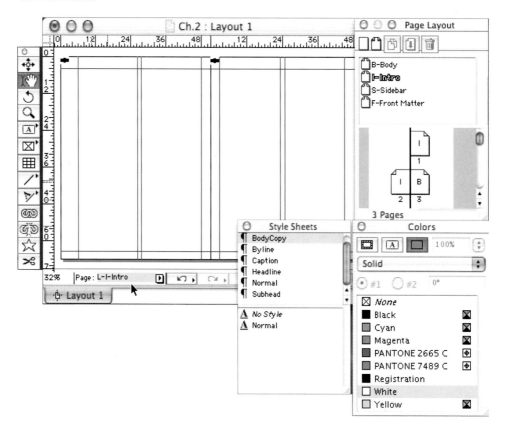

DON'T *RE*-INVENT THE WHEEL #2—APPEND SETUP OPTIONS

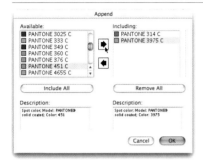

"Steal" from existing files to bolster a newer file. Click Append in five dialog boxes where setup work eats up time: Style Sheets, Colors, H&Js, Lists, and Dashes & Stripes. Then double-click the filename you're taking from to choose just the things you want in a second Append dialog. Select the colors or styles and so on in a list on the left. Then click the right-pointing arrow to send them over to your side. Descriptions for selected items help you choose. Shift-click to select a range of items in the list, or Cmd- or Ctrl-click to select non-adjacent ones. Return a selected item back to the left side with the left-pointing arrow. Luckily, you don't have to repeat this process to also import colors, H&Js, and the like. When you click OK, a warning announces that all other types of appended items will automatically be included, no extra charge!

Shortcuts for Commonly Used Setup Commands in the Edit Menu

	Mac and Win	Mac	Win
Style Sheets	Shift-F11		
Colors	Shift-F12		
H&Js		Cmd-Option-J	Ctrl-Shift-F11

"WHAT, WE NEED THAT LOGO *AGAIN*? " GET A LIBRARY

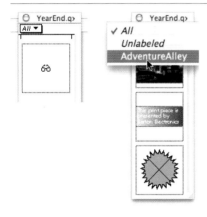

Make a library to store Quark things you may reuse— logos, boilerplate text boxes, and combinations of items—as in a reply form. It's an external file (*.qxl), so it's easy to share with others. Set up a library with Cmd-Option-N or Ctrl-Alt-N (File> New> Library), and give it a name and place. Now fill up this empty palette by dragging in one or more selected items using the Item tool—you're making copies, not moving items. Double-click on a library item to name it. You can use category names—Logos, Pictures, Forms—and then just view all-of-a-kind items, such as all your logos. Or make a long list of unique names. Use the popup menu at the top (Labels button/Win) to choose viewing a custom label, All, or Unlabeled items. When you find what you want, drag it onto the page, making a copy. To remove a selected library item, press the Delete key.

Don't Forget Your Map

QUARKXPRESS

WORKSPACE

Navigating Quark and your project is a lot like sleeping. There's no glory in it, but it's what we spend a lot of time doing. That's why tips for these low-level tasks

Don't Forget Your Map
quark interface tips

are so crucial, because you want to fly through them. After all, when you zoom in and out, scroll or change pages, you haven't advanced your project one iota. But just try to make a great layout without these moves. Dig in here to find some indispensable tricks to add to your bag—like getting temporary access to the Item tool anytime, so you can just hang out in the Content tool. Another great one—being able to keep using a tool repeatedly without having to reselect it each time. And last, an equivalent set of must-have tips for guides—margin, column, and ruler guides. All in all, these are some of the most compelling shortcuts, because you'll use them over and over again.

ZOOM IN OR OUT TO A SPECIFIED PERCENT—NO MOUSING

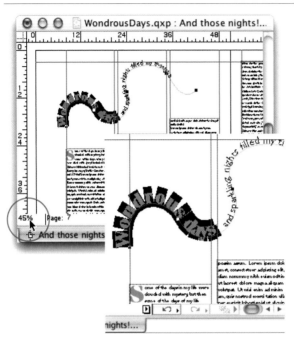

You know that view percent field in the lower-left corner of the layout window? You can use it to zoom in and out, but it's not much fun if you have to use both mouse and keyboard to do it. Ah! But you can highlight that field using the keyboard, then type the percent and be zoomed to your spot, in no time flat. Just press Control-V or Ctrl-Alt-V to highlight the percent field, then type your number (no % sign needed), and press Return or Enter to go there. To get to Thumbnails view, type "T". Double your value by first selecting an item or a bit of text in the area where you'll be working. Then, you'll zoom right to it. Note that Quark now saves your view percent so that when you open a file, that view percent is in effect.

  ## ZOOMING WITH BIGGER OR SMALLER STEPS

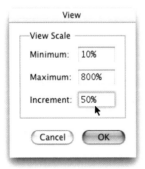

Sometimes it's handy to just click the Zoom tool, rather than drag out the tool, to go farther in or out right in the same area. By default, when you click, the view changes by 25%. You can set the Zoom tool preference for a different percent. To quickly get to the Tools preferences, double-click in the toolbox on the Zoom tool, which highlights the tool icon in the right panel. Click the Modify button to display the View dialog. Increase or decrease the Increment—I like 50%. Less clicking is always refreshing. Now when you click, your view really changes. And remember, if you change the increment when you have no files open, your change is good for all new files from now on!

FASTEST ZOOM

Learning how museums make curatorial decisions in constructing art exhibitions and how they incorporate technology to transform their services to the public. Six Sunrise System interns, graduate and undergraduate students are

When it comes to keyboard shortcuts, zooming is one of *the* most important shortcuts. Not because zooming is hard to do, but because you're doing it all the time. Every extra bit of time it takes you to zoom in or out can probably be magnified hundreds of times in the course of designing and producing a single project. So instead of going back and forth to the tool box to get the tool, access the Zoom tool instead from the keyboard. This is one shortcut you'll be ecstatic you learned, once you see how much time you're going to save. Then, you can really feel like you're on a roll, no stopping you. And, to get the greatest benefit and zoom the fastest, don't just click the tool—click and drag out an area on the page to zoom there.

	Mac	**Win**
Zoom in	Control-Shift click Control-click	Ctrl-Spacebar-click
Zoom out	Control-Option click	Zoom out: Ctrl-Alt-Spacebar-click

*If Control key activates Context menu.
**If Control key activates Zoom.

See also "Get Back the Zoom Tool Shortcut that Quark 5 Stole (Mac only)" (next tip).

   GET BACK THE ZOOM TOOL SHORTCUT THAT QUARK 5 STOLE (*MAC ONLY*)

Control Key
Activates: ● Zoom   ○ Contextual Menu
Control–Shift activates the opposite function.

Here's a dilemma for Mac users. Have you been using the Control key for years to access the Zoom tool? Now in Quark 5 and 6, it doesn't work! The Control key instead brings up the Context menu. However, you can still get back your favorite shortcut easily. And, if you do this just once, it's fixed for all files, new *and* old, even if you don't close all your files first. Press Cmd-Option-Shift-Y or double-click the Zoom tool in the toolbox to open Preferences. In the list under Application preferences, click on Interactive and, in the panel opposite, at the bottom, you'll see the button called Control Key Activates: Zoom. Click there to restore your old shortcut. But remember, when you want to use the Context menu, you'll have to press the Control-Shift keys instead.

See also "Fastest Zoom" (previous tip).

TOGGLE BETWEEN 100% AND 200% VIEW

Although 100% view is the most useful view, where you'll usually see a full half-page at a time (for a standard page), there are many times you need to zoom in to 200%—for reading and editing small or italic text, or sometimes for checking alignments. For those lucky enough to have a large monitor, 200% may be more useful as your default view—100% seems too far away. But in any case, going between these two views is a must. To quickly shift between 100% (Actual Size) and 200% view, use Cmd-Option-click or Ctrl-Alt-click. Be sure to point your mouse at the place you want to zoom to *first*, then do the keystrokes to go *there*. When you zoom out, it doesn't matter where you click if your mouse is pointing to the page or pasteboard (not rulers, toolbox, or palettes).

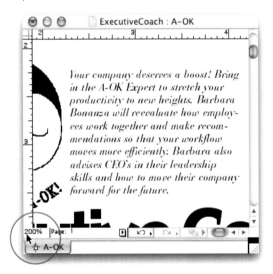

GO TO FIT IN WINDOW? YOU'RE ZAPPED TO ANOTHER PAGE! *%#@+$*!!

Do you feel disoriented when you land on the wrong page after going to Fit in Window (Cmd-0 or Ctrl-0)? It's not hard to do. If you've scrolled your page and now have even one pixel showing at the top of your window that belongs to the page or spread before, then Quark considers that previous page to be the one you're on. And that's where you land when you reduce your view. If you look at the page number by the page popup menu, lower-left screen, or at the Page Layout palette, Quark thinks you're someplace else! Because Quark stacks pages and spreads vertically in one large work space, there's a dividing line that separates each page or spread from the ones above and below. Make sure you can't see that dividing line at the top of your window so you won't feel like you've landed in a strange land.

GRABBER HAND IS THE BEST SCROLLING TIP EVER

She stood there for a moment pondering whether she was perhaps overlooking something. But then, in a flash of recognition, she knew it was all there waiting.

If you don't know this one, you're in for a treat because Quark's scroll bars are very clumsy, especially the vertical one. It's almost impossible to predict how far a scroll will take you, because the distance you scroll the page depends on the number of pages in your layout. In any event, having to use both a horizontal and a vertical scroll bar is a time-sink when you can be merrily scrolling on the diagonal and get there faster. And it's so easy.

With any tool except the Zoom tool, just press and hold Option or Alt while dragging and you've got the hand cursor—Quark's hidden tool. Push, pull, swing it, or drag it, and you're connecting between two points on your page faster than you can say "Grabber Hand." Let go of Option or Alt, and you're back with the tool you just had.

WATCH THE ACTION ON THE FLY WITH LIVE SCROLL

 Although the Grabber Hand is the best scrolling tip, there are times when you've got a long way to scroll, especially across the spread, and the hand tool is just not up to the task. Here's when the scroll bars have their time to shine, except for one small detail—you can't see where you're going, so you go t-o-o far or not far enough. Live Scroll to the rescue! By just adding one little old key, you can see the page scroll *as you drag*. Press the Option or Alt key as you grab that scroll box, and you'll stop exactly where you need to—no guessing games. If you find you really like this feature, you might as well make it permanent by turning on Live Scroll, an Interactive Application preference (Cmd-Option-Shift-Y or Ctrl-Alt-Shift-Y).

See also "Scroll 'n' Go" (Chapter 1).

 SEE BOTH PAGES OF THE SPREAD

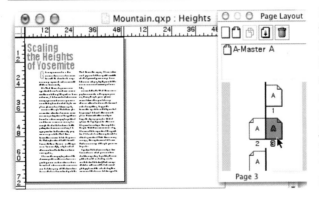

Have you ever found this frustrating? You've got a Facing Pages layout in a reduced view, like Fit in Window, and you change pages. But instead of seeing the entire spread of two pages, you're looking instead at just that one right page? Usually you choose the Fit in Window view just so you *can* see the big picture. Having to scroll that page over to the right to see both pages can be annoying. So whether you like to change pages via the Go to Page command (Cmd-J or Ctrl-J), the Page Layout palette, or the page number popup in the lower left of the layout window, when you're in a reduced view, select an *even-number* page. The facing pages vista can be inspiring.

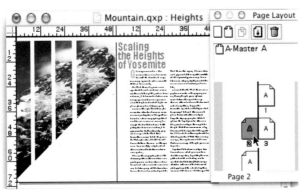

FAST LANE CHANGES—ER, PAGE CHANGES

Getting from page to page is awkward. The Page Layout palette takes up space. Then there's the page number field and popup menu in the lower-left corner of the window. But it doesn't always work when you highlight the number, type a page number, then press Return or Enter. So you find yourself scrolling through a long row of page icons. Cmd-J or Ctrl-J is pretty good for the Go to Page command, but try these:

Extended keyboard:

- Previous page or next page:

    Shift-Page Up or Shift-Page Down (top of the page)—drop Shift to go a screen at a time*

- Go to first page or last page (top of page):

    Mac: Shift-Home or Shift-End (End, only, to go to the bottom of the last page)

    Win: Ctrl-Page Up or Ctrl-Page Down

Not using extended keyboard (Mac):

- Previous page or next page: Control-Shift-K or Control-Shift-L (Drop Shift go by twos)**
- Go to first page or last page: Control-A or Control-D

*Mac users have a second option: Cmd-Page Up or Cmd-Page Down.
**Memory tip: Look at the keyboard. "K" is on the left of the two, i.e. negative, back, etc.*

 GOING BETWEEN A LAYOUT PAGE AND MASTER PAGES

Tweaking the master pages can take time—it's a work in progress. So you often have to go back to the masters when you're on a layout page. Here are some speedy tips for getting there, and if you like master pages, you may be using *multiple* master pages and want to cycle through them:

	Mac	Win
Go between a layout page and master pages	Shift-F10	Shift-F4
Go to next master pages	Option-F10	Ctrl-Shift-F4
Go to previous master pages	Option-Shift-F10	Ctrl-Shift-F3

UNDO—UNDO—UNDO—UNDO…

Redo Key: Cmd+Shift+Z

Maximum History Actions: 30

You can breathe a sigh of relief—Quark 6 offers multiple levels of the Undo and Redo commands! The easiest way is still using Cmd-Z or Ctrl-Z ("E-Z Undo," I always say), but now you may like the Undo History popup menu at the lower-left edge of the layout window, right next to the page popup menu. By default, the Undo menu holds up to 20 actions that can be undone—but not out of sequence. If you want to undo the fourth action back, you'll have to undo the three that came after. Redo is now Cmd-Shift-Z or Ctrl-Y and also has a Redo History palette, right next door to the Undo History popup. To extend your Undos and Redos up to 30 actions, or change the Redo shortcut, go to the Undo Application prefer-ence—Cmd-Option-Shift-Y or Ctrl-Alt-Shift-Y.

GET PICTURE WITH THE ITEM TOOL?

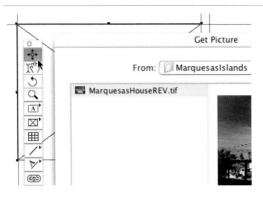

Everyone knows that the Item tool is the move tool. It's the tool that knows the boxes, *not* inside and out, but just the box—no content. So why is it that while you must always have the Content tool to Get Text (some things are sacred), when it comes to pictures, anything goes. Sure, go ahead, use the Item tool to Get Picture (Cmd-E or Ctrl-E), it works fine! There's no logic, but happily it's less to do when you're getting a picture. You probably won't have to change tools.

TEMPORARY ACCESS TO THE ITEM TOOL ANY TIME

On last St. Cadmouse's day, Miss Evelyn P. Istman was found missing from her ancient home along the Thames River. At the age of 103, she had been living alone and attending to matters of state. Just before nightfall, it was learned, she went out to her rose and gardenia garden that has just recently come into full bloom and had apprehended an interloper on her property.

At any time, with any tool except Zoom, you can get to the Item tool but skip that trip to the toolbox. Typically, you have the Content tool—format, edit text, and adjust pictures. But to quickly move a box, just press the Cmd or Ctrl key and presto, you've got the Item tool for as long as you're pressing the mouse down. Ever try to move a guide with the Content tool when you're over a selected picture box? Now you know how. Or, got the tool you need next but you forgot to select or deselect an item? No stopping to run to the toolbox just to get the Item tool to select or deselect. And no *second* trip back to the toolbox to reselect your original tool. No, you just press that magic key, click on or click off, then forge ahead.

CONTENT TOOL IS NOT JUST FOR CONTENT

Quark is finicky about some details and could care less about others. The Content tool is a good example. It's supposed to know contents—the text or picture *inside* a box—but not a lot more. Yet, with the Content tool, you can scale a box or move a line by dragging or nudging! You can select multiple items (use Shift or marquee), move them, or even group them (Cmd-G or Ctrl-G) with the Content tool! But, by some other logic, to copy and paste a line or multiple selected items, you need the Item tool. And here's a gem. With the Content tool, you can cut or copy any item—box and all. Cmd-Option-X or Ctrl-Alt-X to cut. To copy, just replace the X with a C. So there you have it, the new user is befuddled, but those in-the-know lap it up, and life is easier in the end.

TOOLS WITHOUT THE TOOLBOX

You can get to be such a Quark-geek that you virtually never go to the toolbox. Instead, rely on the keyboard to take you down and up the toolbar. But doing a fast switch between the Item and Content tools is what we do most, so naturally there's another shortcut just for that—Shift-F8. Although you can get to the Item tool temporarily, pressing Cmd or Ctrl, there are some things for which Quark simply insists you have the correct tool or you just can't do it—the Item tool to nudge a box a few points in any direction and the Content tool to get some text and nudge a picture inside a box. Of course, occasionally you might need some other tool. Follow the chart, and give these shortcuts a try!

	Mac	Win	Mac and Win
Go to Content tool			Shift-F8
Go between Item and Content tools			Shift-F8
Go down toolbar	Cmd-Option-Tab or Option-F8	Ctrl-Alt-Tab or Ctrl-F8	
Go up toolbar	Cmd-Option-Shift-Tab or Option-Shift-F8	Ctrl-Alt-Shift-Tab or Ctrl-Shift-F8	

FASTER ACCESS TO "FLY-OUT" TOOLS

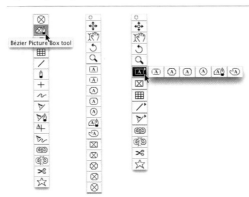

Bézier Picture Box tool

Are you sometimes caught second-guessing where that "fly-out" tool is buried in Quark's toolbox? Or maybe you keep using one of those hidden shaped text or picture box, line, or text-on-a-path tools? Here's a great tip to expand Quark's toolbox so that the tool you need is visible on the toolbox. Just press and hold the Control key (for both Mac and Windows) as you press your mouse down and drag out to select a fly-out tool. When you release the mouse, that tool has been added to the top level of the toolbox. If you don't delete your preferences file, your enlarged toolbox will be displayed every time you launch Quark. To tuck that tool back in, just Control-click on the tool icon. If you're really obsessed, you can do this 18 times to display all 28 tools at one glance.

KEEP A TOOL FOREVER!

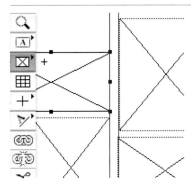

Have you ever noticed that when you use almost any tool *except* The Big Two—Item and Content—you get only a single shot at it, and then it's gone? It's morphed right back into the tool that you used last. But you weren't finished yet? You've drawn a box and want to do another, but now you're back with the Content tool? You've rotated an item, but to do it again, it's back to the toolbox? These are familiar stories in the legends of Quark, but there's a shortcut in shining armor who can solve your problems in no time flat. When you go to the toolbox to select a tool you want to use more than once, press Option or Alt as you click the tool. Now you can draw lines and boxes, rotate items, and make multiple scissors cuts to your heart's content.

See also "Save Endless Time When You've Got Lots of Links" (Chapter 7).

   SEE THE PAGE WITHOUT THE MESS

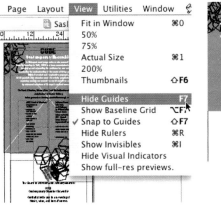 

Quark is a busy visual environment. You've not only got the margin, column, and maybe ruler guides, as well as all the text and pictures on the page, but there are also all those boxes with their dotted-line edges, when they're not selected. It's a wonder you can see what you're doing! I find myself constantly using this shortcut to get a quick take on the state of the page or spread, especially when I'm in the Fit in Window view. Press F7 to quickly hide all the non-printing stuff and the box edges. Call it "Print Preview." This tip works great with the turn-off-greeking tip.

See also "It's Greek to Me—Get the Real Thing Instead" (Chapter 1).

STRATEGIC GUIDES ON MASTERS ENSURE EXACT POSITIONING

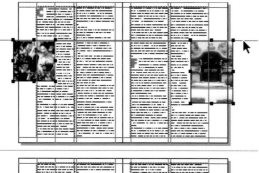

Everyone knows that putting text and pictures on master pages means they'll show up on every page. But putting a ruler guide on a master page can be just as useful to indicate an exact place where the tops or bottoms of items can snap-to on some or all layout pages. Let's say you want a layout where various-sized pictures will hang from the same point on every spread. By marking that spot with a horizontal guide that goes across the spread, you can snap all your picture boxes to it. Go to the master pages, but don't drag out a spread guide. It won't work. Because spread guides on masters don't show up on layout pages, you've got to make two separate ruler guides for the left and right masters—and line them up exactly. Check the Y position of each ruler guide on the Measurements palette to make sure they match up.

SNAP-TO-GUIDES IS FOR 99% OF THE TIME, BUT...

Snap-to-Guides (Shift-F7) in the View menu is on by default. That's good because almost every time you move a box or a line, you're snapping at least part of it to a margin, column, or ruler guide. When you're just pixels away, the guide keeps the item aligned by sucking that thing in like a vacuum cleaner—clean, neat, and fast. But sometimes that magnetic pull is just what you *don't* need. Maybe you're using a ruler guide to line up body copy by the baseline across columns. But just as you get that baseline close to the guide, the text box snaps instead to another guide. You can nudge the box one point in any direction by pressing an arrow key a few times when the Item tool is selected. Or quickly turn off the snap-to by pressing Shift-F7. But don't forget to turn it right back on, you'll need it.

POSITION A GUIDE NUMERICALLY WITH X AND Y

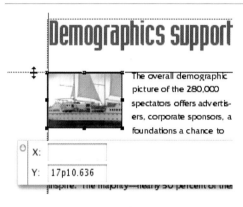

Have you ever wanted to put a guide at an exact location on the page? Let's say you have a picture on the page and you want to top align other pictures to it. If you use the Space/Align box, you may end up moving the original item instead. A perfectly positioned ruler guide easily does the trick. Start by noting on the Measurements palette the Y coordinate of the selected picture, in picas or inches, no matter how many decimal places. Then, with any tool, drag out a ruler guide from the top ruler and read its changing Y position on the Measurements palette as you drag. When the number it displays exactly matches the number you noted for the picture box, let go. Now snap in the other items and they will be identically aligned. The tip also works for spread guides. For vertical guides, use the X coordinate.

DELETE ALL HORIZONTAL OR VERTICAL GUIDES IN ONE FELL SWOOP

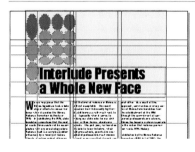

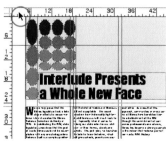

Some people just love using guides. You can temporarily forget numbers and just snap things to a guide to align them. But, before you know it, you've got a ton of guides on your page. This tip is great because you won't have to decide which is worse—dragging each guide back into the ruler or leaving your workspace a mess. Instead, with one swoosh of the magic wand (oops, that's Photoshop!), you can kill them all with one blow, well okay, maybe two. First, scroll your page so there's no pasteboard between the page and the horizontal and vertical rulers. Then, simply Option-click or Alt-click on the top or side ruler and the guides are history—that is, just the horizontal guides or just the vertical. But, it's just a small step over to the other ruler and repeat the shortcut again. By the way, this only works for pages, not spreads.

LIMIT GUIDE CLUTTER—SET A VIEW THRESHOLD

You often use a guide when you're zoomed in and can really see what's going on. Then you zoom out to a larger view and behold, your page is ridden with guide clutter because you've already dragged out a few others. Guides you make when you're zoomed in, however, don't need to be visible in a more reduced view. Press Shift as you drag the guide out from the ruler. When you're done using the guide, no need to delete it, because it's nowhere to be seen when you zoom out. But zoom back there again, at the original view percent *or higher*, and it's right there where you left it!

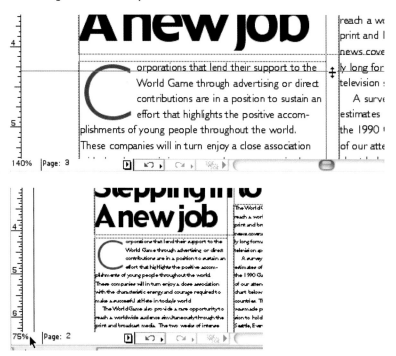

PLOWING THROUGH THE GUIDE MANAGER MAZE

Quark's Guide Manager (Utilities menu) let's you divide up a page or spread into equal units, marked by ruler guides. There are many choices (read "ways to go wrong"). Start out on a page with a single column (using ruler guides with column guides is confusing). In the Guide Manager, choose Horizontal or Vertical for guide Direction, then Current Page or All Pages. Avoid the Spreads options, unless you want guides on the pasteboard. Most likely, you'll want to use Number of Guides rather than Spacing; you can't use both. To divide the *entire* page into three equal areas, enter "4" for Number of Guides, then choose Entire Page/Spread for Origin/Boundaries Type. Then click Add Guides. The outside guides fall on the page edges. The Remove Guides button is on the dialog's other tab—Remove or Lock Guides. Then flip back to the Add Guides tab. So how do you put guides just in the live area *within the margin guides*? Clicking the Use Margins check box is not the answer. Instead, choose Absolute Position from the Type popup, and for your Left/Right or Top/Bottom values below, enter the X position of your left and right margins (for .5" left/right margins, left is .5" and right is 8"), then click Add Guides.

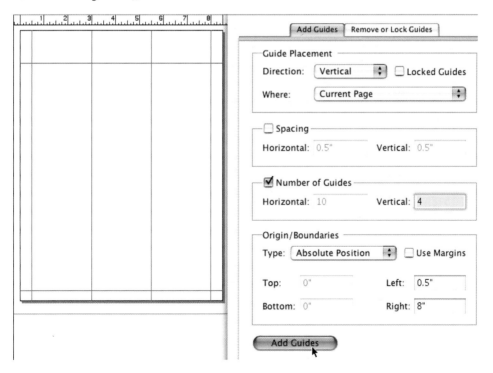

Parts Is Parts

**LINES
&
BOXES
ZONE**

Even though you tend to go to other programs to create drawings for your layouts, there are many times when you can use Quark's drawing tools for a

Parts Is Parts
lines & boxes tips

quicker solution. Lines alone offer a world of opportunity with many styles to choose from. Not to mention that you can create an infinite array of line styles in the very rich Dashes & Stripes editor—thinner, thicker, bigger or smaller gaps, dots or dashes; stripes of equal or unequal weights; and on and on. But don't stop there. Quark's Bezier tools, all those line and box tools that feature a draftsman's pen as part of the tool icon, can be wielded to make almost any kind of line or box— anything from a heart to complex shapes you have to see to believe. And if they're boxes, then you get to fill them with text or pictures. Once you get into these drawing tools, there's no telling when you'll come out.

 **WHEN YOU WANT A STRAIGHT LINE, DO IT RIGHT**

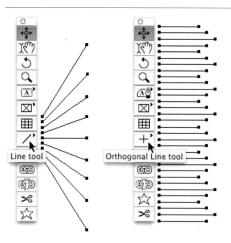

Although the default Line tool draws "straight" lines, it's the *Orthogonal* Line tool that draws the lines we use most—horizontal, vertical, and 45°. It's easy and fast, no keys required, just click and drag. When you need that line longer or shorter, just drag the handle, it keeps the line at the same angle. By contrast, the default Line tool can be forced into drawing perpendicular lines, but it mostly likes to draw straight lines at other angles. It can draw like the Orthogonal tool but only if you hold down the Shift* key. And if you extend or shorten that line, you need the Shift key again. So make life easy for yourself, go get the Orthogonal tool *once* by dragging out to that fly-out tool. From now on, it will be the default tool in your toolbox.

* If your mouse wanders and the line snaps to the next 45° rotation, use Option-Shift or Alt-Shift. But Shift is fine in most cases.

 RESIZE LINES AT THE SAME ANGLE

	Favorite food	Best scene	Destination
John	Steak	Bar	Lots of people
Zinnia	Artichokes	Yoga	Here
Babette	Pizza	Party	Aspen
Judith	Lobster	Culture-anything	New York City
Lawrence	Greek	Symphony	Walking to a concert
Eddie	Rice	Garden	Mr. Ranier

How do you extend or shorten lines drawn at any angle with the default Line tool? If you drag a handle, the angle changes. But it works when you press the Shift key! How about for a set of lines? Grouping is the answer. Drag a marquee to touch all the lines with the Item or Content tool, then Cmd-G or Ctrl-G (Item> Group). Now with one set of handles, you can size the lines together fairly easily. With horizontal or vertical lines, just drag a center handle to resize. But to resize and keep grouped lines on some other angle, your only choice is proportional sizing, dragging a handle with Cmd-Option-Shift or Ctrl-Alt-Shift. The lines keep the angle and width (weight), but the spacing between them changes proportionally. If the original spacing is important, then use Step and Repeat to make a new set of lines at a fixed distance (Cmd-Option-D or Ctrl-Alt-D).

FIVE WAYS TO CHANGE A LINE "WIDTH" OR WEIGHT

In Quark, "width" is line weight, which you often need to change. It's easy to make a mistake because the quarter-point, half-point, and one-point rules all look the same on screen at 100% view. Don't use Quark's Hairline width with high-resolution output. It's only .25pt—too thin. Specify .25pt instead. You can change line weight and other attributes in five places. The Style menu is slowest. The Line Modify dialog (Cmd-M or Ctrl-M) is great for setting attributes for multiple-selected lines, as well as for coloring and runaround. Other options are handier in the Measurements palette. That leaves the Context menu (Control-click on a line/Mac or right-mouse-click/Win). It pops up right where you are, has all the attributes, including the Modify command, and even lets you change a line Content into a text path! Last, if you just want to change the weight visually, use the keyboard.

Using Set Increments from the Width Menu: Hairline, 1-2-4-6-8-12

	Mac	Win
Increase	Cmd-Shift->	Ctrl-Shift->
Decrease	Cmd-Shift-<	Ctrl-Shift-<

Using 1pt Increments (Add Option or Alt)

	Mac	Win
Increase	Cmd-Option-Shift->	Ctrl-Alt-Shift->
Decrease	Cmd-Option-Shift-<	Ctrl-Alt-Shift-<

MATCH A LINE LENGTH TO A BOX WIDTH

Try a different look for your boxes using a heavy line, top and bottom, the width of the box, but little to no weight for the sides. First draw your line, set a good weight, then select the box. In the Measurements palette, double-click the X value and copy it (Cmd-C or Ctrl-C). Then switch back to the line. Choose Left Point in the Modes menu. Then paste the number into the X1 field (Cmd-V or Ctrl-V). Do the same for the box Y value, pasting into the selected line's Y1. Then, copy the box's W value and paste that into the line's L— with the default "mode" of Endpoints, you won't see the "L" (Length). For the line at the bottom, first copy the box's H. Select the top line you just positioned, go to Step and Repeat (Cmd-Option-D or Ctrl-Alt-D), set Horizontal Offset to 0 and for Vertical Offset, paste in your number.

GET IDENTICALLY STYLED LINES EVERY TIME

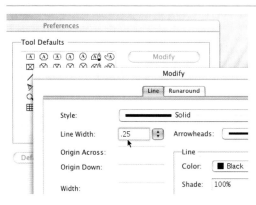

If you've got one line in your layout, chances are you'll have a bunch. For consistency, you might want them to look the same, so set up a default line style. It's easy. If you've read parts of Chapter 1, "Setup Tips," you know that when you have a file open and set a tools preference, your choice is good *just for that layout*. If you want that default for all new layouts, close your current files, then set the preference. Double-click the Line or Orthogonal Line tool in the toolbox to open the Tools preferences. You can click Similar Types to select all the line tools or Similar Shapes to include the corresponding Text-Path tool. Then click the Modify button, and choose the Style, Line Width, Color/Shade, and perhaps Arrowheads. Now all your lines will share the same look the instant you draw them in any new file.

YOU LOOK DASHING!

Add some flair with subtle or crazy lines using Edit> Dashes & Stripes. Vary a line style by duplicating it, then give it a name. Or choose New Dash or Stripe. Make one stripe or dash by dragging in the ruler—the more you drag, the wider it gets. Add another somewhere else. Change the gap space by dragging a dash or stripe with the hand cursor. Or delete by dragging it beyond the drawing area. The Repeats Every field, below, sets the frequency of the repeat. Higher numbers increase the gap. Fit your line style evenly to your line or box length with Times Width. Or use Points for a fixed interval. Check Stretch to Corners to fit the line style symmetrically to your box, which I recommend! Try the Endcap styles. Looks good in the Preview area? Apply your line style to a box frame with Cmd-B or Ctrl-B, or to a line from the Measurements palette.

DESIGNER FRAMES

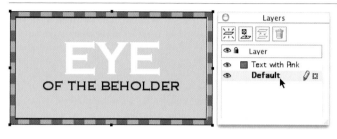

Here's a contemporary look with two-color dashes and gaps of equal length. Duplicate the Dotted line in Edit> Dashes & Stripes. Then type," Designer Frames." Below that, there's one black bar with the right arrow at 60%. Move the arrow left to 50% so the dash and gap lengths are equal. Position field says 50%? Click OK, then Save. With a box selected, open Item> Frame (Cmd-B or Ctrl-B). Set a width, at least 2pts, and select Designer Frames style. Lower down, choose a darker color for your frame and another for the gap, then OK. For extra drama, add one or two boxes whose frames surround the original box. Draw a box to the outside, about a .5pt frame width, with box background color None. Then duplicate the box (Cmd-D or Ctrl-D), and size and position it so that it fits the inside dashed-line edge. Zoom in to check for gaps. The Layers palette makes it easier.

   ## DRAWING MORE THAN ONE

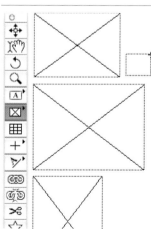

Let's say you want to draw a bunch of boxes of different sizes, making an arrangement of them as you go. Now, you could draw one box, then duplicate it (Cmd-D or Ctrl-D), size it, and move it, and then repeat all those steps for each box in your design. But, you know, sometimes it's just easier to draw them the way you want them in the first place. But Quark takes away your box tool after you draw one. :-(This tip solves that problem by letting you keep your tool and draw as many as you want without the annoyance of return trips to the toolbox. Just press Option or Alt when you click the box tool in the toolbox to select it. Now you've got continuous use of that tool.

PERFECT SQUARES AND CIRCLES

Mekel
Demglal tograghics
Corporations that lend their
suppol to the World Cames
through advertising or direct contributions are in a position to sustain an
effort that highlights the positive accomplishments of young people throughout the
world. These companies within turn enjoy a
close association with the characteristic
energy and courage required to make a
successful athlete in today's world.
The World Cames also provide a
rare opportunity to reach a
worldwide high audience
simultaneously

Square and circle boxes can give a layout a very geometric look, which can be sporty, punchy, and contemporary. As you're drawing a rectangle or oval box, press the Shift key and that square or circle just snaps into place. You can also take any existing rectangle or oval box and turn it into a square or circle by Shift-dragging a handle. Then when you fill a square or circle picture box with an image, the shape of the box immediately pops out on the page. Using a square and especially a circle *text* box takes more work. Don't use paragraph breaks. If necessary, use a paragraph *special character* (§ or ¶) so that the text can continue on the same line. Then size down the type—the smaller the size, the more closely the text approximates the box shape. Justify the text to push it out to the edges.

NO "X" ON THAT NICE, COLORED PICTURE BOX

Making colored shapes on your page puts more color in the layout. Text boxes can have colored backgrounds with the text overprinted or reversed out. Box backgrounds can also have *blended* colors! But when you have color in an empty picture box, there's an X running through it and your page looks busier. It's an extra step to remove it, but it's much easier to see your layout as your work. So just select the box, then go to Item> Content> None. Even faster with the Context menu—Control-click/Mac or right-click/Win. Now the box has a clean-look, *even when guides are on*!

See also "Optical Effects with Blends in Box Backgrounds" and "Put Blends into Lines " (Chapter 11).

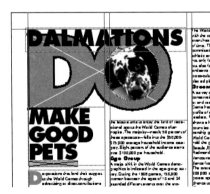

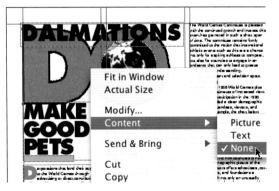

TRY ON A NEW SHAPE!

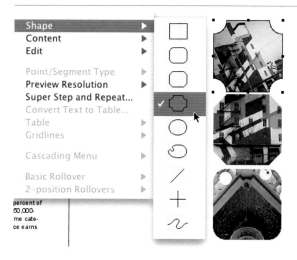

Here's one that's fun and an easy way to create variety in the layout. Change an everyday box into something with more pizazz. Just select any box on your page, then go to Item> Shape> and pick one of the nine shape choices (okay, eight others besides the one you have). You can even change a line into a Concave-Corner box, so long as the line is at least 1pt! And don't forget, when you've settled on a box "look," make sure you repeat the treatment elsewhere so it's not just an unrelated "doo-dad."

MAKE A WACKY OR SUBLIME PICTURE BOX

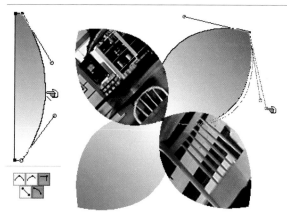

Break out from a blocky look by reshaping a selected box. Pick the Freehand box style ◌ in Item> Shape. Now drag any box handle to reshape it. If necessary, turn on Shape Editing (Shift-F4/Mac or F10/Win). Option- or Alt-click on a path to add points, or on a point to delete it. Drag a selected point or move it with arrow keys, or enter new XP and YP coordinates in the Measurements palette. Change a selected point to a Corner, Smooth, or Symmetrical point by clicking one of three buttons in the palette. With Smooth or Symmetrical points, rotate an endpoint of a handle to change the curve angle or make the curve fuller or flatter by extending or shortening the handle from an endpoint. Convert a straight line segment into a curve by selecting between two points, then click the bottom-row buttons on the palette. Shape the curve by dragging out from between the new smooth points.

DRAW A HEART-SHAPED OR SCALLOPED CURVE

The top and bottom center points of a heart are corner points with curve handles. Start at the bottom, click-drag to the right using a Bezier box tool—use Shift to constrain horizontally. Next, move your mouse northeast and Shift-drag straight up. Then move the mouse back to the left, roughly aligned to both previous points. Shift-drag down. Now, at the heart of the heart, you'll break the handles so the curve goes back up. To make that a corner point, drag from the point pressing Cmd-Control/Mac or just press Ctrl-F1/Win. Press Cmd or Ctrl, and drag back up the bottom left endpoint of that curve handle so it looks like antennas. Now move your mouse farther left and Shift-drag down. For the close, click-drag on top of the first point, looking for the circle-close cursor. Pressing Cmd or Ctrl, reselect that last point and repeat the keystrokes to make it a corner point. Again adjust the handles up and in, like antennas.

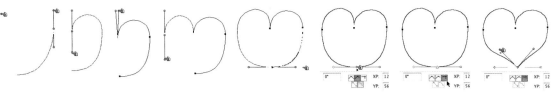

   ## BEZIER DRAWING SHORTCUTS

Here's a bunch of quick ones for making drawing easier.

Move or edit the path as you draw (before or after drawing a point):

- Press Cmd or Ctrl and drag.

Delete your last (selected) point:

- Delete or Backspace.

Completing a Bezier line:

- Change tools, can use Shift-F8/Mac and Win, and Cmd-Option-Tab or Ctrl-Alt-Tab.
- Constrain Bezier straight lines to horizontal, vertical or 45°angles: Shift-click.
- Constrain the handles of Bezier smooth points to horizontal, vertical or 45°angles: Shift-drag.

 Break a handle to make the curve go back the other way:

- Mac: Cmd-Control-drag the handle.
- Win: Ctrl-F1 to change selected point to a corner, then press Ctrl to drag the handle.

 Go from a smooth point into a straight line:

- Click the square end of the out (leading) handle with Cmd-Option or Ctrl-Alt, then make your next corner point.

BEZIER EDITING SHORTCUTS

Editing paths is as important to the end result as drawing. Here are some good ones.

Change a Point *After Drawing Is Complete*: **Select the Point, Then Change…**

	Mac	Win*
To corner	Option-F1**	Ctrl-F1
To smooth	Option-F2	Ctrl-F2
To symmetrical	Option-F3	Ctrl-F3

Change a Path Segment: Click on It First with Item or Content Tool, Then Change…

	Mac	Win*
To a straight-line segment	Option-Shift-F1	Ctrl-Shift-F1
To a curved-line segment	Option-Shift-F2	Ctrl-Shift-F2

Then drag out the line segment *between* the new curve points.

* **Win**: *Change on last point drawn can also be made while drawing.*
** **Mac:** *Change a point to corner while drawing by dragging a handle with Cmd-Control.*

 FLIP HORIZONTAL AND FLIP VERTICAL

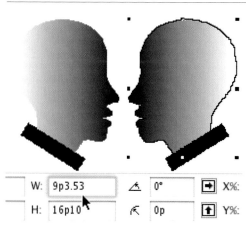

There *is* a way to reflect a Bezier or Freehand shape, but it's not direct. Unlike the nice 'n' easy arrow buttons on the Measurements palette for flipping an image inside a picture box, reflecting the shape or box itself takes a bit more doing. First of all, if you're seeing points on the shape, press Shift-F4/Mac or F10/Win to be in non-editing mode. Now you should see the eight item handles that surround a selected shape. To flip horizontal, copy the W (width) value in the Measurements palette and for vertical, copy the H. Then drag a center handle across the shape to literally turn it over. Oh, but you're not sure when to stop dragging once you get on the other side? Never fear, after you're somewhere on the other side, then just paste the W or H value back into the shape and press Return or Enter. Neat trick!

MOVING A SHAPE OR EDITING POINTS?

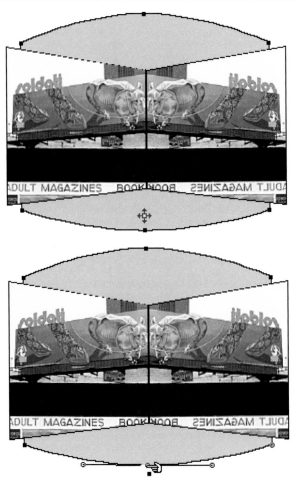

Trying to move the path, but changing the curve instead? Or you want to pull out a straight line segment, but you're moving the whole path instead? First check Item> Edit> Shape. Is it on or off? If you're not editing shapes, turn it off. Use Shift-F4/Mac or F10/Win to go back and forth. Next, you gotta notice the cursor. To move an item, look for the Item tool cursor ✛ when you're on the path, not over a point. If necessary, press Cmd or Ctrl to get that cursor—even if you have the Item tool. To edit a path, find the pointing-finger cursor with a dot ☞ when you're over a point. To move a path segment, position your mouse over the path to see the pointing finger with a \ ☞. Deleting points is easy. Just Option- or Alt-click on a point to remove it. The cursor looks like a circle with an "X" through it. The point is now gone, but the rest of the shape is still there.

FOR COMPLEX SHAPES, MERGE

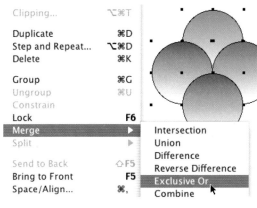

Clipping...	⌥⌘T
Duplicate	⌘D
Step and Repeat...	⌥⌘D
Delete	⌘K
Group	⌘G
Ungroup	⌘U
Constrain	
Lock	F6
Merge ▶	
Split ▶	
Send to Back	⇧F5
Bring to Front	F5
Space/Align...	⌘,

Intersection
Union
Difference
Reverse Difference
Exclusive Or
Combine

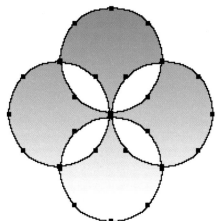

You can create very unusual shapes that are made from combining multiple items with the Item> Merge commands. Select two or more items, including boxes, lines, or Bezier shapes. Do a quick Duplicate (Cmd-D or Ctrl-D) to keep a copy handy, because the merged item replaces your starters. There are six commands (seven if you count joining points), but your most likely choices are Union, Exclusive Or, and Combine. Union makes one shape following the outside outlines of the selected shapes. Exclusive Or and Combine are similar— the areas where shapes overlap become see-through windows after merging. But with Exclusive Or, there are editable corner points where the shapes originally intersected. So there's more to work with. Because the merged shape has the attributes of the item farthest back, you might Send To Back (Shift-F5) the item whose background color, frame weight, and color you want for your merged shape.

Fine Tuning

SELECTIONS
& TRANSFORMATIONS

Let's face it—Quark is a boxy program. Virtually everything in Quark is a box or is in a box. And if it's not a box, it's

Fine Tuning
selection & transformation tips

another item that works very much like a box. You'll find a lot of hidden power in your Quark work when you master all the ins and outs of manipulating items—selecting, moving, stacking, grouping, using the Measurements palette, transforming items (sizing, rotating, skewing), and deleting. Just for instance, do you know how to select a buried item without tearing apart your layout? Can you move a selected item in one direction only—and do it two different ways? Try moving one item in a group without ungrouping. Then there's a ton of ways to make the Measurements palette calculate for you. Make an item or just its contents three times its size or one quarter, move it over .125", or use the palette to align items. Can you size type and pictures incrementally and stop just when it looks good? These are just some of the gems you'll find here that will make your work more creative and fun!

SELECTING A BURIED ITEM

One of the pitfalls in an object-oriented program such as Quark is that you have items overlapping, or stacked, and you can't select the one you want. You click there, but something else gets selected. Happens all the time. Some people use the Bring to Front and Send to Back commands just to get to that buried item. Or worse, they start dragging the top items out of the way. But you don't have to move a thing to the side, front, or back. When you click, but don't select, just click again in the same spot, pressing these keys:

- **Mac:** Cmd-Option-Shift

- **PC:** Ctrl-Alt-Shift

Now each time you click with these keys, your cursor selects the item at the next level back in the stacking order. It doesn't change the order, but you can get to anything on the page, no matter how deep it's buried or what layer it's on.

DESELECT ALL ITEMS

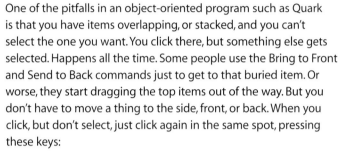

Sometimes it's handier to deselect all items using a key rather than clicking off—especially when you *can't* click off because you are zoomed way in and you've got nothing but items in view. It's usually when you're pretty far along with your project and have plenty of items on your page. Maybe you need to click off because you want to edit or format text with the Content tool, but the Item tool cursor is still displayed because multiple items are selected. Can't click off? When the Item or Rotation tool is in gear (or the Content tool, if more than one item is selected), try Plan B, your second line of defense—the humble Tab key. Just one hit of Tab and instantly all handles have vanished. Did everyone go on vacation?

NUDGE AN ITEM ONE POINT IN ANY DIRECTION

You want to move a selected item a little bit more. It's almost there, but sometimes it's hard to be totally precise with the mouse. Or, in another quandary, the snap-to-guide keeps pulling your item in too far. These are excellent times to use the arrow keys to nudge a selected item a few points in any direction—north, south, east, or west, so to speak—but *only when the Item tool is selected!* (With the Content tool selected, you're moving an image inside a box or the insertion point in text.) Each hit of an arrow key moves the item 1pt, regardless of the view you're zoomed to. If you add Option or Alt when you press an arrow key, your item moves in a ¹⁄₁₀pt interval. Arrow keys are an excellent alternative to Shift-dragging to move an item on the same axis, horizontally or vertically.

HIDDEN COMMANDS—BRING FORWARD AND SEND BACKWARD (*MAC ONLY*)

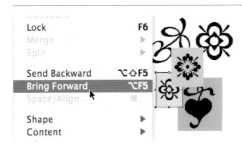

Stacking order means that items in the same spot are arranged in front-to-back order, like stacked objects on a table. A headline on a picture is a text box in front of, and on top of, a picture box. Change the stacking order of a selected item so it moves higher or lower in the stacking order (on a given layer) with the Bring to Front (F5) and Send to Back (Shift-F5) commands in the Item menu. But what about Bring Forward or Send Backward? They're just one step forward or back. Windows folks already have these commands in the Item menu. Not on the Mac—*but* press Option when you view the Item menu to see the "hidden" commands. Or go all the way with keyboard shortcuts—Option-F5 (Bring Forward) or Option-Shift-F5 (Send Backward). The Context menu is easiest of all—press Control and select from the popup menu.

CONSTRAIN A MOVE WITHOUT DESELECTING

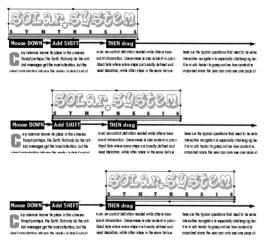

Because so much in graphic design is about alignment, it's a lifesaver to move an item in one direction only, so that it stays aligned horizontally or vertically to its original position. Constrained moving is really great with Step and Repeat, setting the offsets to zero, then Shift-dragging the duplicate to move it so it stays aligned to the original.* The infamous Shift key, the constraining key in computer graphics, keeps an item "in line." No shenanigans! But it's tricky. When you hold down the key, then drag, it deselects! That's because Shift-clicking adds to a selection, or *deselects* it if the item is already selected. You have to fool Quark so it doesn't realize you're Shift-selecting. Press your mouse down, *then* add the Shift, *then* drag. With the Content tool, use Cmd-Shift-drag or Ctrl-Shift-drag.

Once you've set offsets to zero, use Cmd-D or Ctrl-D to make the copy right on top, throughout that session of Quark.

KEEP 'EM TOGETHER

You often want to keep several items together, easily and repeatedly—for a product catalog, for example. Each catalog item has a photo, a caption, and another text box with all the specs and prices. And maybe a logo. When you're juggling these product sets in a layout, save time by not having to select all the things that go together each time. Instead, Group them once. Click on one, then Shift-click to add in each one. Or simply make a marquee by dragging from a blank spot with the Item or Content tool and touch those items you want to select. Then do Cmd-G or Ctrl-G to Group. Now all items in the group are selected when you click just one. To Ungroup, use Cmd-U or Ctrl-U.

SIZE ITEMS TOGETHER

When you have a bunch of text or picture boxes that you want to size *together,* use grouping—it's almost perfect. Say you have a large finished poster that you now want to make a smaller 8.5 × 11" flyer. Instead of recreating all the items on a smaller scale, collect them altogether using Shift-and-click or a marquee (drag from a blank spot to touch those items you want to select). Then use Cmd-G or Ctrl-G to make them a group *with one set of handles.* You can resize a grouped set of items visually and proportionally by dragging a handle while pressing Cmd-Option-Shift or Ctrl-Alt-Shift. There's only one catch—the frame widths of your boxes (if not zero) don't scale, nor do line widths. If that's not a problem, then grouping *is* perfect.

From Contemporary People stock photo CD by Dynamic Grapics. Courtesy Chuck Boysen, Director of Marketing.

See also "Save Page as EPS Saves the Day" (Chapter 12).

MOVING AND SIZING ITEMS WITHIN A GROUP

Just because you've got a group (Cmd-G or Ctrl-G) doesn't mean that you can't work with an individual item in that group. Perhaps you grouped each picture with its caption, then discovered that one caption is too far down. Without ungrouping, you can select one item, move it, or even resize it with the Content tool. To move an item with the Content tool, press and hold Cmd or Ctrl to temporarily access the Item tool. Actually choosing the Item tool won't work! Size an item proportionally by dragging a handle while pressing Cmd-Option-Shift or Ctrl-Alt-Shift. When you need to use the Content tool to do what it does best— adjust a picture in a box or edit/format text—first *deselect* the group, then click back on the item you want to change.

ZOOM AROUND THE MEASUREMENT PALETTE

Getting to know the Measurements palette *intimately* is one of the first jobs a designer or production person ought to take on. It will serve you well because this thin palette is the one you use over and over again, every time you work in Quark.

	Mac	Windows
Open or close palette	F9	F9
Open palette	Cmd-Option-M	Ctrl-Alt-M
Select first field if palette is already open	Cmd-Option-M	Ctrl-Alt-M
Highlight font field	Cmd-Option-Shift-M	Ctrl-Alt-Shift-M
Select next field	Tab	Tab
Previous	Shift-Tab	Shift-Tab
Execute	Return	Enter
Deactivate highlighted field	Cmd-period	Esc

MEASUREMENTS PALETTE *CALCULATES* MOVING AND SIZING

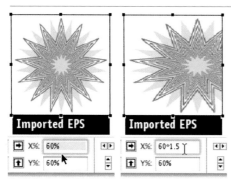

Imported EPS

X%: 60%
Y%: 60%

Imported EPS

X%: 60*1.5
Y%: 60%

The Measurements palette is a calculator. It can't handle your taxes, but it can calculate distances and scale factors. Say you have a box on the page and you want it to be 2p6 (or .417") farther to the right. In the X field, type "+2p6" (or +.417") after the current number. Then press Return or Enter to execute. To move it left, subtract the number, "−2p6." To move it down or up, add to or subtract from the Y value. For sizing, you can increase or decrease the current dimensions in the W or H field by adding or subtracting, as in "+3p3" (or −.125"). Or to scale by some percent, type "*.5" (multiply by 50%, reduce) or "*1.25" (enlarge to 125%). If you have a picture selected, you can modify the X% and Y% fields by any amount, such as +20 (%), −40, *2.5 (multiply = 250% larger) or /3 (divide by 3).

ALIGNING BY X AND Y

The pros and production geeks align items by X and Y for three reasons. Quark's Space/Align dialog is a muddle. Using the Measurements palette is fast and ready to go. Best of all, you choose which item stays in place and which one moves to align—a privilege Space/Align doesn't offer. Top- and left-aligning are easy. Select the item that stays put— item #1. In the Measurements palette, highlight and copy the Y value to top-align and X to left-align. Select the #2 item. Paste into the same field you used to copy, then Return or Enter. You're done. For bottom- or right-alignment, copy the Y or X of #1, then select #2 and paste into the same field. Now they're top- or left-aligned. For #2, the one that's aligning, subtract its H from its Y. Then add the H of #1 *to* the Y of #2. On second thought, just use X and Y for top- and left-alignments!

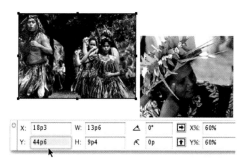 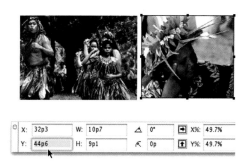

   WHEN RULES NEED TO TOP ALIGN TO OTHER ITEMS

This tip isn't for paragraph rules, but for lines you draw with the Orthogonal (perpendicular) Line tool. The problem with a line is that there's no way to specify its location except from its vertical center line. Because the thickness of the line lies on either side of that center line, a picture can't be top-aligned to it. Ah, but you can *if* you change the line to a box having the same dimension in H or W as the line "width" or weight. So when it comes to production, select each line and in the Measurements palette, change the Line Modes popup from Endpoints to anything else. Copy length L and paste it into the W for a selected horizontal box or H for vertical. The other box dimension is the line width. For 12pt, type "p12." Now the upper-left corner of the box can align by X or Y to another item.

LOCATE AN ITEM FROM THE BOTTOM OF THE PAGE

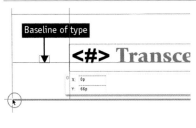

I like to position the page footer and page number at some pica unit from the bottom page edge. Moving the zero point to the bottom of the page makes it easy! Zoom way in to the lower-left corner of the page. Then drag from the intersection of the rulers in the top-left corner of the layout window to the lower-left corner of the page. You see a floating perpendicular axis as you drag. On the Measurements palette, watch the dynamic X and Y locations of the axis. When it says 0 and 66p (11" standard page), release the mouse. Because X and Y still refer to the box origin, upper-left corner, put a horizontal ruler guide down for the baseline of the footer at 1p6 (.25") from the bottom. As you drag the guide, watch the Y location until it says –1p6 or –.25". Now position the baseline of the footer on the guide.

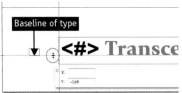

   ## SIZE A BOX *AND ITS CONTENTS* PROPORTIONALLY

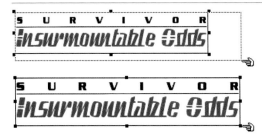

Trying to size an image or graphic by the numbers is a very long-winded process. Try one number after another, typing the percent twice each time in the Measurements palette, once for X%, again for Y%. If you eventually hit it right, you're still not done. You've got to get the box to the same size. Instead, grab a handle of the box while pressing Cmd-Option-Shift or Ctrl-Alt-Shift as you drag out to make it bigger or drag in to make it smaller. Try the same thing with an *unlinked* text box—the box and the type get proportionally bigger or smaller. It's quite useful if you're trying to get the type to fit a specific space on the page, like the width of two or three columns. When you let go, you can check the point size in the palette, which reflects its scaled point size.

⬤   **SIZE TYPE OR PICTURES INCREMENTALLY**

Sometimes you're not sure how you want it until you can *see* it right. Here's a tip to help you try on various sizes to see which size fits best—without dragging. Hold down all three power keys and repeatedly press > to go larger or < to go smaller.

- **Mac:** Cmd-Option-Shift-> or <
- **Win:** Ctrl-Alt-Shift-> or <

With pictures, you can have the Item or Content tool. The X% and Y% change in 5% increments (and the box stays the same size). With text, you must have the type highlighted with the Content tool. The size changes in 1pt increments.

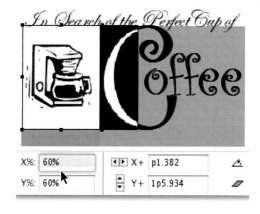 

   TRANSFORMING BOXES

Use the Measurements palette to numerically control box attributes by typing new numbers or using calculations. On the left half of the palette, the Item side, change the box Width (W) or Height (H), or rotate a box and its contents. Rotate *just* the contents on the Content side, the palette's right half. Size type there, or use X% and Y% to size images and graphics, but not the box itself. In the lower-right corner, skew an image within a box. With rotation and skewing, the direction indicated by the icon is a positive number, in .001 degrees. To rotate clockwise or skew northwest, type a negative number. Change the corner radius of a picture box or, with the black arrows, flip its contents horizontally or vertically. Do these also—plus skew text—in Modify (Cmd-M or Ctrl-M) or double-click the box with the Item tool or, with the Content tool, Cmd- or Ctrl-double-click.

See also "Measurements Palette *Calculates* Moving and Sizing" (this chapter).

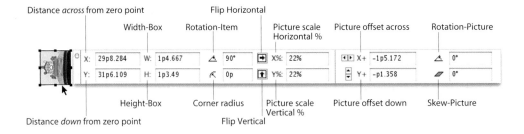

Distance *across* from zero point — Width-Box — Rotation-Item — Flip Horizontal — Picture scale Horizontal % — Picture offset across — Rotation-Picture

| X: | 29p8.284 | W: | 1p4.667 | | 90° | | X%: | 22% | | X+ | −1p5.172 | | 0° |
| Y: | 31p6.109 | H: | 1p3.49 | | 0p | | Y%: | 22% | | Y+ | −p1.358 | | 0° |

Distance *down* from zero point — Height-Box — Corner radius — Flip Vertical — Picture scale Vertical % — Picture offset down — Skew-Picture

ROTATE AN ITEM FREELY OR IN FIXED INCREMENTS

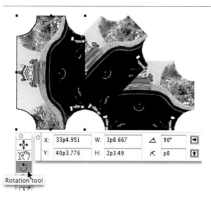

Rotation tool

Grab the Rotation tool (Option- or Alt-click the tool to use it more than once). Press your mouse down at the point around which you will pivot your selected box or item. Choosing this point is a key advantage of using the Rotation tool over entering a number in the Measurements palette. Then drag your mouse away from that spot. With your mouse still down, drag the mouse clockwise or counter-clockwise to rotate that thing in thousandths of a point. (If you drag with your mouse close by the pivot point, it's hard to control because each tiny mouse move is many degrees.)

Pressing the Shift key, the constraining key in computer graphics, you can constrain the rotations to 45° intervals—0°, 45°, 90°, etc.—some of "our most popular" rotations.

EXPERIENCE THE REAL THING, NOT THE BOX

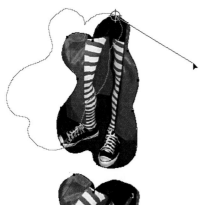

Here's where "the pause that refreshes" pays off. When you rotate an item using the Rotate tool, usually you press down, drag out, then swing counter-clockwise or clockwise—with not a moment to lose. And what do you see as you rotate the item? A black-outlined empty box? Hmm…hard to imagine what it's really going to look like. Instead, after you press down to mark the point of origin, pause for a second. ("Look both ways and then proceed.") That pause gives Quark a chance to collect the image in RAM so that when you rotate, you see the image, graphic, or text that's inside, not just the box. Hurray!

See also "Rotate an Item Freely or in Fixed Increments" (previous tip).

DELETE AN ITEM WITH THE CONTENT TOOL

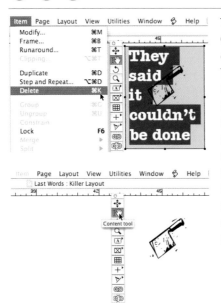

This tip is definitely on my short list wherever I go. Quark can be so finicky about some things. For example, you need the Content tool to do Get Text. But then it can be so lax about other things, like *not* needing the Content tool to do Get Picture. However, deleting an item is one thing Quark is strict about. *Thou shalt select the Item tool to delete an item.* So there. Well, the dictum does seem impervious except for one little fact. From the Item menu, there's a Delete command with a keyboard shortcut! So when you're in the Content tool, which is at least 50% of your time, you can delete an item by simply pressing Cmd-K or Ctrl-K ("K" for "Kill the ball," in racquetball).

DON'T ACCIDENTALLY DELETE A LOCKED ITEM

Seems contrary to all common sense, but in fact it's true—you *can* delete a locked item! Heavens! What's this world coming to? Well, in Quark, locking has a very specific meaning. A locked item can't be moved and can't be sized. But anything else is okay. You can edit the text, you can color the box, you can delete the contents, and you can delete the box. So this is just a fair warning of what you can expect if you don't watch out!

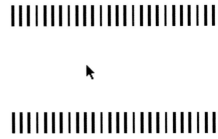

COMIC RELIEF—DELETE WITH MARTIANS OR MELTDOWN

This tip might even fit into the category of "party pleaser"— it's so unexpected! Definitely an inside-track effect. Draw a big picture or text box or select one on your page. On the Mac, your delights last longer if the item is on the right side of the screen. Then press…

- **Mac:** Cmd-Option-Shift-K
- **Win:** Ctrl-Alt-Shift-K

…and see what happens! (Okay, you can undo.)

Enjoy the Scenery

IMAGES →

If type is the King of Page Design, pictures are Queens. Everyone's probably had their fair share of all-text layouts.

Enjoy the Scenery
picture tips

Formatting is tedious, and you work hard to make the page lively. But plunk down a few colored pictures—it's swing time! We've got tips here on how and what to import, fitting pictures to their boxes, cropping, and sizing multiple ways. And how to deal with scanned and digital images without killing image resolution. Those differences between bitmaps and vectors are profound with many prices to pay if you're not careful—the worst being fuzzy images and type! Then, lots of tips on picture effects, warping, making them negative, coloring them, faux duotones, and skewing. Tips on making clipping paths in Quark—we can finally see what we're doing with the new full-resolution preview for images and especially for imported EPS graphics! Finally, importing images to keep file size low and updating pictures. Here's a chapter you can really sink your teeth into. Happy imaging!

DID YOU KNOW YOU CAN IMPORT A PDF?

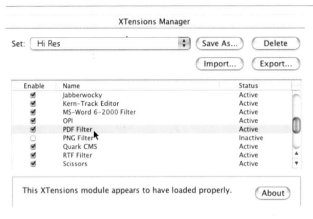

Yes, finally you can import a PDF into Quark and make one there also. To import, just use Get Picture and click the PDF Import tab at the bottom of the dialog, then enter the page number you want (if there's more than one). To export a file, go to File> Export> Layout as PDF. It's the PDF Filter, a Quark XTension that's on by default, which makes it so easy. You might find one day that it doesn't work, however, if you happened to turn it off in XTensions Manager or switched to a different XTensions set. Go check the XTensions Manager (Utilities menu). Click in the Enable column to turn it back on. But you'll have to relaunch Quark for the XTension to take effect.

   GOT A TWO-COLOR JOB AND FOUR-COLOR IMAGES?

You're doing a two-color newsletter or three-color brochure, and your client gave you full color images. You could go into Photoshop and do the mode conversion to grayscale, but why bother. You're just getting started. The pictures could change, all kinds of things could happen that would make that work unnecessary. Don't bother. Instead, do an on-the-fly color conversion. Got your picture box selected, with the Get Picture dialog open and your picture file selected? Then, for the Mac, Cmd-press and hold until you see the image in your box; for Windows, Ctrl-click the Open button. That full color image now looks just like a grayscale TIFF for your comp—and it even prints that way. But in fact, the file on your hard drive is still full color. That's the only thing you've got to remember if and when the picture makes it to final production—go convert it!

DRAG AND DROP PICTURES FROM YOUR DESKTOP
(*WINDOWS ONLY*)

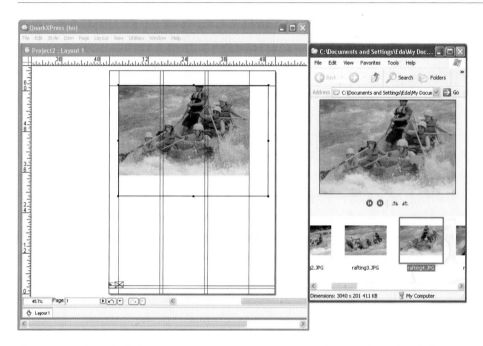

If you have a bunch of pictures to import, open Windows Explorer or, from the desktop, open the folder with the picture files and position the window off to the side of the screen so that the filenames show. Back in Quark, size the window down so that you've got a few inches. You can further clear that area by collapsing any palettes—double-click the title bar. Now you should be able to see that window with the picture files on the side. Go to Fit in Window (Ctrl-0) or a more reduced view so you can see the greatest number of picture boxes. Then just reach out and touch that first picture file and drag and drop it into a box! Repeat until done.

FIT TO BOX AND BOX IT UP

Quick-fitting an image to its box proportionally is a neat way to get an oversized image to a manageable size in one leap—great for those 8 × 10" mug shots that need to be only 1 × 2". You've always been able to do Cmd-Option-Shift-F or Ctrl-Alt-Shift-F ("F" for "Fit to Box"). In Quark 5, it became a command in the Style and Context menus—Fit Picture To Box (Proportionally). Here's the idea. Make a picture box on your page roughly the size and shape you want when done, perhaps sized to the width of a column or two. Get Picture, press the Fit to Box keys, and now it's the right size. But the box doesn't fit on all sides. Because it's a proportional fit, it fits one dimension only. So here's the second tip—do Fit Box to Picture, very fast from the Context menu (press Control/Mac or right-click/Win). Now it's just right!

CROPPING—UP CLOSE AND PERSONAL

Don't go changing copy that the editor or client gave you. But "hands off" doesn't apply to pictures. Artistic license is a must! Leaving space around the subject psychologically distances the viewer from the subject. Lay photography, rampant in not-for-profit and government work, is the worst—grass, ceiling fans, the car next door, you name it. Instead, crop in on images so they seem to explode at the edges, heightening the drama. If a subject is in three-quarter view, crop the back tightly and leave more space in the direction the subject's facing. Crop off the top inch or two of someone's head—it's not a lobotomy. Just drag the picture box handle in on the image—no keys. Then, with the Content tool, drag inside the box to position the image dynamically. Polish it with the arrow keys to nudge it a bit more, with the Content tool in hand.

GET THE PICTURE CENTERED

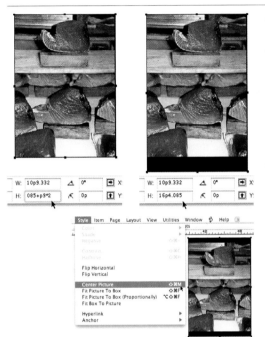

Centering an image or graphic in a box seems simple, but it's quite difficult to do—that is, without the Center Picture command (Style menu) and the shortcut Cmd-Shift-M or Ctrl-Shift-M. Very useful if you want to have a flat or blended color surrounding your image. I prefer a bar of color at the top, or top and bottom, but not on the sides. For a bar at the top and bottom, do the Fit Box To Picture command (Style menu). Then use the Measurements palette to extend the box down two times the height of one bar. After the H value, type, "+p9*2" (or +.125"*2). Then press Return or Enter. Finish with Center Picture and color the box background. For a bar above, drop the *2 and just add the height of the color bar to H. Then change the Y+ field to that same number, "p9" (or .125").

EYEBALL IT

Yosemite National Park

When it comes to sizing images and graphics on the page, numbers are great for the second, third, and fourth ones in a set. But for the first one, you want to see it the right size, not guess at a number. When you type a percent, and that's actually one percent typed two times (X% and Y% in the Measurements palette), you're guessing—one number after another until "it's good enough." Instead, drag the picture by any handle, pressing all three keys—"lean on the keyboard"—Cmd-Option-Shift or Ctrl-Alt-Shift. Special perk—the box and image are both sized together. The handle *opposite* the one you drag stays fixed. To size a picture to the width of a column, when the picture is snapped to the left column guide, drag from a handle on the right side. Keep a picture centered in your layout—drag from the top or bottom center handle.

NEED THE PICTURE BIGGER, BUT NOT THE BOX?

This is one I use all the time. I often draw a picture box the size I want for the layout. Bring in a picture, do a Fit to Box. But now the picture needs to be bigger to successfully fill that box, allowing for some cropping. You can size just the image and not the box, in 5% increments by pressing:

- **Mac:** Cmd-Option-Shift-> or -<
- **Win:** Ctrl-Alt-Shift-> or -<

Sound familiar? It's exactly what you do to size type in 1pt increments! Word of warning—your best quality image comes with no sizing, 100%. With a 300ppi image, however, you can safely size up to about 120% and still have acceptable quality. Based on a 150-line screen (lpi) or less, a 225ppi image is all you need for most brochure and magazine work.

THOU SHALT KNOW THY BITS AND PIECES

Bitmaps and vectors, photographs and graphics—the most fundamental concepts in computer graphics are no place for fuzzy thinking or you can ruin a great layout. A bitmap image, like a TIFF, consists of rows of dots or pixels, having a *fixed* resolution, measured in pixels per inch (ppi) and output to dots per inch (dpi). By contrast, vectors, like a "true" EPS, or drawn objects, have *no* resolution. They're just a set of instructions and the quality is determined on output by the resolution of the printer. An EPS from Illustrator, Freehand, or CorelDRAW can be scaled to any percent in Quark, big or small, and it's fine. But scale a TIFF image in Quark to 200%—a 300ppi resolution drops to half (150ppi)! As for the faux EPS—if it looks like a photo, it's a bitmap, whether or not the label says EPS—buyer beware! And if it's a real EPS but has an imported bitmap within, the same rules apply.

ULTIMATE SYSTEM FOR AVOIDING BAD RESOLUTION

A major dilemma in laying out pictures—when you scan images, you don't know how big or small you'll use them in the layout. If you enlarge them in Quark, they can be ruined and with reducing, there can also be problems. Try this three-pass system. Scan all pictures at 100% at 72dpi—the low-res is faster with this method and the 100% scale makes the math easier! Import them into Quark, and scale each one to fit the layout. On a hard copy, record the percent of enlargement or reduction, reading the X% and Y% in the Measurements palette for the selected box. For enlarged pictures, rescan them at the percents used in the layout, at 225ppi or higher. Re-import them into the same boxes, no additional scaling. *If pictures are digital to start,* try sizing them up or down in Photoshop with resampling *off.* You can gain resolution by sizing down or, if you have 300ppi, you can increase the dimensions, but don't go below 225ppi resolution (for 150lpi output, that's usually fine). For pictures you've sized smaller, rescanning isn't necessary if you've used hi-res images to start. However, if you have multiple hi-res images sized down, printing can really slow down.

   ## FUZZY TYPE IN YOUR PHOTOSHOP IMAGE?

If you want to add text to your image in Photoshop, but it's going to be straight type—no Gaussian blurs or other filter effects—add that type in Quark! Then you'll know the type will output properly, be vector-based Postscript, and not have fuzzy, anti-aliased edges. The fact is, there are numerous ways to go wrong with type in Photoshop. Best bet is to save the file as EPS, *but* you must never, never open that image back up in Photoshop. The text layer rasterizes and becomes a bitmap at the resolution of your image. Instead, if there are changes, go back to your master .psd file, make the change, and save a new EPS to replace the first. But other reasons to do it in Quark? You can move the type around independently of the image, and when there are text changes, there are no trips back to Photoshop.

GRAPHICS AS FUN-HOUSE MIRRORS

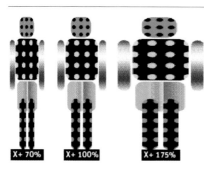

X+ 70%   X+ 100%   X+ 175%

This is one of those weird effects—sizing a box and its picture together *non-proportionally*. You're more likely to use this one with an EPS graphic, not a TIFF. Photographic images, being snapshots of the "real world," usually require fidelity. But graphics are pure metaphor and rarely attempt to be realistic—and when they try to be, they usually fail miserably. The beauty of graphics is their boldness, their ability to make a point with impact by emphasizing the main thing. That makes them good subjects for non-proportional scaling, besides having no resolution issues to deal with. Go ahead, Cmd-drag or Ctrl-drag a handle of an imported true EPS. As you drag wide, the graphic, well, puts on weight. Drag it narrow, the graphic quickly loses it. Someone please Cmd-drag my hips—in!

ACCESSING IMAGE EDITING COMMANDS *(MAC ONLY)*

The following two tips are fun ways to work with images in Quark using the image editing commands from the Style menu. However, on the Mac, there's one hitch—a Display application preference setting that imports TIFF images at 32-bits (color depth). Change this setting (Cmd-Option-Shift-Y) to 8-bit. Then import the image again and you'll be able to use the Negative and Contrast commands. Don't worry, the original picture file on your hard drive won't be altered. The 8-bit preference is only for *screen display*, and it doesn't affect the bit depth when printed. On a different front, Mac users get more options using the image editing dialogs. Use Cmd-Z to undo your last move so you can try something else without closing the dialog. Apply your choices with Cmd-A.

See also **"Negative and Positive Together"** and **"Faux Duotones #1" (next tips).**

NEGATIVE AND POSITIVE TOGETHER

Very cool effect to pair positive and negative images. Duplicate a picture box on top of the original by pressing Cmd-Option-D or Ctrl-Alt-D. In Step and Repeat, set the offsets to zero, then click OK. Move the copy over so it's butted—copy the Width (W) field in the Measurements palette. Select the duplicate, add the W to the X position (or add the Height (H) to the Y). Now they're side by side. Make one negative with Cmd-Shift-Hyphen or Ctrl-Shift-Hyphen. Black turns white, red turns cyan, green turns magenta, and so on. Then flip it horizontally using the Flip Horizontal arrow on the palette. Try a checkerboard of four! Works for TIFF (not 1-bit), JPEG, GIF, plus a few more—but not EPS. Using these image editing commands only affects the way the images are displayed and printed from Quark. Picture files on your drive are unaffected. It's better to use Quark's image tools for comping and do the final in Photoshop.

   FAUX DUOTONES #1

This spectacular and unusual effect is not a duotone. Think of duotones as images in which two inks, usually black and a spot color, are mixed together in some proportion. In a classic duotone, the image is a grayscale of that mixed color, going from white down to black, so it looks pretty realistic. By contrast, the faux duotone is like a grayscale image with a veil of flat color dropped on top. In essence, all the white in the image is replaced by the second color. This is easier to do in Quark than in Photoshop! First, set up your spot color in Edit> Colors (Shift-F12). Then import a grayscale TIFF image into a selected picture box. Now for the surprise finish—in the Colors palette, change the box background color to the spot color. Presto, your image is utterly transformed. For a softer look, use a tint of the background color.

FAUX DUOTONES #2

For an even more surreal effect, let's do another tip for grayscale images, using black and a spot color or two different spot colors. With your grayscale TIFF image in a selected picture box, go to the Colors palette (F12). Click the top-middle button to apply a color to the *image*, and, with the button on the right, apply a *second* color to the box background. Wow! If you're using black and one color, try making the box background color black and the image the second color. Either of the two colors can be tinted. Word of warning from my service bureau—if pictures like these are going into a multi-page layout that will later be imposed at the printers (making printer spreads, not reader spreads), the background color drops out! It's not Quark's fault—the imposition software is to blame.

  TURN A BORING IMAGE INTO A GRAPHIC

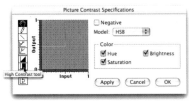

Make lackluster images experimental and fun using Quark's Contrast dialog. Select your picture, which can be any of the file types named previously. Press Cmd-Shift-C or Ctrl-Shift-C to open Picture Contrast Specifications. Try out any of nine buttons along the left edge. The Posterize button reduces all the tonal and saturation values (color or grayscale) to just six gray/color levels. The Poster*izer* lets you set 10 levels that you can adjust in the graphing area. Click the Inversion Button to flip the graph of input and output—similar in theory to Negative, but different results. For a totally wacky, psychedelic look, draw an up-and-down mountainous graph with the Pencil tool. Use Apply, then reset the image with the Normal Contrast tool, six down from the top. Again, you'll get better quality with comparable techniques in Photoshop.

See also "Negative and Positive Together" (this chapter).

SKEW A GRAPHIC OR IMAGE WITHIN A BOX

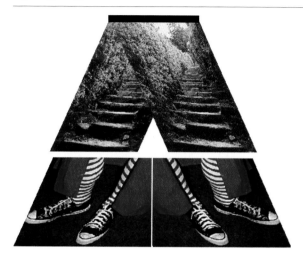

Give an image a more emotional and intense look by skewing it—changing it from a rectangle into a parallelogram. You can make the effect more subtle by skewing just the image, not the box. Select your picture box, then in the Measurements palette, way over in the far lower-right corner, enter a number of degrees for Picture Skew. If you've got other tricks you want to do in the Modify dialog, you can also do your picture skew in the Picture tab (Cmd-M or Ctrl-M). It doesn't take much to make a statement—10 to 15 degrees goes far, unless you want a really exaggerated effect. The last step is optional. You can leave the edges of the image as a parallelogram, or size down the box from the sides so that the overall shape of the picture still looks rectangular.

MAKING A CLIPPING PATH

Quark clipping paths (Cmd-Option-T or Ctrl-Alt-T) drop out a light or white background around your subject—even without a clip path from Photoshop. (For Photoshop paths saved with TIFF, EPS, or JPEG images, select Embedded Path in Type popup or with TIFF, also Alpha Channel.) Otherwise, select Non-White Areas. Decreasing Outset and increasing Threshold do the lion's share of dropping background pixels. Decrease Outset by small amounts using a negative number to remove pixels at the path edge. Tolerance affects the number of background gray levels that drop out overall. If you have too many points, increase Noise and Smoothness in small amounts. Click OK, then you can manually fine-tune the clipping path, just like a runaround. Press Option-Shift-F4 or Ctrl-Shift-F10 (Item> Edit> Clipping Path) to see the clipping path right on the page. Drag the path (pointing finger with "\" cursor) or a point (with a "■" cursor). Click on a point and adjust its handles or change the type of point from the Measurements palette.

SHORT TIPS FOR CLIPPING PATHS

From Contemporary People stock photo CD by Dynamic Graphics.
Courtesy Chuck Boysen, Director of Marketing.

Putting that image on another color? Before you open Clipping Paths, apply the box background color you're planning on using behind your outlined image. Having that background in place lets you see how good your clipping path is when you click Apply in the dialog. Those light pixel halos at the edges of your subject really pop out with a colored background!

Holes in your images? Many times the subject you're outlining with a dropped out background has areas within that also need the background dropped out, like pretzels. Easy to do—just uncheck Outside Edges Only in Clipping Paths dialog.

Fill the shape of your clipping path with another image.

Here's an attention grabber—how many times have you seen the shape of an outlined image filled with another image? It takes only two-steps. First, in Clipping Paths, get your path set up, then click Invert and Apply. You should see the background of the image, but the foreground subject is dropped out. Click OK, then do Step and Repeat, setting offsets to zero, to make a duplicate box #2 on top. Do Get Picture to import another image into that box. Then send #2 to the back using Shift-F5 so #2's image is now only visible through the empty clipping path of the first box, now on top.

FULL-RESOLUTION PREVIEW FOR IMAGES

At last! Quark 6 gives you full-resolution preview. In the past, making clipping paths in Quark was for comping only, because how could you make an elegant edge from a 72dpi preview? Now images can be seen looking their best, even when you zoom in on them, assuming they're 225 to 300dpi. However, there is an uneasy twist—getting to the preview has two levels. First, go to Preferences (Cmd-Option-Shift-Y or Ctrl-Alt-Shift-Y), click Full Res Preview, an Application preference. Then uncheck Disable Full Resolution Previews on Open so that all your pictures will automatically import with the *potential* for hi-res preview. But if you have a lot of pictures, you might also want to check Selected Full Resolution Previews. If not, choose All Full Resolution Previews. Now, whether or not the picture displays at hi-res also depends on the View menu setting: Hide Full Res Previews. If this says Show instead, your imported pictures display at 72ppi. Finally, if you're not sure what resolution your pictures are at, just select one or more, then go to Item> Preview Resolution> Low or > Full Resolution, and make your choice.

See also "Full-Resolution Preview on the Fly" (next tip).

   FULL-RESOLUTION PREVIEW ON THE FLY

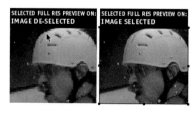

Although full-resolution preview is a huge step forward, like most great things, moderation may be needed. Why? Let's say you're doing a product catalog or just have a lot of pictures. If they're all viewing at full strength, that could certainly slow down Quark's performance as you scroll, change views, or change pages. How about turning on the preview only when you need it? Go to preferences (Cmd-Option-Shift-Y or Ctrl-Alt-Shift-Y) and click the Full Res Preview preference under Application preferences. On the right, click Selected Full Resolution Previews under Display Full Resolution Preview. From now on, only pictures that you've selected preview at full res. Practical! Set the Full Res Preview for any image on import (or from Item> Preview Resolution> Full Resolution).

See also "Full-Resolution Preview for Images" (previous tip).

LOWER THAN LOW—KEEP THAT FILE SIZE DOWN

72 DPI DISPLAY   36 DPI DISPLAY

Ever do a product catalog? Or an annual report? When you import a lot of pictures into a Quark file—even though those representations on your page are low-res bitmaps (72dpi) linked to hi-res files on your drive—all those low-res bits add up and your Quark file can put on weight! Keep your file size down and speed up scrolling by importing those images at 36dpi. In the Get Picture dialog, select your picture file, then press Shift and click Open. (Mac users, keep pressing Shift until you see the image on your page.) Now that set of dots on your page, though not quite as clear, is adding only half the calories to your file size! The file on your hard drive is the same as it ever was.

  ## QUARK, SERVANT OF MINE, ALERT ME TO PICTURE CHANGES

Some pictures in this project have been modified. Do you want to update them?
Note: Only modified pictures will be updated. There may also be missing pictures, select Usage in the Utilities menu to view and update these.

No   Yes

Here's one way you can slough off a bit. By setting a little preference, you can put Quark to work checking for pictures that have been changed or are missing. Go to Preferences by pressing Cmd-Option-Shift-Y or Ctrl-Alt-Shift-Y. Click the General (Print Layout) preference. Then check Verify under Auto Picture Import. From now on, when you open that Quark file and the linked picture files have changed (but retain the same filenames), Quark alerts you and asks you if you want to update them in one fell swoop. Click OK. Or, if you want to examine each instance, click Cancel and go to Utilities> Picture Usage after the file opens. Of course, if you want this feature to be in effect for all new files you create, close all open Quark files *before* you go to Preferences.

UPDATE THAT PICTURE AND RETAIN CROPPING AND SIZING

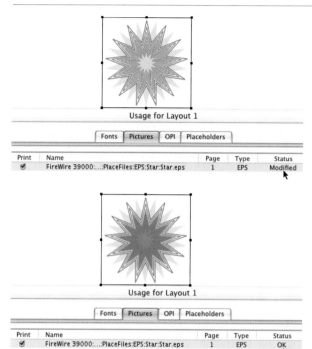

Usage for Layout 1

	Fonts	Pictures	OPI	Placeholders			
Print	**Name**				**Page**	**Type**	**Status**
☑	FireWire 39000:...:PlaceFiles:EPS:Star:Star.eps				1	EPS	Modified

Usage for Layout 1

	Fonts	Pictures	OPI	Placeholders			
Print	**Name**				**Page**	**Type**	**Status**
☑	FireWire 39000:...:PlaceFiles:EPS:Star:Star.eps				1	EPS	OK

You've got a bunch of pictures on your page that have been sized, cropped, rotated, skewed, reversed, inverted, or whatever the heck you did to those things. And now many of them have newer versions (with the same filenames). Oh dear. If you use the Get Picture command, you'll have to first record the modifications you made to each picture so you can reenter them again (in the Measurements palette or image editing commands in the Style menu). But halt everything—spare yourself the grief. Instead, update all your images in Utilities> Usage, Picture tab (Option-F13/Mac or Shift-F2/Win) and everything you've done to those images is remembered. Just select the file or files in the list whose Status says Modified, then click Update. After getting your okay, Quark brings in the new and keeps the existing sizing, cropping, rotating, and whatever. You can relax.

Gas Keeps You Goin'

Text is the backbone of virtually every designer's job. Just think how much time you spend importing text, linking text, cleaning up text, highlighting text,

Gas Keeps You Goin'
import text & word processing tips

formatting text, editing text, deleting text, searching text, and maybe even proofing text. In short, you're coming and going text. Which is why I devote three whole chapters to the subject, including some of the longest in the book. This chapter deals with the most tedious end of that spectrum. The farther down the line you go, the more interesting type becomes. With a great style sheet, you can practically fly through text formatting. But back to now. Yes, importing, linking, and doing those word processing things are boring. And that's precisely why you need these tips more than practically anything else—so you can get through them faster and onto other more fun and creative exploits. If you just allow all those people who give you text files to run amuck, your type will look like it belongs in Word. (What an insult!) Take charge, make that type look good. Digging into the trenches is the only way out.

WHEN GETTING TEXT, LINK FEWER BOXES

Text placed on page	LINKED BEFORE SIZING	
When the text is large in point size, then it takes a lot more boxes and a lot more clicking to put all the text on pages. But if you	follow the tip and size the type down before you make your first link, you'll have less to do and can go on to the next thing on	your to-do list— maybe even go home early d!

Text placed on page	SIZED BEFORE LINKING	
When the text is large in point size, then it takes a lot more boxes and a lot more clicking to put all the text on pages. But if you follow the tip and size the type down before you make your first link, you'll have less to do and can go on to the next thing on your to-	do list—maybe even go home early!	

Typically, people use larger type when they're trying to write something. But put that same text into a multi-column layout and the point size should be smaller, because now you've got columns, not text running the full width of the page. So why link a bunch of boxes on multiple pages when you get text, and then find, after you size down the type, that you have more boxes and pages than you need? Instead, get text into that first box but before you link, size down the type. Click the Content tool in the text box. Then do Select-All (Cmd-A or Ctrl-A, or click five times) to highlight not only that text, but also all the text *in the file* that you can't see yet on the page. Pick a smaller point size. Now when you start your linking, you'll have fewer boxes to draw and link, and fewer pages to add.

SAVE ENDLESS TIME WHEN YOU'VE GOT LOTS OF LINKS

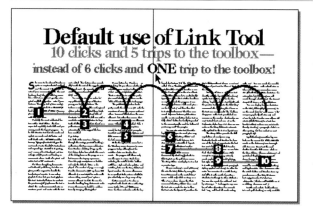

Default use of Link Tool
10 clicks and 5 trips to the toolbox—
instead of 6 clicks and ONE trip to the toolbox!

Linking can be a snap or real tedious. By default, you can make a single link with two clicks and then you lose the Link tool— instead, you've got the Item or Content tool, whichever you had last. If you have a lot of text to link and you keep having to return to the toolbox to pick up the Link tool, it's aggravating. Instead, keep the Link tool for as long as you like by pressing Option or Alt when you click to select the tool in the toolbox. Now you can just do a single click on each box to flow text there. Click on the first box, then the next box, then the next, and so on. No stopping.

WORRY-FREE LINKING AND UNLINKING

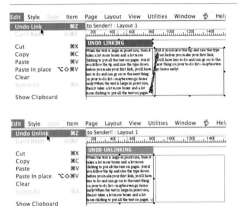

After all these years, Quark has finally changed our lives for the good on a small but important point. When you use the Link or Unlink tool, you can now undo! Yes, it seems so natural, so right that you wouldn't even bat an eye. Yet, it has never been true before Quark 6. I used to counsel my students to save before linking or unlinking, then use the Revert To Saved command to recover from a series of bad links or a drastic unlink. After all, one unlinking click on the head or tail feathers of the link arrow between two text boxes not only breaks the link, but all the following text is instantly swept up from your pages and replaced with that red "X" saying "more text to link." Now, however, we can proceed blithely through the roses without a care in mind. (Why did they wait so long?)

YOU'RE LINKING AND YOU'RE OUT OF PAGES

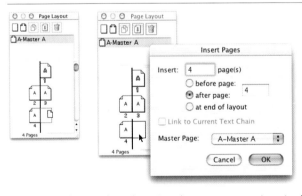

Unless you're using the Automatic Text box or doing a one-page layout, you'll be adding pages when you start linking. Shortcut to the Insert Pages dialog to add a bunch of pages at one time, pick the master page they'll be based on, and specify exactly where those pages will be added— before or after the page you name or at the end of the layout.

This is way shorter than dragging the master page icon in the Page Layout palette down into the pages area for each page you want to add. Instead, drag the master page icon down into the pages area, but only once and do it while pressing Option or Alt. Then once you're there, release the mouse *before* Option or Alt and the Insert Pages dialog pops right open. Easy!

   ### DON'T LET YOUR BODY COPY GO WANDERING

I came to recognize these ago-
nized conversations from the
moment I picked up the phone.
When I heard the pained voice
on the other end of the line, I
knew that once again, I was in
for a hard time. My energy level
dropped as I sank into the nearest chair by the residential phone
in my office. What was it now, I
wondered. Instantly I knew that
again, I had managed to disap-
point her badly. It always
seemed to come from out of the
blue, I never could anticipate the
timing, though I tried; although
thinking as it was usually
after I had left some message

question on her voice mail.
Dreams of another time
in the Chinese Gardens.

Writers often combine various text elements into one text file instead of having to track a bunch of small files—one for body copy and others for captions, sidebars, etc. But when you lay out that text in a series of linked boxes, you've got trouble waiting to happen. Ever done a job with no editing changes? So you're adding a few more lines on page one, failing to notice that a few more lines of body copy have been pushed back into your first caption box and the first few lines of that caption have now drifted into the second caption box, etc. Trouble, trouble, trouble. Save yourself headaches. After you link text boxes, before you do anything else, check to see what follows the main story. Cut and paste each caption, sidebar, or whatever into its own text box so it stays put.

   ### TO UNLINK OR NOT UNLINK?

You need a picture area with a text box filling the column that's part of a larger text chain. If you unlink the box from the text chain—oops! All subsequent boxes are drained of text. (You can Undo!) Instead, delete the text box with the Item tool or change its content (Item> Content> Picture). Presto! The text in that box passes into the next box in the chain. Here's another one—you want to make a sidebar or pull quote with a box that's now occupied with body copy. You can Shift-click on the box with the Unlink tool to unlink it from the text chain and force that text into the next linked box. Now you've got an empty text box to work with. Finally, check the last box in the chain to see if text is overset. See a red "X?"

HIGHLIGHTING ALL THE TEXT THAT'S THERE? DON'T DRAG

Clear	
Select All	**⌘A**
Show Clipboard	
Find/Change	⌘F

Everyone uses the Select All command to highlight all the text of a story for formatting, first clicking the Content tool in any text box of the story. But when it comes to highlighting all the text in a headline or caption, don't you often resort to dragging the Content tool across the text? Not a great idea, because you don't just do it once, you do it all the time. That's a lot of stress on your hand. Did you know that every time you drag the mouse, you're constricting the blood vessels in your wrist, which over time accelerates the onset of those repetitive motion symptoms we all dread? So here's one place where you can use better ergonomics, at no extra cost. Just do Select All with Cmd-A or Ctrl-A after you click the Content tool on the box, and presto—all the text is highlighted. Nothing like it.

DON'T DESELECT THE TEXT TO SEE WHAT YOU DID

This is absolutely one of the neatest things about Quark and entirely unique in page layout software, to my knowledge. When you've highlighted some type and made some styling choices, you want to see how it looks without the highlighting. But don't click *inside* the box to deselect. Okay, that does the job, but when you want to make further changes, you've got to re-highlight the text after you've had a look. Remember that every single extra motion is magnified into dozens or hundreds of moves through the life of a job. Instead, click *outside* the box to deselect the box and see the text without highlighting, then click back on the box, and the *highlighting is remembered* for your next styling move!

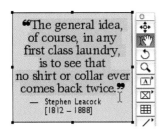 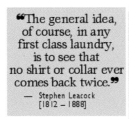 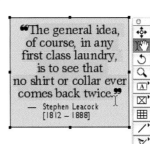

SELECTING A WORD, LINE, OR PARAGRAPH AND MORE

Selecting a word, a line, a paragraph, and a story:

	Mac and Windows
Word	Double-click it
Word with punctuation following	Double-click between the word and the punctuation
Line	Triple-click
Paragraph	Double-click twice (four clicks)
Story	Click five times; Cmd-A or Ctrl-A

Selecting text backward and forward using arrow keys:

	Mac and Windows	
Previous character	Shift-left *arrow*	
Next character	Shift-right	
Previous line	Shift-up	
Next line	Shift-down	
	Mac	**Windows**
Previous word*	Cmd-Shift-left *arrow*	Ctrl-Shift-left *arrow*
Next word*	Cmd-Shift-right	Ctrl-Shift-right
Previous paragraph*	Cmd-Shift-up	Ctrl-Shift-up
Next paragraph*	Cmd-Shift-down	Ctrl-Shift-down
To start of line	Cmd-Option-Shift-left	Ctrl-Alt-Shift-left
To end of line	Cmd-Option-Shift-right	Ctrl-Alt-Shift-right
To start of story	Cmd-Option-Shift-up	Ctrl-Alt-Shift-up
To end of story	Cmd-Option-Shift-down	Ctrl-Alt-Shift-down

The phrase "previous paragraph" is shorthand. If your insertion point is in the middle of a paragraph, this shortcut selects to the beginning of that same paragraph. If your insertion point is at the very beginning of a paragraph, it selects the entire previous paragraph. Next paragraph selects to the end of the current paragraph, etc. Previous and next word work similarly—previous selects from the insertion point to the beginning of the same word. If you are before or after a word space, it selects the entire previous word.

EASY TEXT EDITS OVER PICTURES—OPAQUE TEXT BOX EDITING

OPAQUE TEXT BOX EDITING OFF | OPAQUE TEXT BOX EDITING ON

☑ Opaque Text Box Editing

In Quark 6, text boxes no longer have a white background color—instead, it's None. That's good news. When you put text over an image, you won't have to remove that box color every time. But, when it comes to editing that text, it can be a strain. Get the best of both possible worlds—keep your see-through text boxes on top of pictures, but automatically give them white backgrounds when you edit the text. Go to Display application preferences with Cmd-Option-Shift-Y or Ctrl-Alt-Shift-Y, and check the option Opaque Text Box Editing. Now, when you edit, your lovely transparent text box that's sitting on a picture magically turns white! And even if your type is white, your text is still readable. Pretty cool.

See also "Set Picture Box Background Color to None" (Chapter 1).

   ## DRAG AND DROP TEXT—ALWAYS AND SOMETIMES

She walked ahead of him, without any thought of whether he was **following** her. Well, he'd show her—why not just ditch into the next side street and see how long it would take her to **notice**? then maybe she wouldn't take him for granted anymore. Yea, that sounded like a good idea, at least at the time. He felt **pretty glum.**

☑ Drag and Drop Text

Did you know you can edit text by using drag and drop with the Content tool instead of cutting and pasting? Set this up for all time by first closing all open Quark files. If you have a file open when you change the preference, drag and drop is good for *this file only*. Press Cmd-Option-Shift-Y or Ctrl-Alt-Shift-Y to open Application preferences. In the Interactive Application preference panel, check the Drag and Drop Text option. Once on, you can not only drag and drop highlighted text, you can make a copy simultaneously by Shift-dragging it. Note that you can do drag and drop only within a single story.

Mac users also have the choice to just do drag and drop on the fly:

- **Cut text as you drag:** Cmd-Control-drag
- **Copy text as you drag:** Cmd-Control-Shift-drag

MOVING THE INSERTION POINT USING ARROW KEYS

Use with Arrow Keys	Mac	Win	Mac and Win
Previous character			left *arrow*
Next character			right
Previous line			up
Next line			down
Previous word	Cmd-left *arrow*	Ctrl-left *arrow*	
Next word	Cmd-right	Ctrl-right	
Previous paragraph	Cmd-up	Ctrl-up	
Next paragraph	Cmd-down	Ctrl-down	
Start of line	Cmd-Option-left	Ctrl-Alt-left	
End of line	Cmd-Option-right	Ctrl-Alt-right	
Start of story	Cmd-Option-up	Ctrl-Alt-up	
End of story	Cmd-Option-down	Ctrl-Alt-down	

   ## DELETING CHARACTERS—SIX SHORTCUTS

Being adept and fast when editing makes the whole thing go a lot faster. Stopping to use the mouse is a real time sink. So get to know these shortcuts for highlighting type, moving the insertion point, and here, deleting characters. That way you can get to the fun parts sooner.

Element to Delete	Mac	Win
Highlighted characters	Delete	Backspace
Previous character	Delete	Backspace
Next character	Shift-Delete	Delete
Extended keyboard	Forward Delete (keypad)	
Previous word*	Cmd-Delete	Ctrl-Backspace
Next word	Cmd-Shift-Delete	Ctrl-Shift-Backspace

* Selects the entire word if the insertion point is in the word or in the space after it.

TYPING DUMB QUOTES—INCH AND FOOT MARKS

The Smart Quotes Interactive preference is on by default, and it gives you curly quotes instead of inch (12") and foot marks (1'). That's great most of the time, but what do you do when you actually need to have the inch and foot marks? Go back to the preference and turn it off, type, then turn it back on? Goodness no! Do this instead:

	Mac	**Win**
Foot mark	Control-'	Ctrl-'
Inch mark	Control-Shift-'	Ctrl-Alt-'

   GETTING A QUICK ZAPF DINGBAT *(MAC ONLY)*

Sometimes adding a Zapf Dingbat gives a little extra sparkle to the page. Then again, it's a drag to have to manually change the font. This tip lets you do it all with no highlighting and no mousing. It's perfect for bullets! Just type the combo-keys at an insertion point using Cmd-Option-Z to change the font to Zapf Dingbat. Then type the letter of your favorite dingbat from one of the four sets of characters:

- Typing the letter with no extra key
- Typing the letter with Shift
- Typing the letter with Option
- Typing the letter with Option-Shift

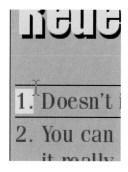 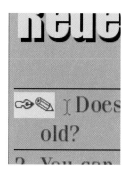 

PROOFING TEXT? SKIP THE PICTURES

When you're proofing text edits and typography, you've got to look at the *printed* page—the screen just doesn't work for final edits. But, when you print, why wait for the pictures on your pages to be imaged? Instead, go to the Options tab of the Print box (Cmd-P or Ctrl-P) and at the bottom left, for Picture Output, choose either Low Resolution or Rough instead of Normal. The Low Resolution setting prints the 72dpi bitmap that Quark uses to represent your image on the page. You get a look at your image next to your text, but not at the full resolution that comes from referencing the original picture file on your drive or network. The Rough setting is another step down from Low Resolution. Selecting Rough just puts a box with an "X" through it for every picture on the page, along with your text. Either way, you'll get faster hard copies, and that's all you need for this stage of your workflow.

MAKE SPELL-CHECKING GO FASTER AND DO MORE

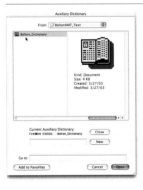

If you tend to use the same technical words, industry jargon, or foreign language words in your text, make things easier and more accurate when it comes to spell checking. Rather than stumble over certain words repeatedly, add them to an Auxiliary Dictionary so Quark will bypass them unless they're misspelled. Go to Auxiliary Dictionary to open an existing dictionary or make a new one by typing in a name and clicking New. Whenever you spell check, open the dictionary *first* so you can add words to it. Otherwise, the Add button is dimmed. To add a word, just click Add or better, press Cmd-A or Alt-A. Another approach—correct all misspelled words. Then, if the remaining "suspect" words are legitimate and you want to add them *all* to the dictionary, press Option-Shift-Done or Alt-Shift-Close.

SPELL CHECKING FROM THE KEYBOARD

Checking spelling isn't exactly a fun task, but it's sure necessary. In fact, you should do it once or twice for each job—after you've imported *all* the text, and again, as a final step, especially if there have been text edits. So when you can make the spell checker less drudgery with a few shortcuts, it's worth remembering!

Open Check Spelling Dialog (Utilities Menu) To

	Mac	Win
Check word	Cmd-L	Ctrl-W
Check story	Cmd-Option-L	Ctrl-Alt-W
Check layout*	Cmd-Option-Shift-L	Ctrl-Alt-Shift-W

* If you have more than one layout in your file, you can't check the entire project at one time.

Check Spelling Tasks

	Mac	Win	Mac and Win
Replace word			Double-click correct word in list
Skip word	Cmd-S	Alt-S	
Look up*	Cmd-L	Alt-L	
Done	Esc or Cmd-. (period)	Esc	

*Sometimes adds more words than originally offered.

   ## SKIPPING PORTIONS OF YOUR DOCUMENT WHEN YOU SEARCH?

Searching has been one of the worst and most *inexcusable* pitfalls in Quark. If you just want to search your current story (the linked frames of one word processing file or one unlinked box), you'll want to press and hold Option or Alt to see the Find Next button become Find First. Clicking Find First starts your search at the top. Then continue with Find Next. But why doesn't Quark "wrap around" its searches? No good reason. In Quark 6, they took a small step in that direction. Now, if (and only if) you click the Layout option to search all text in the current layout, the program brings up a dialog asking if you want to start at the beginning when it comes to the end. Good work guys but why not go all the way and just make the wrapping dialog come up for *any* search that's incomplete?

MAKING TEXT LOOK LIKE TYPESETTING WITHOUT ANYONE NOTICING

TWO SPACES AFTER PERIODS

White or brown birthday cake, this was a big decision. Somewhere along the line, my mother discovered this great bakery where they could make rabbit-shaped cakes with white frosting and white cake, and pink jelly-bean eyes. Or dark brown teddy bear-shaped cakes of chocolate through and through. Invariably, I went with the chocolate (taste winning over looks, but the bunny was as cute as could be.)

ONE SPACE AFTER PERIODS

White or brown birthday cake, this was a big decision. Somewhere along the line, my mother discovered this great bakery where they could make rabbit-shaped cakes with white frosting and white cake, and pink jelly-bean eyes. Or dark brown teddy bear-shaped cakes of chocolate through and through. Invariably, I went with the chocolate (taste winning over looks, but the bunny was as cute as could be.)

Face it, there's only one word space, not two, after a period or other punctuation. Some people will kill over this. We're not in typewriter days anymore with mono-spaced type like Courier. Since 1985, we have the proportional type of true typesetting where using two spaces was never the rule. So instead of arguing about it with your clients or bosses, be a clandestine rebel. Go ahead and remove those "double" agents—globally. Open Find/Change with Cmd-F or Ctrl-F. Type two spaces in the Find field, then one space in the Change field. Press Option or Alt to Find First, then click Change All. Run the search repeatedly until no more changes are found. With each search, the number of spaces goes down by one. To close the dialog, press Cmd-Opt-F or Ctrl-Alt-F.

Essential Searches for "Text Cleanup"

Remove	Find	Change
Multiple word spaces	(2 word spaces)	(1 word space)
Multiple returns	\p\p	\p
Multiple tabs	\t\t	\t

REPLACE UNSIGHTLY <u>UNDERLINES</u> WITH *ITALIC*

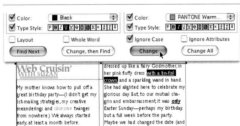

"Searching on attributes" is great for getting rid of those nasty underlines that cut through the descenders of letters (g, j, p, q, y, etc.), making little knots on the page—a hold-over from typewriter days. Replace underlines with italic. In the Find/Change box (Cmd-F or Ctrl-F), uncheck Ignore Attributes to expand the palette. Under Find on the left side, check Type Style. Click the U two times to make the search conditional on the Underline style. On the Change side, again check Type Style, then click "I" twice to make italic the required result. To replace underlines that also occur with other attributes, such as bold, click *once* on the styling button for each added attribute, both under Find and Change, so the search will also find bold, underlined words and replace with bold italic.

See also "Use True Fonts, Not Bold and Italic Type Styles" (Chapter 8).

CLEAN UP TEXT THAT'S PASTED INTO AN EMAIL

has already been classified by the Immigration and ¶
Naturalization Service as an O-1. ¶
¶
His recent work at the Chicago Center for Fine Arts, ¶
building on earlier efforts over the course of his twenty-¶

Tilde   Tilde

already been classified by the Immigration and Naturalization
Service as an O-1. His recent work at the Chicago Center for
Fine Arts, building on earlier efforts over the course of his twen-
ty-year career, underscore his stature as an extraordinarily talented ¶
individual will not only benefit the field of visual communica-¶
tion, but will also advance national development programs the individ-

Tilde

When "you've got mail," the copy for your layout has often been typed or pasted into the email and it needs help. Email text often has a return character at the end of each line, not just after paragraphs. Pour that into a layout and it looks like %#@*+$! Luckily, blank lines indicate where the "real" paragraph breaks are. To fix this up, do three passes, automated with the Find/Change command using Cmd-F or Ctrl-F. First, search out the blank lines. Copy and paste two consecutive returns from the text or type "\p\p" into the Find field. Type a tilde (~) or another obscure character into Change. Press Option or Alt to Find First, then Change All. Now it looks like one big paragraph, but you still have a return at the end of each line. Press Cmd-I or Ctrl-I to see the invisible characters. Do the lines end in a word space or not? Remove all the return characters with Find: \p, replacing with either a word space, if you need one, or nothing if you don't. Find First and Change All. Last step—restore the "true" paragraph breaks. In Find, type "~" and in Change, type "\p". Change All. Miraculous!

REMOVE STRANGE CHARACTERS IN YOUR TEXT

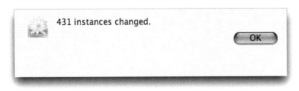

When text has been gone cross-platform or been pasted in an email, you can get some pretty strange looking characters in your copy. Never fear, they are quickly removed. Just copy and paste any word or stray character from the text into the Find field. But take a good look at these anomalies. Sometimes they are substituted characters for something that got lost—such as the apostrophes have been replaced with commas, or perhaps an open or close quote mark now displays an "æ" mark. If so, then search for the wrong character and replace with the correct one. You'll often need to look at each case and avoid Change All. But sometimes these characters simply need to be removed—empty open box characters at the start of lines, for example. Leave the Change field empty or possibly replace with a word space. Then Find First and Change All—the weirdos are gone.

YOU JUST DID CHANGE ALL, THEN REALIZED YOUR MISTAKE :-(

What a relief, after you thought you made a horrible mess in the Find/Change box by clicking Change All when you shouldn't have—and you can't even consider using Revert to Saved because you haven't saved the file for over an hour—you can relax. The Undo command (Cmd-Z or Ctrl-Z) can reverse an almost unlimited number of changes you just made with one little ol' fateful click on the Change All button. Thank goodness! But you do need to close the Find/Change box first, before using Undo. Redo is Cmd-Shift-A or Ctrl-Y.

REPLACE EDITORIAL STYLE TAGS WITH STYLE SHEETS

Converting your editor's style tags or codes into style sheets puts you way ahead. If you have <subhead> tags preceding your subheads, on the same line, you can automatically remove the tags while applying the subhead style. Before you set up your search, apply the body copy style to all the text, starting with Cmd-A or Ctrl-A (Edit > Select All). Open the Find/Change box with Cmd-F or Ctrl-F and uncheck Ignore Attributes. Under Find at the top, check Text, then copy and paste the tag or code, like <subhead>, from the text into the Find field. Under Change, also check Text but leave the text field blank so the tag will be removed. Back under Find, click Style Sheet and choose the body copy style. Click Style Sheet again on the other side, and choose the subhead style. After searching, all the subheads look typeset and the tags are all gone!

 CHANGE ALL THOSE 11PT HOBO SUBHEADS TO 10PT BRUSH

Use the Find/Change command to make styling changes lickity-split. (But if you're using style sheets, just edit the style when you want to change the look.) To give a fast facelift to a set of deadbeat subheads or other type elements— *automatically*—open the Find/Change box (Cmd-F or Ctrl-F). Uncheck Ignore Attributes to expand your search options. On the left under Find, click the check boxes and existing styling attributes you want to change. On the right under Change, click the check boxes and new type attributes you want instead. Skip the Text option at the top, but do check the Font, Size, Color, or any of the type style buttons—Plain, Bold, Italic, and the like. Press the Option or Alt key, and click Find First. Look at a few instances to be sure you set up your search correctly, then choose Change All.

See also "Replace Unsightly <u>Underlines</u> with Italic" (this chapter).

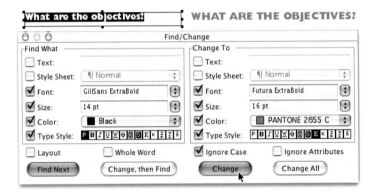

MAKE SNAZZY BULLETS WITHOUT GROANING

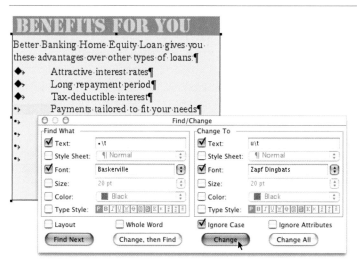

You can automatically convert every bullet in your brochure into a colored Zapf Dingbat or another picture font. Open Find/Change (Cmd-F or Ctrl-F) and in the Text field under Find, type in the bullet character (Option-8 or Alt-Shift-8) or whatever character is used in your story. Then, in Change, type the letter you want to use for your Zapf Dingbat ("n" for square bullet). Uncheck Ignore Attributes to expand the search options. Under Find, click Font and choose from the popup menu the font used for your existing bullets. Switch over to Change, and again click Font, but choose Zapf Dingbats or other picture font. You can also replace black bullets with colored ones using the Color popups. Press Option or Alt to Find First, then choose Change All to quickly transform all your plain-Jane bullets into eye-catching attention-getters.

See also "Getting a Quick Zapf Dingbat" (Chapter 8).

BE THOROUGH—SEARCH TEXT ON MASTER PAGES

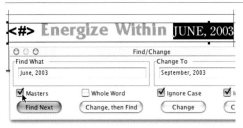

I know you guys are out there, putting in e-n-d-l-e-s-s hours, making l-o-n-g projects with multiple formats, and naturally using multiple master pages. But do you know that your Find/Change searches (Cmd-F or Ctrl-F) don't automatically include master pages? It's a small extra step to hop through all your master pages with any search.

Doing complete passes with searching is the most sensible method so you don't have to keep track of which story or master you've searched. After searching the layout, leave all the same settings in Find/Change, but now go to any of your master pages. The check box in Find/Change that just a minute ago said Layout, now says Masters. Check that, then press Option or Alt and click Find First, then Change All or examine numerous instances first, not a bad idea. Quark will search the current master page and then move on to all of the others.

WILD CARD SEARCHES FOR NUMBERED LISTS

Got a manual with a ton of numbered lists? Jazz up those numbers with a contrasting font and color. But what a job to locate and highlight every number! With wild card searches, your worries are over. To search for a variable character, type the string "\?". For numbered lists, make a character style sheet with your font and color. Then in Find, search for each one digit number, followed by a period: \?.—better yet, because this search finds the last letter and period of each sentence, add a return character before: \p\?. Uncheck the Text field under Change to keep those characters. Below, still under Change, click Style Sheet and choose your character style. To search for two digit numbers, use \?\?. or \p\?\?.—and if there's a tab before and after the two-digit number, use \t\?\?.\t.

SEARCH FOR SPECIAL CHARACTERS

Search For	Mac	Windows	Displays in Field *or* Can Just Type This
Tab	\t	Ctrl-Tab	\t
Paragraph marker	Cmd-Return	Ctrl-Enter	\p
New line marker (soft return)	Cmd-Shift-Return	Ctrl-Shift-Enter	\n
New column (single down arrow)	Cmd-Enter	Ctrl-keypad Enter	\c
New box (double-down arrow)	Cmd-Shift-Enter	Ctrl-Shift-keypad Enter	\b
Current auto-page number	Cmd-3	Ctrl-3	\3
Next linked-box page number (continued on)	Cmd-4	Ctrl-4	\4
Previous linked-box page number (continued from)	Cmd-2	Ctrl-2	\2
Flex space*	Cmd-Shift-F	Ctrl-Shift-F	\. (Mac) \f (Win)
Backslash	Cmd-\	Ctrl-\	**

P.S. If this list seems too much, just copy and paste into the Find field.

* Fixed space you specify in Character preferences.

** For Mac & Win, you can also just type "\".

Your Own Bumper Stickers

FAROUT

FONTS

AHEAD

This chapter gets you to the heart of any well-designed page—typesetting. Without exquisite type handling, your gorgeous graphics will crumble with clay feet.

Your Own Bumper Stickers

screamin' type tips

With 50 tips, here's a nitty-gritty gold mine to sink your teeth into—starting with character attributes, which deliver the bulk of the type "look," everything from getting a font fast to penetrating the secrets of the track editor. Type effects will inspire you with gradient type, hanging punctuation, perfect drop caps, grunge type, and more. How about those authentic geek type things—soft returns, dashes, and spaces to make your pages look truly professional, down to the last em- and en-dash. Then dig down in the trenches to deliver true "typography" for maximum readability—paragraph attributes, including tips on leading, paragraph spacing, and global word spacing. Can't forget about hyphenation, one of the most important and least understood features in Quark. Finally, everyone's favorites—tabs and indents <ha>, including doing equal-interval tabs. Mastering these tips will take your type to new heights—and not just with baseline shift! What does that mean? More people will actually read more of your message. That's progress!

GET THE FONT YOU WANT WHEN YOU TYPE IN A NEW BOX

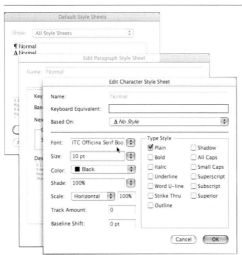

When you make a text box and start typing, would you like that default 12pt Helvetica or Arial text to be more to your liking? You won't find the answer in Quark's preferences for text box tools. But you can control the default type specifications by editing the Normal paragraph style sheet. With no files open, press Shift-F11 (Edit> Style Sheets) to open the Default Style Sheets dialog. With the ¶Normal style highlighted, click Edit to open a second dialog. Click Edit again, in Character Attributes, to change such options as Font, Size, Type Style, and Color. Change paragraph attributes by clicking tabs at the top of the dialog: Formats, Tabs, and Rules. Now in every new Quark file, when you enter text, you'll get your favorite type attributes—or at least your company's favorites! And, it can be just as helpful to do this with a given project or layout open.

AVOIDING LONG LINES FOR FONTS

I'll bet many of you have l-o-n-g font lists. When you're scrolling through dozens of fonts in the Measurements palette, your highlighted type could already have a new face. Every time you want a new font, use the keyboard to highlight the font field in the palette using Cmd-Option-Shift-M or Ctrl-Alt-Shift-M. Then type the first letter or two of the font name. Chances are the font name you want is already displaying. Typing the first letter pops up the first font starting with that letter, and so forth—it's alphabetical. Press Return or Enter to apply. When you don't know what you want, just cycle through your font list. Going down towards Zapf Dingbats, use Option-F9 or Ctrl-F9. Or, going up toward Adobe Caslon, add Shift—Option-Shift-F9 or Ctrl-Shift-F9. Your type automatically changes each time you press those keys. Return or Enter not required*.

	Mac	**Windows**
Highlight font name	Cmd-Option-Shift-M	Ctrl-Alt-Shift-M
Next font down	Option-F9	Ctrl-F9
Next font up	Option-Shift-F9	Ctrl-Shift-F9

Note that once the first font starting with the letter you pressed is displayed, you can use the up/down arrow keys to go up or down the font list. The Next Font Down or Up keystrokes, listed below, don't work in this case.

USE "TRUE" FONTS, NOT BOLD AND ITALIC TYPE STYLES

B Frutiger Bold font

ag bold font

R Frutger Roman with bold style

ag bold style

Century Expanded Regular Italic *font*

ag italic font

Century Expanded Regular *with italic styling*

ag italic font

For print documents, you should always specify bold and italic type by using a font instead of bold or italic styling (Cmd-Shift-B or -I or Ctrl-Shift-B or -I). Most importantly, you're seeing on screen the actual font you'll get when the job is output. So when you use tracking and kerning to tighten up letter and word spacing, your decisions are based on the actual letter forms, rather than a simulated version of those letters. In short, you're not working blind. And, on another front, problems can occur when outputting high-resolution files that don't use true fonts, especially with older imagesetters. Using the real thing gets you more predictable and trouble-free results. Unfortunately, it takes longer to choose a font than press a button or use a keyboard shortcut. So use paragraph and character style sheets so you're only choosing the font once.

GETTING A GOOD POINT SIZE

HELVETICA 10—NO TRACK

Then, slowly, he took her hand as he glanced back at her for one last look, before she faded into the distance of a long lost dream. He had hoped that she might be able to stay with him as he made his way along the treacherous path, but then he knew, it was not to be.

TIMES 11—NO TRACK

Then, slowly, he took her hand as he glanced back at her for one last look, before she faded into the distance of a long lost dream. He had hoped that she might be able to stay with him as he made his way along the treacherous path, but then he knew, it was not to be.

The point size popup menu offers only 11 sizes from 7 to 72 pts, but you can choose any whole number, as well as tenths, and even thousandths of a point. Go ahead, type in a number. Don't even use your mouse. Highlight the font field in the Measurements palette using Cmd-Option-Shift-M or Ctrl-Alt-Shift-M. Press the Tab key to highlight the point size field to type your number. What's a good size for type on a standard page? Serif type (Times, Palatino) sets about a point size smaller than sans serif type (Helvetica, Arial, or Gill Sans). And, with more columns and a shorter line length, the point size should be smaller so you have enough words for a readable line of type. Choose a point size in relation to the length of the line, and based on whether it's serif or sans serif type.

	Serif	Sans Serif
Two-column	10–11 pt	9–10 pt
Three-column	9–10 pt	8–9 pt

   FIND THE PERFECT SIZE—VISUALLY

The best tip around for sizing type til it looks good is keyboard shortcuts. After all, when you're not sure how big that headline or body copy should be, why try one number, then another and another. Instead go larger or smaller incrementally and when it's right, stop! There are two sets of shortcuts to size type up or down. Shortcuts for the "standard" increments that are listed in the popup menu make jumps in point size up or down, with only 11 choices from 7 to 72 pt. So, when you're starting with 12pt text and know it's going way bigger, use the large increment shortcuts. Then, when you're in the ball park, switch over to 1pt increments to fine-tune. Polishing is easy—just add Option or Alt to the previous shortcut.

	Mac	Win
Standard increments*		
Larger	Cmd-Shift->	Ctrl-Shift->
Smaller	Cmd-Shift-<	Ctrl-Shift-<
1pt increments—add Option or Alt		
Larger	Cmd-Option-Shift->	Ctrl-Alt-Shift->
Smaller	Cmd-Option-Shift-<	Ctrl-Alt-Shift-<

*Uses the sizes listed….

QUICK TYPE STYLES

I know I just said above not to use bold and italic type styles but to use true fonts instead—
that's a *production* tip. But when you're designing, it's better not to get bogged down in
production detail because you're not even sure that the design will fly. Besides, design and
production are different mind-sets. It's much easier to use type styles in the design stage.
Applying type styles from the keyboard saves a lot of back and forth mousing. Later on, you
can use Find/Change or Font Usage to switch to the true fonts.

Type Style	Key Letter	Shortcut Mac	Shortcut Win
Plain	P	Cmd-Shift-P	Ctrl-Shift-P
Bold	B	Cmd-Shift-B	Ctrl-Shift-B
Italic	I	Cmd-Shift-I	Ctrl-Shift-I
Underline	U	Cmd-Shift-U	Ctrl-Shift-U
Word Underline	W	Cmd-Shift-W	Ctrl-Shift-W
Strikethrough	/	Cmd-Shift-/	Ctrl-Shift-/
Outline	O	Cmd-Shift-O	Ctrl-Shift-O
Shadow	S	Cmd-Shift-S	Ctrl-Shift-S
All Caps	K	Cmd-Shift-K	Ctrl-Shift-K
Small Caps	H	Cmd-Shift-H	Ctrl-Shift-H
Superscript	+/Mac or 0/Win	Cmd-Shift-+	Ctrl-Shift-0
Subscript	+/Mac or 9/Win	Cmd-Shift- -	Ctrl-Shift-9
Superior	V	Cmd-Shift-V	Ctrl-Shift-V

See also "Use True Fonts, Not Bold and Italic Type Styles" (this chapter).
See also "Change All Those 11pt Hobo Subheads to 10pt Brush" (Chapter 7).
See also "Batteries Not Included—Picture and Font Usage" (Chapter 12).

SUPERSCRIPT OR SUPERIOR—WHICH IS WHICH?

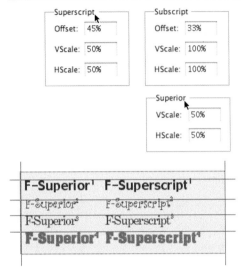

Do you use Superscript with footnotes[5], ordinals (1st), and [®]? Pressing Cmd-Shift-+ or Ctrl-Shift-0 (zero) for Superscript raises up the text, but doesn't make it smaller! But Superior does it all. Use Cmd-Shift-V or Ctrl-Shift-V to raise it up, shrink it down, and automatically top align the footnote or text to the cap height, which is ideal. *But* occasionally, if you're a type geek, you need more control over the offset. Use Superscript, because you can control that distance text is raised up from the baseline and it affects all instances in the file. Press Cmd-Option-Shift-Y or Ctrl-Alt-Shift-Y to open Preferences. Click Character, a Print Layout preference, for Superscript, Subscript, and Superior options.

Change the default 100% VScale and HScale settings to size up or down the superscript (or subscript). Change the amount of the offset from 33% of the point size to a number appropriate to the body copy font.

   ## FAST TRACK TO TRACK AND KERN TO TIGHTEN HEADLINES

Whether you're in the design or production phase, you need tracking and kerning for word and letter spacing. Otherwise, your headlines look, well, flabby. So kick in the track and kern for larger type, say over 16pts, highlighting the text to track, and starting with an insertion point to kern. But when you track or kern with the Measurements palette, does it drive you nuts that it goes from zero to "–10" when you click on that left arrow opposite the track/kern field? Overkill! But if you add Option or Alt when you click, it changes in units of one. Even better, use Cmd-Option-Shift-[or Ctrl-Alt-Shift-[to remove space in units of one (without Option or Alt for units of 10). To add space, replace "[" with "]". When you use style sheets, you can include a track setting for your headlines to tighten spacing, but kerning must be manually applied.

TRACK BODY COPY TO FIX SHORT LINES

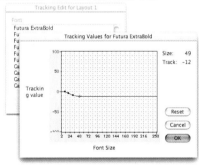

Print a hardcopy first to do this crucial level of proofing. Examine the body copy, looking at the last line of each paragraph. If there's a short last line ending in a three- or four-letter word or, worse, an "ing" or other hyphenated syllable, prepare to tackle. Get rid of short lines and hyphenated syllables with a quick hit of tracking. Highlight the entire paragraph by clicking four times in succession with the Content tool—lickety-split timing not required. Then press Cmd-Option-Shift-[or Ctrl-Alt-Shift-[a few times to tighten up the letter and word spacing until the short line is bumped up to the previous line. Bonus! You've gained a line of space. Don't go to more than a –4 setting without checking it on a proof. Avoid tracking just the last couple of lines or words, which makes the paragraph spacing uneven and more likely requires a higher setting.

   ### TRACK A FONT FOR ALL TIME WITH TRACKING EDIT

Futura Extra Bold

Track your favorite fonts once and for all. Set a sample headline in the desired font. Record your track settings for up to three point sizes, plus a fourth smallest size below which tracking *won't* occur. To track your font for all new documents, close your Quark files. Go to Utilities> Tracking Edit and select your font. Click Edit to display a chart of the font's tracking by point size. Across are the point sizes, down are the track settings, with a horizontal line at zero to initially indicate no tracking for all sizes. Click-and-hold down right on the zero line, near the Y axis to make your first point for the smallest size *below* which no tracking will occur. Move the mouse slightly to adjust the setting until the display, in the upper right, has the desired point size with a zero track value. Repeat for three more point sizes, using negative track numbers. For Futura Extra Bold, I have 14pt—Track 0, 20pt—Track –3, 36pt—Track –5, and 48pt—Track –7.

TWEAK BAD LETTER PAIRS WITH KERNING TABLE EDIT

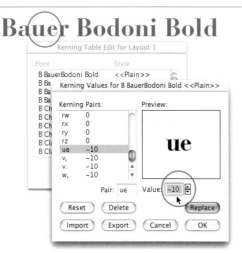

The pair kerning editor can fix bad letter-spacing for specific pairs of letters in a single font, such as AGaramond Italic. For pair-kerning body copy, style a long imported text file in the font you want to edit and at a typical point size. Circle the worst letter pairs on a hard copy. (For pair kerning changes to affect type in all new files, close all Quark projects.) Go to Utilities> Kerning Table Edit, select a font, then Edit. You'll see existing kern pairs available for many fonts. Select a pair on the left to see it displayed opposite with the current Kern Value. Change the amount of kerning below, pressing Return or Enter to apply the new value to that pair and see the display update. Negative numbers tighten space, positive numbers add. If you Option- or Alt-click the up-down arrows, kerning changes in units of one. If no kern pairs are listed, type in a pair, enter a kern value and press Return or Enter. Your kern values for this font are applied to all type over 4pt. To avoid auto-kerning at body copy sizes, increase the point size in the Auto Kern Above option (Character preferences).

 REMOVE MANUAL KERNING

Making a Mess

If you're involved in workgroup publishing or you work in a place that gets lots of Quark files, like a prepress house, you've probably seen some lousy over-kerned type. Kerning on steroids. Getting rid of kerning used to be a royal pain. If you tried to highlight the text, then changed the setting to zero, you were actually removing tracking, not kerning. So then you'd have to click between every pair of letters to reset the kern value to zero—too much work! Happily there's a new command bestowed upon us to solve this very problem. Go ahead and highlight that ugly text, then go to Utilities> Remove Manual Kerning—a big leap in the right direction of quality typography and shorter days.

ADJUST TYPE VERTICALLY WITH BASELINE SHIFT

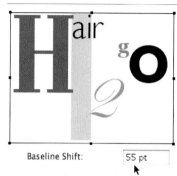

Baseline Shift: 55 pt

Baseline shift is used to raise highlighted type up (positive number) or down (negative number) from the baseline of the type. It's usually applied to small type elements, just a bullet or special character, never to a whole paragraph. For example, sometimes the bullet character is too klutzy-looking next to text in the same font and probably more so when using a contrasting font, such as a Zapf Dingbat or an ornament. So you size down the bullet, but then it's too low and needs a boost. Typically, a bullet is top aligned to the top of the lowercase letters. You can also use baseline shift creatively when designing logos and other specialty type treatments. Because baseline shift is in the Character dialog, it's much easier to press keys.

Baseline Shift	Mac	Win
Up 1pt	Cmd-Opt-Shift-+	Ctrl-Alt-Shift-0 (zero)
Down 1pt	Cmd-Opt-Shift-hyphen	Ctrl-Alt-Shift-9

   ### INCREASE DRAMA WITH REVERSE TYPE

President's Message

If you thought this year was tough...

What would I take to a desert island? Reverse type! That's "white" type on a black or color background—to be exact, it's just the paper color. It's a great way to get dense areas of color on the page, even if it's black. Very effective for positioning two important statements close together without competing. For example, you can put the name of a repeating newsletter column like "President's Message" in reverse, but have the specific headline, "Stormy Weather," appear in positive, black-on-white type. To make reverse type, highlight the type, then in the Character dialog (Cmd-Shift-D or Ctrl-Shift-D), select White for Color. Or in the Colors palette, click the "A" button at the top, then click White below. Give the box background a color so the type pops out, or put the type on a picture—Text Box Background Color is None by default in Quark 6.

See also "Type with Gradients" (this chapter).

SMALL CAPS WITH A TWIST

Wʜᴀᴛ Wᴇɴᴅʏ Wᴀɴᴛᴇᴅ Wᴀs ᴀ Wʜɪsᴛʟᴇ

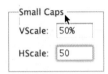

Headlines in small caps can be an elegant touch in a more formal-looking design. Letters that are typed as capitals remain as large caps, while the lowercase letters become small caps. It's easy to just highlight the headline and apply the small caps style (Cmd-Shift-H or Ctrl-Shift-H), but you can get more unusual effects by experimenting with the height of the small cap letters in relation to the large caps. Go to the Character preferences (Cmd-Option-Shift-Y or Ctrl-Option-Shift-Y) and change the Small Caps VScale and HScale from the default of 75%. For tall spiky caps, reduce the percent, or to make the small caps almost the same size as the large caps, increase the number. For variety, try different percents for VScale and Hscale. When you go to Preferences, it doesn't matter whether your type is highlighted because your changes affect *all* small caps text *in the file*.

 TRACK TYPE FOR A WIDE-OPEN-SKY LOOK

Building a Coalition
ᴇᴅᴜᴄᴀᴛɪᴏɴ ɪɴɪᴛɪᴀᴛɪᴠᴇ ꜰᴏʀ ᴛᴏᴍᴏʀʀᴏᴡ

The problem at hand
An unprecedented overhaul over the current 3.0, nearing its second-year anniversary. While the wait has been long, the new offering comes like a

You can now create an index for any publication or group of files comprising one large publication. The Indexer is well-designed for making and editing index entries needed

Along with generating Table of Contents, you will be in full gear with a new links management feature to keep track of all new and graphics placed in a publication and

Although you tend to think of tracking as something to *tighten* word and letter spacing, it can be just as enhancing, for opposite reasons, to *add* space between letters for a very open look. Try it on a running head where you want a nicely designed treatment at the top of each page, but not so obvious that it competes with important headlines placed just below. By adding generous space between letters, you get a very airy feel—attractive but subtle. Dress it up with all-caps to give more contrast to the main headline. But the key is to add *enough* positive tracking to make it look deliberate. Otherwise, it looks like wishy-washy and badly set type. After highlighting the type, press Cmd-Shift-] or Ctrl-Shift-] to add tracking in units of 10. For 1pt intervals, add Option or Alt. To close up space in those large increments, use the "[" (left bracket) instead.

HANGING PUNCTUATION—LARGE QUOTE OR BULLET

❝They that can give up essential liberty to obtain a little temporary safety deserve neither liberty nor safety.❞

— Benjamin Franklin
[1706–1790]

Typographers agree that the page looks better and cleaner when quote marks, bullets, and similar non-alphabetic characters hang outside the text box, on the left, so that the type vertically justifies in a clean line. Doing this in Quark is a bit indirect but not hard. First put a word space before the quote mark or bullet.

Click with the Content tool to make an insertion point between the space and the quote mark. Using repeat hits of Cmd-Option-Shift-[or Ctrl-Alt-Shift-[, you can kern back the space incrementally so that the quote mark is no longer visible—until you print the page. And there it is, hanging out in the margin in all its glory, and you've got a nice, clean vertical left edge.

TYPE IN A BOX WITH A NEW ANGLE

Brand NEW!

Beyond the Blue
By Bethanie Byron

Byron's book recalls the 50's and early 60's when life in the US had a carefree lifestyle, prior to the sex, drugs and roc 'n-roll onslaught, not to mention the Vietnam war, which brought our count

| Text Angle: | 30 |
| Text Skew: | 0° |

Make your type more like a graphic—very useful with a text-heavy layout that's lackluster. This technique works best for accent type, a keyword or phrase, rather than a headline. Start by drawing a text box using one of the six shaped text box tools (Rounded-, Concave-, or Beveled-Corner; Oval, Bezier, or Freehand), or the Starburst tool, at the bottom of the toolbox. To convert the default starburst picture box to a text box, go to Item> Content> Text. Choose Get Text, paste or type in your text. With the Content tool, Cmd- or Ctrl-double-click on the text box to open the Modify dialog. Click on the Text tab and right at the top, type in a new Text Angle. Click Apply to see it change on the page. Small numbers such as 15–25° go a long way. Fill the box background with a color or tint. The ragged edges on the type are just a screen display thing and print out fine.

PERFECTING THE DROP CAP—PART I

Everyone agreed that his statement was shocking. But his intention left room for copious speculation. Had he really intended to insult the Prime Minister? Probably not. On the other hand, it certainly is hard to fathom. Everyone from the Queen on down shook their heads and tittered.

Drop caps are a piece of cake in Quark. Their purpose is to draw the eye down from the headline, giving the reader a little boost into the body copy. A great way to enhance the drop cap is to style the first letter in a contrasting type face—something heavy in weight or having a decorative quality. Then, with your insertion point in the paragraph, go to Formats (Cmd-Shift-F or Ctrl-Shift-F) and click the Drop Caps option, a paragraph attribute. For most uses, set Line Count to drop the cap into 2 or 3 lines. The longer your line length and number of lines, the more lines you can drop into and the bigger the resulting cap. After you click OK, kern the space between the drop cap and the next letter by clicking an insertion point there. Then press Cmd-Option-Shift-[or Ctrl-Alt-Shift-[to tighten, or press Cmd-Option-Shift-] or Ctrl-Alt-Shift-] to loosen.

PERFECTING THE DROP CAP—PART II

Everyo was s left r Had he really Prime Minis other hand, Everyone fr their heads ₐ

Making a delectable drop cap can take a bit more. The spacing that precedes a drop cap is often too big, preventing the cap from making a clean vertical alignment with the lines below. To push the drop cap to the left edge of the box, go to Formats (Cmd-Shift-F or Ctrl-Shift-F) and give it a *Character* Count of 2. Then enter a word space in front of the drop cap and, with your insertion point between the space and the cap, kern back the space until the cap is perfectly aligned to the left edge of the type below. (See the previous tip for kern units.) You may also need to adjust the cap's vertical alignment if it sits too low. It should top align with the cap-heights on the first line. Apply baseline shift to the highlighted cap to move it up or down. To go up by 1pt: Cmd-Opt-Shift-+ or Ctrl-Alt-Shift-0. To go down 1pt: Cmd-Opt-Shift-hyphen or Ctrl-Alt-Shift-9.

PERFECTING THE DROP CAP—PART III

Believe it or not, there's another step that's often required to make a great drop cap. With some fonts, when you drop the cap, it's a bit too large or small. Too small is the worst, the top of the cap is lower than the x-height—the top of the lowercase letters on the first line of copy. And sometimes it sticks up too much, although that can be an interesting look. In either case, you can change the size of the drop cap using the Measurements palette. First highlight the cap, then go to the point size field in the palette and you'll see the cap size as 100%. To enlarge or reduce it, choose a percent over or under 100%. Fine-tuning par excellence!

FANCY TYPE WITH TWO COLORS USING TEXT TO BOX

Make an eye-catching, color-blasting headline by converting text into a picture box, using different colors for the box background and frame. First style your type the way you want it to look—minus the two-tones. Track and kern, you can't do it later. Then highlight the headline—with multiple lines, highlight just the first line. Go to Style> Text to Box, and your type is one shaped picture box. Repeat the process for a second line. Add a frame width. Select the picture box and go to Frame (Cmd-B or Ctrl-B). Then apply different colors to the frame and box background using the Frame and Box tabs of the Modify dialog (for multiple boxes, it's the Group tab). Your letter-shaped picture box can be stretched and squished! In addition to the new picture boxes, you still have the original editable text. Move it to the pasteboard for possible text edits later on.

  TYPE WITH GRADIENTS

For a more dynamic look, fill headlines or other type with gradients, or Quark Blends, by converting them to picture boxes using Text to Box. In the Colors palette, click on the top right button for the box Background Color. Just below, from the popup menu that says "Solid," select a type of blend: Linear, Mid-Linear, Rectangular, Diamond, Circular, or Full Circular. Just below that, there are now two radio buttons for #1 and #2 blend colors. Click a color in the list below, then select the #2 button and choose another color. With the two types of Linear blends, you can enter 90° or –90° in the degree field to blend vertically or 0° or 180° to go horizontally. Or experiment with other angles. To get rid of the big distracting "X" across the letters that indicates it's a picture box, select the box, then go to Item> Content> None.

See also "Fancy Type with Two Colors Using Text to Box" (previous tip).

   TYPE ON A PATH

For text on a straight-line path, click-drag the Line- or Orthogonal Text-Path tool. The latter makes easy lines on 90° and 45° angles. For an irregular path, drag the Freehand Text-Path tool. The Bezier Path tool provides maximum control but it's the least intuitive if you're new to pen tools. Draw a set of straight-line segments with corner points using a click-and-release method, moving the tool to a new spot each time. Curves are harder. Click-drag to draw a smooth point with a set of control handles that set the curve's slope and fullness. Drag in opposite directions—click-drag up, move the mouse, click-drag down—for one curve. The more you drag, the fuller the curve. Control handles should extend about one third the length of the curve segment. End a line by double-clicking on your last point or changing tools. Enter or paste text on the selected path by clicking it with the Content tool. Style as usual.

WRAP TEXT INSIDE A SHAPED BOX

Grab the reader's attention with text in an unusually shaped box—great for a set of testimonials or a "New Item" accent. Draw a square or circle text box (or picture box, for that matter). With the Rectangle or Oval Text Box tool selected, press the Shift key as you drag out. When it looks the right size, release the mouse *before* the Shift. Of course, the oval text box you get without using Shift is also fairly unusual. Use Get Text, type or paste your text in the box. To get the text to visually create the shape of the box, without using a background color or frame weight, size the type down and justify it. More adventurous? Change the shape of a selected text box with Item> Shape, then select from the five shaped boxes. Or, with one of the line types, your box is converted to text on a path!

See also "Make a Wacky or Sublime Picture Box" (Chapter 4).

   ## "GRUNGE TYPE"—VERTICALLY OVERLAPPING TYPE

I believe it was Robin Williams, the desktop graphics author and guru, who coined the term "grunge type" to describe type that looks "on the edge," or maybe she just brought the term to my attention. A funky typeface can have a lot to do with an edgy look, but so can leading. It's called *minus leading,* when type is set so that that the leading value is smaller than the point size and the descenders of one line touch or overlap onto the cap-heights of the line below. In traditional typography, this would be verboten. But in our topsy-turvy world, it has a dramatic, eye-catching look that may be great for headlines or other type. So, for example, if your headline is 20pt, try a leading value of 10 to 14 pt. Of course, this may not gel with a classic, corporate identity, but it's great for a contemporary, agitated look.

 STRANGE TYPE EFFECTS

Here's another funky approach to grunge type— non-proportionally scaled text—though type purists will cringe! The easiest way to judge how far out to go is to scale the type visually. With the headline or other text in its own box, press Cmd or Ctrl and drag a box handle to alter proportions. To scale just one dimension, Cmd- or Ctrl-drag a *center* handle in or out. If your headline shares the box with other text, you can horizontally or vertically scale the *highlighted* headline using Cmd-] or Ctrl-] in 5% increments, or add Option or Alt for 1%. Whatever scale type you last used, horizontal or vertical, is what you'll get using the keyboard. To match those settings for other type, check the Horizontal or Vertical Scale percents used in the sample highlighted text. Press Cmd-Shift-D or Ctrl-Shift-D to open the Character Attributes dialog and note the Scale type and percent.

 THE *REAL* SHADOW TEXT

Shadow style? Here's the real thing. With the text in its own box, do Step and Repeat (Cmd-Option-D or Ctrl-Alt-D). With Repeat Count 1, change the offsets to 0, then close. Now there's a duplicate box on top. Flip the highlighted text vertically, clicking the big up arrow in the Measurements palette. Next set the Runaround to None (Cmd-T or Ctrl-T). Shift-drag it down to vertically constrain the move—press Cmd or Ctrl with mouse down, add Shift, then drag. Stop when the baselines of the two reflected lines are aligned. Set the Text Skew to about (–60°) in the Text tab, Modify dialog. If needed, extend the width of the duplicate box, dragging a center handle. Then move the box horizontally to realign the slanted text. Increase the shadow effect by shortening the box height: Cmd- or Ctrl-drag up the bottom center handle, then again readjust the box position. Tint the shadow text color (Cmd-Shift-D or Ctrl-Shift-D). Effect doesn't work with descenders!

AUTOMATIC LIGATURES WITH CHARACTER PREFERENCE
(MAC ONLY)

Ligatures OFF

Filbert finds the flea and flows the fickle floozy.

Ligatures ON

Filbert finds the flea and flows the fickle floozy.

☑ Ligatures
Break Above: 1   ☐ Not "ffi" or "ffl"

With serif fonts, like Times and Palatino, ligatures can be the finishing touches to elegant typography with a handcrafted look. A ligature is a single character of text combining two letters that flow together. With fonts like the Adobe Expert Collection, you can get up to five ligatures, but even with regular everyday serif fonts, using Quark on a Mac, you can get two ligatures automatically inserted into your text. Go to Character Preferences under Print Layout (Cmd-Option-Shift-Y or Ctrl-Alt-Shift-Y). Click the Ligatures check box to automatically replace all instances of f-i and f-l with the ligatures fi and fl. The Break Above setting is the track value above which no ligatures occur, i.e., wide letter spacing is contrary to ligatures. If you add ligatures when no Quark files are open, ligatures show up in your serif fonts for all new files. Note that Quark can still spell check and search text with ligatures.

FANCY PRICING AND FRACTIONS

Getting snappy prices and fractions is easy as π (pi) and just a matter of two steps. First type a price, $29.99, or a fraction, $7/8$; you can only do one price or fraction at a time. Then highlight that and go to Style> Type Style> Make Price *or* > Make Fraction. It looks great, but your new fraction may need some tweaking. If the denominator is touching the slash mark, add some kerning using Cmd-Option-Shift-] or Ctrl-Alt-Shift-]. Also, if the fraction looks big, highlight it and reduce the size. Easiest way is Cmd-Option-Shift-< or Ctrl-Alt-Shift-<. One or two hits of the shortcut keys does the trick. And lo and behold, you have something that actually looks real life!

  SOFT RETURNS—MORE READABLE HEADLINES

Accounting Errors Run Rampant

Enrun will be facing some very stiff charges this week in Congressional hearings. Reports from the will say that they are prepared to fight this all the way. Consider adding tracting to a

The FCC has stated very clearly that no offense will go unpunished. Spotespan for Enrun said that the company will do what it can to protect its financial situation, and hope that that style with layout controls.

then choose at the from zero. There is to backtract.
Hyphenation t mation from a son place inside the Pa

Accounting Errors Run Rampant

Enrun will be facing some very stiff charges this week in Congressional hearings. Reports

The FCC has stated very clearly that no offense will go unpunished. Spokespan for Enrun said that the

Your formatted headline may be wrapping around to a second or even third line. How editorially readable is it with the current line breaks? Does your headline split up a phrase like, "by the—accounting office?" Or even split up an "a" or "the" from its noun, as in "Accounting Error Causes a—Scandal?" Insert your own line breaks with a *soft return* using Shift-Return or Shift-Enter. The soft return creates a new line but not a new paragraph. That means you don't also get the paragraph spacing or indenting that happens if the headline has those attributes to start. You can also use a soft return to improve the rag of your flush-left type by bringing a word from the end of one line down to the next. But with editing, that line break can occur in the middle of a line. Instead use a discretionary hyphen *before* the hyphenated word.

See also "On the Spot Hyphenation Fixes—Discretionary Hyphens" (this chapter).

LONG AND SHORT DASHES (EM AND EN)

You've heard of M&Ms, and of course Eminem? This is Em and En!

There are at least three major varieties…

Hyphen. When auto-hyphenation is on, Quark automatically inserts them.

Em dash. A long dash that's used to separate thoughts as in "He faltered—but stood his ground." An em is a typographic unit that equals the point size of the type. So an em dash in 10pt type is 10 points.

En dash. A dash that's longer than a hyphen and half the width of an em dash. Think, an "m" has two humps, but the "n" has only one, half what the "m" has. So an en dash is half the width of an em dash. Use an en dash to separate dates and times as in "January 1–December 31" or "2–5 pm."

Whether you like spaces around dashes or not doesn't matter, but be consistent.

	Looks Like	Mac	Win
Standard hyphen, breaking	-	Hyphen	Hyphen
Standard hyphen, nonbreaking	-	Cmd-=	Ctrl-=
En dash, nonbreaking	–	Option-hyphen	Ctrl-Alt-Shift-hyphen
Em dash, breaking	—	Option-Shift-hyphen	Ctrl-Shift-=
Em dash, nonbreaking	—	Cmd-Option- =	Ctrl-Alt-Shift-=
Discretionary (soft) hyphen	(invisible)	Cmd-hyphen	Ctrl-hyphen

See also "On the Spot Fixes—Discretionary Hyphens" (this chapter).

SPECIAL WORD SPACES

Don't end up with Southern Bell on two lines—use a non-breaking space between words of a company or product name. Four varieties of spaces here, from small to large—punctuation, standard, and en, as well as the flex space, which you can specify for any width in Character preferences. And you've got five non-breaking spaces. Of those, all but the standard space are fixed spaces, meaning when type is justified, those spaces don't expand or contract. (Caveat: *only* if you set all three Character spacing settings to "0" for Quark's H&J Standard setting, Cmd-Option-J or Ctrl-Shift-F11.) Use fixed spaces for a constant interval, such as on a fancy menu where the prices follow right behind the entrée listings and are hard to spot! For a "true" industry-standard em space, check Standard Em Space in Character preferences. Otherwise, you get Quark's concoction.

	Looks Like	Mac	Win
Breaking standard space	H H	Space	Space
Non-breaking standard space	H H	Cmd-5	Ctrl-5
Breaking punctuation space	H H	Shift-Space	Shift-Space
Non-breaking punctuation space	H H	Cmd-Shift-Space	—
Breaking en space	H H	Option-Space	Ctrl-Shift-6
Non-breaking en space	H H	Cmd-Option-Space	Ctrl-Alt-Shift-6
		or Cmd-Option-5	
Breaking em space (type twice)	H H	Option-Space	Ctrl-Shift-6
Non-breaking em space (type twice)	H H	Cmd-Option-Space	Ctrl-Alt-Shift-6
		or Cmd-Option-5	
Breaking flexible space	—	Option-Shift-Space	Ctrl-Shift-5
Non-breaking flexible space	—	Cmd-Option-Shift-Space	Ctrl-Alt-Shift-5

LEADING—NOT AUTO LEADING

AUTO LEADING

She stood there for a moment pondering whether she was perhaps overlooking something. But then, in a flash, she knew it was all there waiting.

When she turned the corner, she saw something that made her start. It was so bewildering that she could not even describe it to herself. She turned on her heels, whisked out the door and took off for the nearest phone booth. No sooner had she closed the door and looked in her purse, she realized she was foiled again. No change.

"10 ON 14" LEADING

She stood there for a moment pondering whether she was perhaps overlooking something. But then, in a flash, she knew it was all there waiting.

When she turned the corner, she saw something that made her start. It was so bewildering that she could not even describe it to herself. She turned on her heels, whisked out the door and took off for the nearest phone booth. No sooner had she closed the door and looked in her purse, she realized she was foiled again. No change.

Did you know that leading (pronounced **ledd**-ing) enhances type readability more than point size? Body copy looks more inviting and easier to read when leading is generous. Many people, however, fall back on using Quark's default Auto leading, which is probably the smallest acceptable leading value for body copy. With Auto, a 10pt body copy has 12pt leading, (say "10 on 12"). Try instead a 3 or 4 pt spread between point size and leading, such as 9 on 13. But with headlines, the opposite is often true. When a multi-line head is followed by body copy, leading for that head should be tight so its multiple lines are easily spotted as one unit. A 24pt head with Auto leading gets you close to 29pts of leading. Try leading at 24 to 26pt instead. A few extra points of leading, at that point size, is still tight.

Leading	Mac	Win
Increase by 1pt	Cmd-Shift-"	Ctrl-Shift-"
Increase by .1pt	Cmd-Option-Shift-"	Ctrl-Alt-Shift-"
Decrease by 1pt	Cmd-Shift-:	Ctrl-Shift-:
Decrease by .1pt	Cmd-Option-Shift-:	Ctrl-Alt-Shift-:

PARAGRAPH SPACING, THE "HIDDEN" ATTRIBUTE

Paragraph spacing can be as crucial as leading for delivering a message. Used properly, paragraph spacing expresses the hierarchical organization of the copy. A subhead, for example, needs more space before and less after to visually announce the body copy below. Using equal spacing weakens the editorial message. Unfortunately, paragraph spacing is in the Formats dialog, not on the Measurements palette so it's tempting to use blank lines with various leading values instead. This is a mistake waiting to happen. With multiple-linked text boxes, one of these blank lines will likely fall at the top of a column, causing a drop in the white space that—guess what—goes unnoticed *until printed*! Get to Formats fast: Cmd-Shift-F or Ctrl-Shift-F. Press Tab four times to highlight Space Before, one more for Space After, then Return or Enter to close. When it comes to production, use style sheets to apply paragraph spacing hassle-free.

PARAGRAPH SPACING AND INDENTS—SPECIFY IN POINTS

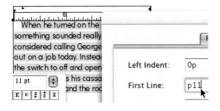

The conventions of traditional typesetting are a great foundation. When you specify paragraph spacing and indents in points, you're talking the language of all other type attributes. Space Before and After are set equal to or an interval of the leading value. A headline with 20pt leading might have 20pts after (full-line space) or 10pts (half-line). For the standard first line indent, use a number equal to the point size so 10pt body copy has a 10pt indent. If you're set to picas, and go to Formats (Cmd-Shift-F or Ctrl-Shift-F), 0p is the default—just add the points after—0p20 for 20pts of spacing, or simply 20. But with inches, it's more awkward. You can enter points by typing "p" then the number of points, or "pt" after the number: p20 or 20pt. When you click OK or Apply, however, the points are converted to a weird decimal number—in this case .278".

See also "Trade in Nasty Numbers—.167", .3125", or .625"—for Picas" (Chapter 1).

RESET QUARK'S DEFAULT *GLOBAL* WORD SPACING OF 110%

Default word space 110%

In the end it

Word space 100%

In the end it

For good-looking type, know this fact—by default, Quark is adding 10% extra space between all words, whether you use Get Text, type, or paste, or whether the type is set flush-left or justified. Check it out. Go to Edit> H&Js with Cmd-Option-J or Ctrl-Shift-F11. With "Standard default" setting highlighted, click Edit and look, on the right, at the 110% Optimum (word) Space setting under Justification Method. The Minimum and Maximum settings automatically affect the spacing and consequently the hyphenating of all justified text, which is fine, but…the Optimum setting at 110% expands *all* word spacing in your Quark file, flush-left or justified. Make this fix for all new files. Close your Quark files, then go to H&Js again. Edit the Standard setting with Optimum word Space set to 100%. Or, if you're squeamish, make a new setting called "100%" to apply to text using Formats or a paragraph style.

TRYING TO SET TABS AND NOTHING'S WORKING?

ProCorp, Inc. Projected Sales
In millions¶

	2003→	2004→	2005→
Corporate→	198→	395→	791→
Commercial→	94→	188→	376→
Chicago→	59→	119→	238→
Region→	→	42→	85→
State-wide→	→	32→	64→
National→	→	12→	24→
International→	→	30→	6→

○ ○ ○   Find/Ch

Find What
\t\t

☐ Layout   ☐ Whole Word

[Find Next]   [Change, then Find]

Ever click Apply in the Tab dialog and nothing happens? Many people who type in word processing avoid the tab ruler. They keep hitting that Tab key to push the text over. When you get that text in Quark, and apply a tab, the text sits there because it's actually at the second or third tab! Be a detective, check this out. Turn on Invisibles with Cmd-I or Ctrl-I (View> Show Invisibles) to see the hidden characters. Watch those forward pointing arrows pop up, each one a tab. Rather than a select-and-delete approach, use Find/Change (Cmd-F or Ctrl-F). Copy and paste two tabs from the text into the Find field, looks like "\t\t." Paste them again into Change , but then delete the second tab. Looks like "\t." Press Option or Alt to Find First, then Change All. Repeat the search until all multiple tabs are replaced by just one. Now you're ready!

TABS—LINE 'EM UP EQUALLY

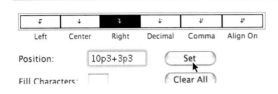

Set tabs at equal intervals and let Quark do the math! With table text highlighted, click Clear All in Tabs (Cmd-Shift-T or Ctrl-Shift-T). Add your first and second tabs, clicking on the tab ruler on the page and noting their locations in the Position field. Click Apply. Does the interval between them seem about right? Subtract the first tab number from the second. Now add that interval to the second tab value in the Position field: 10p3+3p3 (inches: 1.708"+.542"). A third tab pops up on the ruler. (If you moved the existing tab, Undo—Cmd-Z or Ctrl-Z.) Then, crucial step, click the Set button or better, Cmd-S or Alt-Shift-S. That totals the numbers and deselects the tab marker on the ruler so you can make another tab, and not move the existing one. Repeat the pattern—add the interval, Set, add the interval, Set…until you're done!

ALIGNING NUMBERS WHEN SOME ARE IN PARENTHESES

	Fiscal Year Ended	
December 31, 2002		December 30, 2003
2004		2005
$(401,062,375)		$(306,758,503)
(1,599,116)		(4,656,984)
2,563,367		(2,356,0270)
172,258		7,258,158
820,426		991,721
(2,391,575)		(1,325,721)

It's annual report season. How do you get those infamous loss numbers ($29,000,000,000) to align with the gain numbers that *aren't* in parentheses? You can't use right-align tabs! First, loss numbers are usually rounded off, no decimal points. So why think of using a decimal tab? Because it acts like there's a decimal point after the number and lets the close parens hang out to the right. Or try an Align-On tab, which can be used to align on any ol' thing—a close paren, bullet, long dash, question mark, whatever. Just copy your align-on character in the text,")." Then in Tabs (Cmd-Shift-T or Ctrl-Shift-T), click the Align On button and paste or type your character into the Align On field below. After you click on the tab ruler, then Apply, your tabbed text is now miraculously aligning to that whatever. And with loss numbers, the parens still hang out.

BULLET COPY—CODE NAME:"HANGING INDENTS"

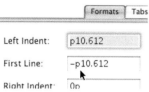

| Formats | Tabs |

Left Indent: p10.612

First Line: –p10.612

Right Indent: 0p

Need hanging indents for bullet copy? Turn on Invisibles (Cmd-I or Ctrl-I) to see if there's a word space or a tab character (right-pointing arrow) after each bullet. If you have word spaces, quickly replace the spaces with tabs using Find/Change—"•" (word space) in Find and "\t" in Change . Bullets are Option-8 or Alt-Shift-8. For hanging indents, highlight your bullet copy and open Tabs (Cmd-Shift-T or Ctrl-Shift-T). See the two small black triangles stacked at the left end of the ruler? To indent the whole paragraph, drag the bottom triangle to the right and the top triangle (first line indent) goes too. But to hang, drag the top triangle *back* to the left edge of the ruler. That's all you have to do. Or specify that indent numerically in Formats (Cmd-Shift-F or Ctrl-Shift-F). The Left and First Line indents should be the same number, except the first indent is a *negative* number.

DESIGNER CHARTS—NO LEADERS, PARAGRAPH RULES

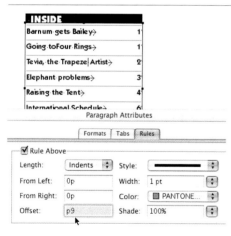

Paragraph Attributes

| Formats | Tabs | Rules |

☑ Rule Above

Length: Indents   Style: ▬▬▬

From Left: 0p   Width: 1 pt

From Right: 0p   Color: ■ PANTONE...

Offset: p9   Shade: 100%

Make cool charts with paragraph rules, not those old-fashioned leader tabs.......... After your tabs are set, no leaders, highlight again, but not the column headers, and open the leading, say 18pt leading for 10pt type, *if* your paragraphs are only one line each. (If not, use tighter leading with paragraph spacing above, instead.) Then open Style> Paragraph Rules (Cmd-Shift-N or Ctrl-Shift-N), and click the Rule Above check box. Set Rule Length to Indents, meaning the rules go the full width of the text box, minus any rule indents, here none. Use a small rule width, like .25pt for light lines. The Offset is tricky. The value is given as a percent, but it works better to enter points. Try the point size of the type, or a bit larger, and go from there—10pt (or p10). Click Apply to check it out. Ideally the rule above should be vertically centered between two lines of text.

   FAKE A RIGHT-ALIGNED TAB

This is a fast workaround to working with tabs *but no tab ruler*! Let's say you've got a title at the top left and you want the date on the right of the same line. Or in a short table of contents (no leader tabs allowed!), you want the topics left-aligned but the page numbers right-aligned. Just throw in a *right-indent* tab between the two—it's a special character. On a flush-left line of text, highlight the word space between the left-aligned text and the characters to be right aligned. Then type Option-Tab/Mac or Shift-Tab/Win to send the following text over to the right, regardless of any other tabs present. Bonus—that text stays at the right edge of the column or box, even if the box width is changed. If you Show Invisibles (Cmd-I or Ctrl-I), you'll see the right-pointing tab character separating the two.

   INDENTING WITHOUT DIALOG BOXES

a**X**, the Clybourn St. Dalmation, was in the habit of running way ahead of her Mom, finding a scrap or two of food, and wolfing it down before you could say. "Get over here!!" However, this was one of the few things about this crazy dog that you just had to overlook.

The Indent Here character is another way, somewhat unusual, to do indents, completely bypassing both the Formats dialog and the Tab ruler. Two small drawbacks—only one indent per paragraph and no leader tabs. By inserting the Indent Here character at an insertion point of your choice, all the *following* lines in the paragraph automatically indent to that point—just press Cmd-\ or Ctrl-\. One of many possible uses for Indent Here is to draw more attention to a drop cap used in a fancy quote or introductory paragraph. Put your insertion point right after the drop cap, then do Indent Here—now that large letter *really* stands out.

CONTINUOUS APPLY IN TAB (OR ANY) DIALOG BOX

This tip is so easy and seductive, you'll slip into a regular habit. It's called Continuous Apply because once you turn it on in any dialog box, whatever you do becomes immediately effective. Well, okay, you might have to click in another field close by to tell Quark you're finished typing. Pressing Option or Alt, click Apply. You'll see the button stay in the "down" position until you click it again, no key. This tip is especially handy when sliding tab markers back-and-forth on the Tab ruler (Cmd-Shift-T or Ctrl-Shift-T), or adjusting the Offset when adding paragraph rules (Cmd-Shift-N or Ctrl-Shift-N). And an extra perk—when you return to that dialog next time, Continuous Apply is still on!

NO-HYPHENS SETTING FOR HEADS, SUBHEADS, CAPTIONS

Headlines, subheads, and usually captions shouldn't be hyphenated. It looks bad and makes it harder to read your most visible messages! Rule out one surefire set of pitfalls and repetitive fixes by making an H&J setting that has hyphenation turned *off*. Do it for all files you make from now on by closing your Quark files first. Of course, it may also be just right for the file you have open. Go to Edit> H&Js with Cmd-Option-J or Ctrl-Shift-F11. Click New, and type this name: No Hyphens. Then uncheck Auto Hyphenation, right below. Click OK and Save. To apply the setting to a headline, click on it once and press Cmd-Shift-F or Ctrl-Shift-F to open Style> Formats. Then select the No Hyphens option from the H&J popup menu. Of course, the best way to automatically apply a no-hyphens setting is with style sheets.

See also "Automate Hyphenation with Styles" (this chapter).

HYPHENS—GETTING TOO MANY OR NOT ENOUGH?

With two columns of *justified text* on a standard page, and plenty of words on a line, you can probably let hyphenation do its thing. But with three or more columns, exercise control using H&Js. Hyphenation and Justification go together like peanut butter and jelly. Without good hyphenation, justified text can have big gaps between words, or letters can be crammed together. In the H&Js dialog, the numbers you plug in for Justification Method determine how much Quark can space out words and letters or cram them together. The more slush room you allow, the fewer hyphens you'll have because Quark only tries to hyphenate when it can't meet your spacing range limits. Quark's default Maximum word space setting of 250% allows word spaces to grow into gaping holes that can be *two-and-a-half times* the normal space. "Rivers of white space" means big gaps between words start to visually connect down the page.

Go to Edit> H&Js with Cmd-Opt-J or Ctrl-Shift-F11. Click Duplicate to make a new H&J setting for justified text, based on the Standard setting. Change Hyphens in a Row, the maximum number of consecutive hyphenated lines from Unlimited to 2 or 3. The Smallest Word (6) and Minimum Before (3) default settings are good. But for Minimum After, 3 characters instead of 2 avoids an "-ly" at the start of a line. For Justification Method, trying 75% Minimum and 125% Maximum reduces those gaps and increases hyphenation. Increase the Maximum Character spacing from 4% to 10% so the word gaps shrink more.

For *flush-left type*, the Hyphenation Zone controls frequency of hyphenation, not Justification Method. If a line ends with a word falling in that hyphen zone, Quark doesn't try to hyphenate. With the default Hyphen Zone of zero, Quark attempts to hyphenate every line. But with a two-column setup, you can afford to have fewer hyphens and allow a more generous *rag* (the in-out profile of the ragged-right edge), so increase the hyphen zone to 1p or 1p6 (.167" or .25").

AUTOMATE HYPHENATION WITH STYLES

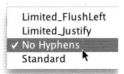

It's not hard to apply an H&J setting to an entire story you highlighted with the Content tool using Select-All (Cmd-A or Ctrl-A). Just do a quick Cmd-Shift-F or Ctrl-Shift-F to open Style> Formats and choose your hyphenation-justification setting from the popup menu. But what do you do when you've got an H&J setting you want to apply to many paragraphs that are sprinkled through the text? Are you going to open the Formats box for every headline and subhead? The resounding answer is *no*! Make a style sheet for each of these paragraph types and incorporate the appropriate H&J setting. Then you can just apply the style and forget about the H&J that's getting handled in the background! (By-the-way design tip: Even if your body copy is justified, use flush-left in your style sheets for the no-hyphen heads and subheads!)

ON-THE–SPOT FIXES—DISCRETIONARY HYPHENS

on·the·pnone·to·tne·rresiaent·or·a·protes-
sional · association · from · which · she · is
resigning, · she · tells · him · in · no · uncertain
terms · how · his · lack · of · leadership · and
forthrightness · may · be · aggravating · an
already · weakened · organization. · Politic
she's·nor.·When·she·was·a·kid.·more·than

on·the·pnone·to·tne·rresiaent·or·a·protes-
sional · association · from · which · she · is
resigning, · she · tells · him · in · no · uncer-
tain·terms·how·his·lack·of·leadership·and
forthrightness · may · be · aggravating · an
already · weakened · organization. · Politic
she's·nor.·When·she·was·a·kid.·more·than

Great-looking type takes finessing. Correct bad line or hyphen breaks in flush-left or justified copy using discretionary hyphens. Bad *line* breaks occur when you need a hyphen. For example, justified copy can have big gaps between words. Hyphenating the last word on a previous line can even out the spacing. *But not with the hyphen key.* Without fail, after some edits, that hard hyphen causes a bad break from the middle of a line! A discretionary hyphen, however—Cmd-hyphen or Ctrl-hyphen—does the same job, but like a good guest, it disap-

pears when not wanted. Bad *hyphen* breaks occur when you *don't* want a hyphen. For exam- ple, in flush-left copy, if two or more consecutive lines are the same length, it's not ragged. But if one line is hyphenated, you can force that hyphenated word to the next line, no hyphenating, by typing the discretionary hyphen right *in front of* the word. You've heard of safe havens? Well these are safe hyphens <ow>.

HYPHENATION EXCEPTIONS—WHERE TO HYPHENATE

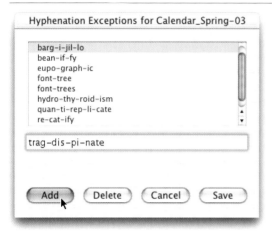

Hyphenation Exceptions for Calendar_Spring-03

barg-i-jil-lo
bean-if-fy
eupo-graph-ic
font-tree
font-trees
hydro-thy-roid-ism
quan-ti-rep-li-cate
re-cat-ify

trag-dis-pi-nate

Add   Delete   Cancel   Save

Proprietary, technical, and industry terms cause problems with hyphenation. Quark uses algorithms for hyphenating, but they're not always right. Control hyphenation for unknown words with Utilities> Hyphenation Exceptions. Enter a word in the field below, typing hyphens or not to include or exclude them. Press Return or Enter to add the word to the list. Here's the bad news. The words you add to Hyphenation Exceptions are stored in the Preferences file and do not cross reference to those added to the Auxiliary Dictionary, used for spell checking. Not only will the spell checker still stop at the words you add in Hyphenation Exceptions, you can't use the Auxiliary Dictionary to indicate preferred hyphenation. And if you enter a word using lowercase, it won't apply the suggested hyphenation to the capitalized word in the text. However, using Hyphenation Exceptions should certainly improve your hyphenation!

See also "Make Spell-Checking Go Faster and Do More" (Chapter 7).

Power, Power, Power

Nothing beats style sheets! After all these years, it still amazes me that you can apply umpteen different looks to type with just two clicks. Of course,

Power, Power, Power
style sheets tips

you still go through that tagging process—this one's a subhead, this one's a caption. But think how much time and aggravation you save not having to manually style those 29 subheads, each with a font, point size, leading, etc. After applying a style to the body copy, two clicks per paragraph is a small price to pay compared to hand-tooling. And if that were the only benefit of styles, it would have been enough! But thank goodness, there's more! Changes. Now that you've got all your paragraphs tagged with the right style, you can afford to make styling changes at the last minute. Don't even touch those paragraphs that are affected. Now certainly that would have been enough. But again, still more. Design consistency is assured because, assuming you've applied the correct style in each case, you know the numbers all match up. So if you're not using styles, the time is now! (Okay, if you only do ads and one page flyers, you're off the hook.)

GO HOME EARLY—HA HA—STYLE SHEETS FOREVER!

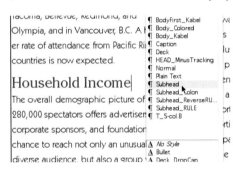

Tacoma, Bellevue, Redmond, and Olympia, and in Vancouver, B.C. A higher rate of attendance from Pacific Rim countries is now expected.

Household Income

The overall demographic picture of the 280,000 spectators offers advertisers, corporate sponsors, and foundations a

Tacoma, Bellevue, Redmond, and Olympia, and in Vancouver, B.C. A higher rate of attendance from Pacific Rim countries is now expected.

Household Income

The overall demographic picture of 280,000 spectators offers advertisers, corporate sponsors, and foundations chance to reach not only an unusual diverse audience, but also a group

Nothing better in desktop publishing than style sheets—lightening-speed text formatting, easier-than-pie style changes, instantly affecting countless paragraphs, and consistent type handling. That's a lot for two clicks. Click on the paragraph, click on the style name—zap, it's formatted. Setting up a style is easy with some sample text looking like the style you want. Because you've got to format the text anyway, might as well make it a style and avoid having to choose those type formats repeatedly. To make a style, start with an insertion point in the text, then Shift-F11 to open the Style Sheets dialog. Click New, slide to Paragraph, and, in the next dialog, name your style. Click OK, then Save. Now open the palette with F11 to apply the style to your sample so this paragraph gets updated also, when you change the style. You can get many of the styles commands with the Context menu.

CHARACTER STYLES FOR POLISHING

QUALITY-DRIVEN GRT is a leading company in its field of consumer electronics. No company surpasses its record for excellence

SERVICE-ORIENTED GRT has a record for fastest response time when customers call with problems. Get your problems solved instantly.

■ Technology-Powered GRT has been at the forefront of consumer electronics since the early 1980's. No one comes close

Character styles are the icing on the cake of paragraph styles, which do most of the work since they include paragraph *and* character attributes. Character styles are like polishing those exceptions within a paragraph. For example, say you have a bulleted list of items, each beginning with some key words to flag the reader. You apply a paragraph style that gives you hanging indents, font, size, and the like. But to make the first few words of the bullet in a contrasting font, you either do it manually or apply a character style, by highlighting the text and clicking on a character style listed at the bottom of the Style Sheets palette. To make a character style, design some sample text to base your style on, click in that text, and press Shift-F11 to go to the Styles dialog. Click New, drag down to Character, and name the style in the next dialog.

APPLYING STYLES—LOOK MA, TWO HANDS ARE BETTER THAN ONE

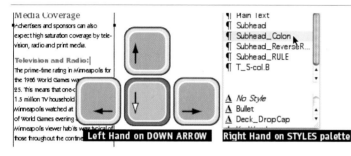

Do you use a lot of arm motion to apply styles, going back and forth between the text and the Styles palette? Grazing your eyes over the page, maybe you're also overlooking a few subheads.

Try this. Click the Content tool in the story, then choose Select All (Cmd-A or Ctrl-A) and apply the body style. Then click in the top paragraph. If you're right handed, put your cursor over the Style Sheets palette and *keep it there*. Open the palette to see all the style names and avoid scrolling the list. With your left hand, click the down arrow on the keyboard repeatedly, moving the insertion point down one line with each click, applying a style there or passing. To apply, move your right hand slightly to get to the style name in the palette. It looks like this—down, down, down, click, down, down, click, and so on. If you're left handed, switch hands.

APPLYING STYLES—WHEN THEY DON'T WORK

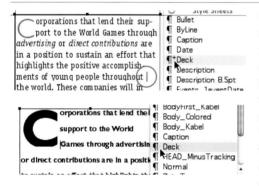

Unfortunately, all is not perfect in Quark's style sheet world. Sometimes you apply a style and the paragraph looks just the same. In the Styles palette, the style name is highlighted but there's a "+" in front of the name to indicate that the text styling doesn't match the style sheet definition. You have only one choice. Force the style to apply by pressing Option or Alt as you click the style name again. But that wipes out any local formatting in the paragraph, like italic, bold, or a different font. Then reapply those formats manually. There are two steps you can take to minimize this occurrence. First, make sure the text comes from MS Word, where a style (Normal style) is applied automatically *before* you import it. Second, when you choose Get Text, be sure Include Style Sheets is checked in the dialog.

See also, "If You Know What's Good for Ya, Include Style Sheets" (this chapter).

MODIFYING STYLES—QUICK CHANGES TO STYLE SHEETS

Style sheets are works in progress. Because a style is based on sample text, adjustments are sometimes needed if it doesn't fit all instances. When you come to the 34th subhead, you might decide that the point size should be smaller. That's the beauty of styles, you can easily make a change in the 11th hour. All you have to do is Cmd-click or Ctrl-click on the style name in the Styles palette (F11 to open) to jump to the Style Sheets dialog with that style highlighted. In fact you just type in quick succession—Cmd-click, Return/ Mac or Ctrl-click, Enter/Win to be in the Edit Style Sheet dialog for that style. And, once you edit that style using the Edit button for Character Attributes or, for paragraph attributes, the tabs at the top—Formats, Tabs, and Rules—all paragraphs with that style are immediately updated when you click OK and Save.

BASED-ON STYLES—WATCH THEM CASCADE

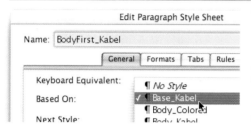

With lots of styles, based-on styles are a great production method. Simple idea—multiple styles that are related are based on a single style that has the shared attributes. In a two typeface treatment, those subheads, captions, bylines, and what not could all be based on a single style that supplies font, alignment, color, scaling, and so on. Then at the last minute, when you need to change those common attributes, you just change the definition of the base style, and all the based-on styles follow suit. Create a Base style with the common attributes in Style Sheets (Shift-F11). Then set up each based-on style by choosing the Base style from the Based On popup menu in the General panel of Edit Style. Choose the attributes that are unique to that style, such as point size. Though it's not an intuitive way to set up styles, you'll be glad when changes are afoot.

SQUEAKY-CLEAN! STYLES "TAKE" AND FONTS ARE TRUE

Here's a tip from Toby Zallman, a l-o-n-g-t-i-m-e Quark user and friend, who spent many years typesetting in a real typesetting shop. She sometimes prints out her clients' text files in a word processing program, then saves them as ASCII text, about as raw as it gets—no bold, no italic, no nothing. When she gets the text in Quark and applies styles, they go in nice 'n' easy. Then, with *character* styles, she reapplies all the italic and other local formats, as she looks at the hard copy for reference. Of course, all her styling uses true fonts so no italic or bold styling ever reaches her pages. It's a sure method and totally professional. Now are you going to try it?

See also "Character Styles for Polishing" (this chapter).
See also "Use True Fonts, Not Bold and Italic Type Styles" (Chapter 8).

   COMPARE TWO STYLE SHEETS

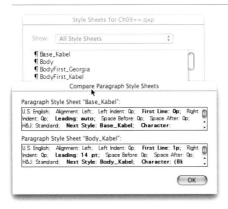

This feature is so buried that you need a microscope, or this book, to find it! When you've got a lot of styles and a long list in the Styles palette, you may discover that you have some very similar styles. You might even apply them to the same paragraph in turn and can't tell what's different about them. And maybe they're *not* different! Check it out. Go to the Styles Control Room (Shift-F11), and select the two styles you want to compare using Cmd-click or Ctrl-click to select the second one. They must both be the same type—paragraph or character. Then, get this, press the Option or Alt key so that the Append button now says Compare. You struck it rich! Click while it's hot! Amazingly enough, up pops the Compare dialog with a complete report on the attributes of each style. Well done, Watson!

   RECYCLE YOUR STYLES

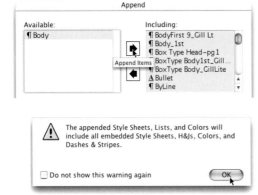

Setting up style sheets isn't hard, but why repeat your efforts? Here comes a project that's related to one you did and needs a similar look. It's a promotional campaign, or your corporate identity. Append styles so you can reuse what you've already got. Press Shift-F11 to go to Styles-Central. Click Append, then double-click the Quark filename with the style sheets you want. The Append Style Sheets dialog opens with a list of styles in that file, with descriptions, and a blank list on the right for your "shopping cart." Select the styles you want, using Shift and Cmd or Ctrl to select multiples. Then click the right arrow to drop them in your cart. The Append Conflict dialog box then asks you to choose what to do when the style you're importing has the same name as one you already have—Rename, Use New, Auto-Rename, or Use Existing. Click Repeat For All Conflicts to bypass all those approvals.

 ## IF YOU KNOW WHAT'S GOOD FOR YA, INCLUDE STYLE SHEETS

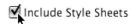

Here's a little known feature that seems totally obscure when you encounter it in the Get Text dialog—Include Style Sheets. By default, the option is not checked, but it should be. It's crucial to getting styles to work correctly in Quark. Once you check it, Quark remembers, unless you delete your preferences file. But if the option is left unchecked, any text file you import and apply styles to will not "take" the style—*without force*. Yes, you can press Option or Alt when you apply the style ("Okay brotha, either put up or shut up") and make that style listen up. But watch it take revenge by also removing all the local formatting you lovingly gave it. ("Why you dirty rat!") So you see, the lesson is, Include Style Sheets *or else*!

 ## FORMAT TEXT ON THE FLY AS IT'S IMPORTING

If your client uses styles in her word processing program, you're in luck! When you import her text file, final or not, her style names are added to your Style Sheets palette. Then make new styles based on that text, now styled. Just add one letter to each original style name, maybe a hyphen at the end. Then delete her styles. When you click Delete, you're prompted to replace that style with another one—yes, choose your equivalent style name. Paragraphs tagged with the deleted style now have the new style instead. If the text file isn't final, go back and remove the hyphens from your style names. Then, when the final text comes in and you choose Get Text, you can immediately reassign all paragraphs tagged with her style names to your styles. In the Append Conflict dialog, click Use Existing after checking the Repeat For All Conflicts (this time around) option.

  WHEN YOUR CLIENT'S STYLES GET INTO YOURS

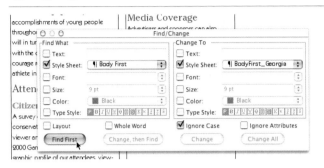

This is no X-rated tip. But maybe you've just got text and discovered, to your shock and horror, that the text… (Is pornographic? No!) That the text already has styles applied and your styles list is now doubled! My, oh my. You have two choices. Follow the previous tip, deleting each old style and replacing with your new one. Another approach—Use Find/Change (Cmd-F or Ctrl-F) to do the replacement. Uncheck Ignore Attributes to expand the dialog. Click the Style Sheet check box on both sides. On the Find side, choose the first style name you'll replace. On the Change, select the one you'll use instead. Press Option or Alt, and click Find *First*, then Change All. Then choose the second style to replace, then the third…. Pretty soon you…are…asleep…. Sweet dreams!

   STYLE AS YOU TYPE WITH NEXT STYLE

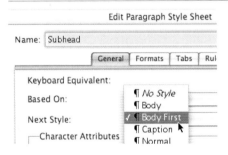

Many graphic designers (especially on Macs) don't have a word processing program, such as Word. So naturally, when you do need to type some text, you use Quark. Impress your friends and clients—set up your style sheets, and then you can write and style at the same time— multi-tasking! It's called Next Style, and it works *only* when you're typing, so don't get all excited about cutting your time applying styles. First, set up your styles (Shift-F11). After naming, check out the Next Style below. "Self" means the same style, but pick the one that's more likely. For your Headline style, how about using the Subhead style for Next Style? And for Subhead, use Body text. Then type your headline, applying the Headline style. Press Return or Enter, and you're automatically in the Subhead style. Type your subhead, press Return, you're typing in Body Text style—and only one trip to the Styles palette!

HEADLINES WITH STYLE

Headlines usually need tracking to trim down excess letter and word spacing that happens in large desktop type. You can fuss over every head-line to get it just right, or you can cut that time in half—because tracking is an attribute that can be included in your style sheet (although not kerning). How much tracking do you need? Highlight the headline, then Option- or Alt-click several times on the left-arrow button on the Measurements palette next to the track control. Or press Cmd-Option-Shift-[or Ctrl-Alt-Shift-[to close up space until it looks good. Then Cmd-click or Ctrl-click on your headline style in the Style Sheets palette (F11), quickly followed by Return or Enter, to beam up to the Edit Style Sheet dialog. Click the Edit button inside the Character Attributes area. Enter the negative Track number for that headline. OK, OK, Save. Now when you apply the headline style, it's rocking.

  INDENTING—TWO STYLES: ONE WITH, ONE WITHOUT

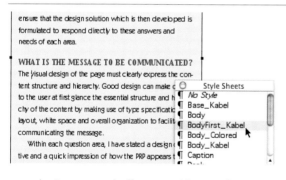

Have you ever noticed at the begin-ning of a story and after a subhead, most designers don't indent, *even if* all the other body copy paragraphs are indented? It makes sense. Indenting is a way of telling the reader, "Heads up—new paragraph." But in these two special positions, you don't need a flag, it's already obvious to the reader. And you get a much nicer squared-off corner without indenting. So how does that translate into style sheets? Two styles for body copy, not one. If you've already got your body style set up, get another one by clicking on the style name in the palette (F11) by pressing Control/Mac or right-click/Win, then choose Duplicate in the Context menu. You're whisked away to the Edit Style Sheet dialog, where all you have to do is enter a new name, Body First, click the Formats tab above, and set the First Line indent to 0. (Okay, you also have to apply the style!)

PARAGRAPH SPACING—BLISS WITH STYLES, AGONY WITHOUT

Paragraph spacing is key to making your editorial message clear. Subheads need spacing before and maybe a bit after. In-column headlines need space after. Too bad, paragraph spacing didn't make the Measurements palette. Some people, not you, do bizarre workarounds, just to avoid the dialog. Using double returns has a major pitfall—blank lines fall at the tops of columns, causing a drop down in the column alignment. They sure jump out at you on the printed piece! But when you include paragraph spacing in your style, the rest happens painlessly. Add paragraph spacing to an existing style by Cmd-clicking or Ctrl-clicking on the style name in the palette to open Style Sheets. Press a quick Return or Enter to edit the style. Click the Formats tab for Space Before, Space After. More intuitive—apply paragraph spacing (Cmd-Shift-F or Ctrl-Shift-F) to your sample text before you create your style.

   TABS—ONCE AND FOR ALL

Nobody likes tabs, so don't go there… often. With styles, keep your tab exposure to a minimum. A quick in and out, and the rest is practically automatic. Style your first table with font, point size, and so on. Then Cmd-Shift-T or Ctrl-Shift-T (T for Tabs). After you set your tabs and your table is glowing, click in the body of the table. Press Shift-F11 to open Style Sheets. Click New…Paragraph. Quark picks up all the attributes, including tabs, leaders, everything. Try this style naming—T5-col.B. T stands for Tab, so all tab styles list together. It's got 5 tabbed columns, and it's the table Body style. Now click in the column headers paragraph and set up a new style—T5-col.H for Header. With consistent naming, it's easy to spot the style you need. Import your next five-column table, highlight, apply T5-col.B, click in the column headers, apply T5-col.H.

See also the tips on tabs and indents (Chapter 8).

STYLES FOR WIDOW AND ORPHAN CONTROL

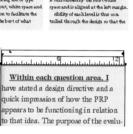

Widows? Orphans? (Is this *Oliver Twist*?) Widow and orphan control lead to Good Typography—because the first line of a paragraph widowed at the bottom of a text box or the last line orphaned at the top *will not be tolerated*. Two lines minimum, fair and square. Start with your subheads. In Style> Formats or the Formats tab of the Edit Subhead Style Sheet box (Shift-F11), click Keep Lines together and All Lines in ¶ so your two-line subhead stays together. Then add Keep with Next ¶. For a minimum of two lines of body copy following the subhead, apply to the body or its style sheet the attribute Keep Lines Together, then Start: 2 End: 2. Warning: Flush bottom layouts are *not permitted* when widow and orphan control rules. In every case, the last line at the bottom will be automatically moved to the top of the next linked box or column. Do you understand?

PARAGRAPH RULES WITH STYLES ARE A SNAP

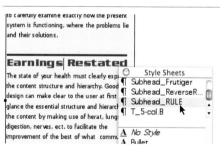

Paragraph rules pop your heads or subheads and add pizazz when you lack pictures. Rules above or below a paragraph are done with typesetting. When text is edited, the rule moves with the paragraph, no hand-tooling. And you can use rules in a style! Set it up once, use it again and again. Create a sample paragraph first. Click a headline or subhead with the Content tool. Press Cmd-Shift-N or Ctrl-Shift-N (Style> Paragraph Rules). Click Rule Above or Rule Below or both. For length, choose Indents so the rule goes the width of the box, minus any indents you enter. Or choose Text so the rule extends as wide as the longest line. Set other choices. Offset is given as a percent, but points are easier. For Rule Above, try the point size p14 or 14pt, then click Apply. For Rule Below, try half the point size. Now set up your style….

SUBHEADS REVERSED OUT OF A BAR—PARAGRAPH RULE STYLE

exactly how the present system is functioning, where
the problems lie and their solutions.

HealthCare Policy

The state of your health must clearly express the content structure and hierarchy. Good design can make
clear to the user at first glance the essential structure
and hierarchy of the content by making use of head

Style Sheets

¶ Subhead_ Colon
¶ Subhead_ReverseRULE
¶ Subhead_RULE
¶ Subtitle

Edit Paragraph Style Sheet

ne: Subhead_ReverseRULE

General | Formats | Tabs | Rules

☑ Rule Above

Length:	Text	Style:	▬▬▬
From Left:	0p	Width:	14 pt
From Right:	0p	Color:	■ PANTONE...
Offset:	–p5	Shade:	100%

Reverse type lightens up a page with color. This reverse is done with a paragraph rule. It takes some fussing to set up, impractical to do case by case. But you don't have to— paragraph rules can be in your style. Start with some sample text on the page, and base your style on that. Click the Content tool in a subhead, and make sure it has a descender (as in g, p, y). Add one, if necessary, to make your sample representative. Then press Cmd-Shift-N or Ctrl-Shift-N (Style> Paragraph Rules). The sample shown here has a Rule Above, Length: Text and a thick line Width in color. For 14pt Frutiger Black, I chose a 14pt line Width and an offset of –p5 (–.069"). Then flip over to the Formats tab in the dialog, and add some para- graph spacing. If your rule is dark, make the subhead text white before making your style.

PARAGRAPH RULES HANG OUT

Here's an unusual look you might want to try. Your paragraph, maybe a pull quote, intro copy, or other specialty text, is indented on the left, right, or both sides. Above and perhaps below, you've got a paragraph rule going the full width. Looks easy, but it's got a little twist. Start by indenting your text in Formats, Cmd-Shift-F or Ctrl-Shift-F, noting the amount of the indents. Click Apply. Then, without closing, switch over to the Rules tab. Click Rule Above, Below, or both. Set Length to Indents. Now enter those same left and right *paragraph* indents here for the *rule* indents (From Left and From Right)—*but*, make them negative numbers. Finish with Width, Color, and Offsets (in points). Click Apply. Your text should be indented from the rule, which goes the full width of the box! Now make it a style sheet.

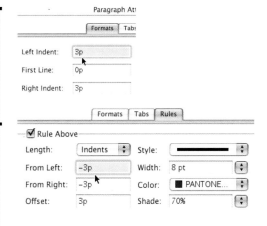

THE ART

OF TYPE

"Well-printed books are just as scarce as well-written ones, and every author should remember that the most costly books derive their value from the craft of the printer and not from the author's genius."

George Bernard Shaw

Paragraph Att

| Formats | Tabs |

Left Indent: 3p

First Line: 0p

Right Indent: 3p

| Formats | Tabs | Rules |

☑ Rule Above

Length:	Indents	Style:	▬▬▬
From Left:	–3p	Width:	8 pt
From Right:	–3p	Color:	■ PANTONE...
Offset:	3p	Shade:	70%

Livin' la Vida Layout

LAST EXIT BEFORE LAYOUT

When all is said and done, it's the layout that goes out the door and into the hands of your client or boss. This meaty chapter covers all the tricky

Livin' la Vida Layout

can't-live-without layout tips

aspects of assembling the parts. Start with one of Quark 6's most exciting features—layout spaces. Then discover more than seven great ways to make your layout fit, including desperate measures. Know how to send that head or subhead to the top of the next column or box? Getting those lines of body copy to line up across the spread? Takes a few tricks. Moving and removing pages, and more. Then, there's a plethora of ways to align and space items for a pleasing finish, not to mention making scads of multiples with a single click or two. Getting runarounds to go all the way around, and around irregular silhouettes and graphics. Finally, you come to some of the least known capabilities in Quark—layers and tables—having only first appeared in Quark 5 and enhanced a lot in Quark 6. With one chapter, the kingdom can be yours!

LAYOUT SPACES FOR DIFFERENT VERSIONS AND PAGE SIZES

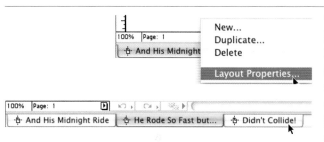

The operational word for layout spaces—*repurposing*. Don't go back and forth between multiple files of related projects, such as in an ad campaign, to reuse content. In the past, when the page size changed, you started a new file. Now Quark 6 can accommodate any number of layouts of varying dimensions and orientations—all in the same file or *project*. Instead of documents, you now have *layouts*, along with Print Layout preferences, not Document preferences, and a Layout menu for making new layouts and setting Layout Properties, including Layout Type (Print or Web). Try this. When you're designing and want another look, instead of starting over, just Duplicate the current layout (Layout> Duplicate). Now you have all the same content, but with a new set of master pages. You can have a new layout in no time by just rearranging the items. Navigate between layouts using the tabs down in the lower-left screen.

   TITLE BAR BLUES—PROJECT 1: LAYOUT 1: HUH?

You launch Quark 6, look at the title bar and… what's all that *stuff* up there? See the previous tip for a complete explanation. But, because you can now have multiple *layouts* (what we would've called "documents" in the past) in one big *project* (what we would've called a .qxd file before), you've got to name not only the New Project (Ctrl-N)—when you save the file, .qxp—but also each new layout that you make. If you have only one layout, your title bar will read "(your file name): Layout 1." No big deal, but at least you won't be banging around trying to find out how to get rid of the annoying "Layout 1." (I admit to this initial reaction!) Guess what, even if you only have one layout, you can use it to give your filename a subtitle! Name your layout from Layout> Layout Properties, or use the Context menu.

SYNCHRONIZE TEXT (OR NOT) IN DIFFERENT LAYOUTS

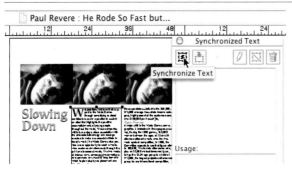

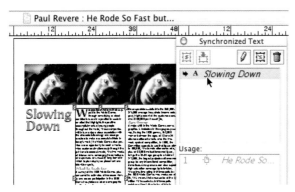

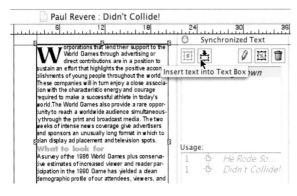

Synchronizing text means you edit text once for an entire project (in other words, multiple layouts in one file as described above), and all synched text in other layouts instantly updates. Select text with either the Item or Content tool, then click the Synchronized Text button, top left of the Synchronized Text palette (Window menu). The entire story is added to the palette as a named entry, not just what's highlighted. Now add this text to another layout by clicking the story name in the palette, selecting an empty box on the page, then clicking the second button, Insert Text into Text Box. If you duplicate a layout, synchronize all text *first* before duplicating—otherwise, it's not automatically synched. If you add synched text to existing text in a box, the new synched text replaces what's there. To un-synchronize text, click the Unsynchronize All button or delete the selected story entry—trash-it/Mac or X-it/Win in the palette. The text story stays on the page but is now *custom* text—editing it has no effect on other layouts.

FITTING THE TEXT TO THE LAYOUT

You know the Fit Picture to Box command? Well how about a Fit Text to Layout command? Sorry, nice try. The tough part is making it fit *without compromising the design*. But here are a few ways to pull out all the stops and make it fit kosher-style, not klutz-style. What's known as "tricks up the sleeve"—from best to worst.

Tracking short lines. First line of attack, recommended even if fit is not a problem. Look at the last line of each paragraph and see if there's a hyphenated syllable or short word, alone on the line. If so, highlight the entire paragraph, four clicks, then remove a few units of tracking until the short line pops to the previous line.

See also "Track Body Copy to Fix Short Lines" (Chapter 8).

Reduce paragraph spacing. If you've used paragraph spacing for body copy, reduce the amount of the space. A fast fix with style sheets.

Reduce point size or leading *slightly*. Again, use your style sheets to make very small changes until it fits. This technique is best used for stand-alone projects, one-time designs—not a newsletter or quarterly report.

Make pictures smaller. Consider reducing slightly those pictures that are less important. Just a bit. Or reduce the runaround down to 9pts (.125").

Tracking body copy. First *sneaky* way to fit more in, and the only good way. To reduce letter or word spacing for body copy consistently, edit your style sheets. Cmd-click or Ctrl-click on the body style name in the Style Sheets palette (F11) to open the dialog. Reduce tracking, a character attribute, in very small increments, perhaps tenths of a point, though it can be as little as .001pt.

Reduce slightly the page margins. Go to the master pages and choose Page> Master Guides.

Apply 98% horizontal scaling for body copy. This is common, although not my favorite, because it changes the aspect ratio of the type. Again, use style sheets to add the character attribute.

Desperate measures. Case by case. Here's where you stoop to the bottom line—whatever it takes, short of deleting text. What is the client or audience least likely to spot? For example, you've got a ton of tabbed charts, but a few of them need a small adjustment to the last tab. Go ahead, do it manually—make sure no one's watching. Extend a text box a tiny bit beyond the right margin. Extend a text box down below the bottom margin a smidgeon to fit in the last line of the paragraph. You get the picture. Don't ask. Don't tell.

CONTROLLING THE LAYOUT WITH SPECIAL CHARACTERS

This summer a small group of Southwest College students has been engaged in a most interesting endeavor—learning how museums make curatorial decisions in constructing art exhibitions and how they incorporate technology to transform their services to the public.↓

Development¶
Starting June 19, each over five weeks, the ir gathered here in the la style conference room to talks by a wide ranş and technology profes both inside the Colleg business community a large. Thorp, who has provided the vision fo got things off to a stro:

You can shorten a text box from a bottom handle to force a headline to the top of the next linked box. But sometimes the Next Column and Next Box characters work better. Make an insertion point in the text, right before the headline you want to send on. Press Enter on the *keypad* and it's done. With a subdivided text box, the headline goes to the top of the next column, *same* box. Either way, press the up arrow on the keyboard to send the insertion point back to where you started. Turn on Invisibles (Cmd-I or Ctrl-I)—there's a single down-arrow character, which you can delete to remove the break. If you have *subdivided* text boxes, you can send the headline to the next *box*, using Shift-Enter (keypad), making a double-down arrow. With the Auto Text Box, you can have a sequence of articles with headings at the tops of pages! Bravo!

WITH SUBHEADS, ALIGNING BODY COPY TAKES TRICKS

College and from the business community at large.

Baseline

Museum Practices

Six interns are participating full time in this nine-week interdisciplinary program titled "Technology Content

gathered here ir
style conference
to talks by a wid
and technology
both inside the
business commu
who has provid

Right Indent:	up
Leading:	14 pt
Space Before:	p12
Space After:	p2
Alignment:	Left

Getting body text to align by the baseline makes a cleaner and more approachable page, although there are good designs that can't be accomplished with this goal. If all we had was body copy, layout would be a cinch. Subheads, especially two-liners, make it tougher. But it can be a cinch. First, the subhead leading must equal the body leading. So if the body is 9 on 13—9pt with 13pt leading—then the subhead can be 9, 10, 11, 12 or 13pt on 13pt leading and in bold, italic, or a contrasting font. (*But*, if your subheads are bigger than the body, use baseline grid to avoid non-alignment when subheads fall at the tops of columns—see next tip.) Second, the paragraph spacing must equal one line of leading, with more space above than below. For 13pt leading, use 11, 12, or 13pt Space Before and 2pt, 1pt, or no Space After.

BASELINE GRID—TEXT ALIGNMENT ACROSS THE PAGE

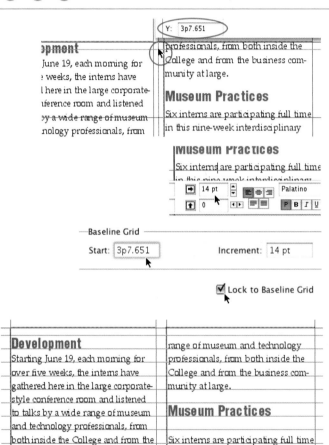

Keep text aligned by the baseline across the page or spread with Lock to Baseline Grid—especially good with text-heavy layouts, where non-alignment is noticeable. Text snaps to the grid, a set of horizontal guides set at a fixed interval down the page. First, where will the baseline grid start on the page, measured from the top edge? If you've moved the zero point on your rulers, reset them ("zeroing-out") by double-clicking in the small square at the intersection of the two rulers. Then drag from there to the baseline of the top line of body copy, noting the Y value on the Measurements palette. Enter Y into the Start value, under Baseline Grid (Paragraph preferences—Cmd-Option-Shift-Y or Ctrl-Alt-Shift-Y). For Increment, enter the body copy leading. Then apply Lock to Baseline to the body copy and subheads, preferably using style sheets, in Formats (Cmd-Shift-F or Ctrl-Shift-F). It's unnecessary and distracting to show the grid (Option-F7 or Ctrl-F7).

VERTICALLY JUSTIFYING TEXT

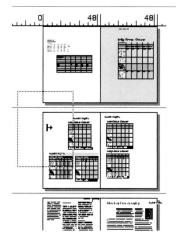

Inter ¶ Max—0p

His summer a small group of Southwest College students has been engaged in a most interesting endeavor—learning how museums make curatorial decisions in constructing art exhibitions and gathering.

How they incorporate technology to transform their services to the public will be a further area of research, which will bring them to a greater awareness of the museum-technology interface.

Inter ¶ Max—1p

His summer a small group of Southwest College students has been engaged in a most interesting endeavor—learning how museums make curatorial decisions in constructing art exhibitions and gathering.

How they incorporate technology to transform their services to the public will be a further area of research, which will bring them to a greater awareness of the museum-technology interface.

14-pt. LEADING
7-pt. PARAGRAPH SPACE

Vertical Alignment

Type: Justified

Inter ¶ Max: 1p

Vertically justifying text in a box so it goes from the top to the bottom regardless of the number of lines or the box height is questionable at best. Sometimes with a flush-bottom layout, however, you have to resort to "desperate measures," instead of using more kosher methods (as in the two tips above). To get this authoritative look, go to Item> Modify by double-clicking the box with the Item tool. Or, with the Content tool, Cmd- or Ctrl-double-click. Click the Text tab, and from the Vertical Alignment Type menu, select Justified. If you leave the Inter ¶ Max setting at 0, the leading increases equally. But if you want the needed space only to be added *between* paragraphs, enter an Inter ¶ Max setting. If your setting is too low, leading will still be affected to achieve justification. Avoid a paragraph return on the last line, which offsets the justification.

REARRANGE YOUR PAGES IN THUMBNAILS VIEW

You can use the Page Layout palette or Page> Move Pages to move pages to new positions. But did you know that you can also rearrange pages in Thumbnails view? Press Cmd-Ctrl-V or Ctrl-Alt-V to highlight the View % field in the lower-left corner of the layout window. Or just double-click it. Type "T" for thumbnails, then press Return or Enter. On the Mac, you can see the type better in thumbnails if Text Greeking is turned off in the General Print Layout preference. Then, with Item or Content tool, grab a page and move it to a new location. Use the Shift key to select a range of pages or use Cmd-click or Ctrl-click to select non-consecutive pages. If you see a right-pointing arrow cursor before you release, you will shuffle the remaining pages down. If you see a down-arrow cursor, your page will push the next spread down one.

TWO WAYS TO REMOVE PAGES

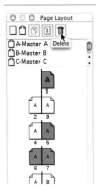

Having to remove pages is common. Aside from budget cuts and project reductions, you typically end up with more pages than you need due to importing text and linking when the text is still at a large point size. Naturally, you end up adding a lot more pages than you really need to get all the text on pages. Once you size down the type, you've got extra pages. You can remove pages from the Page> Delete Pages command, when you're on a layout page, not a master. Specify in the dialog which pages to delete. If you're a fan of the Page Layout palette, select a range of page icons using Shift-click. Or use Cmd-click or Ctrl-click to select non-consecutive page icons. Then click the Trash/Mac or X/Win button at the top of the palette to delete.

TEXT RECOMPOSING WHEN OPENING SOMEONE ELSE'S FILE?

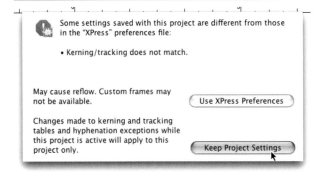

Workgroup publishing is a fact of life. Typically your work is reviewed by someone else, or you get files from other designers. What happens when you open another person's Quark file? The Nonmatching Preference alert dialog opens to warn you that the file you are about to open may contain *dangerous* material. Just kidding. It only contains different track or kern tables or different hyphenation exceptions. I have a feeling that it's more than that because I get it all the time with my own files! To open that file without causing the text to reflow, just click the button *Keep Project Settings*. If you click Use XPress Preferences (your application settings, not the document's), the text will likely reflow on opening. Other things that can cause text recomposing are corrupt fonts or fonts on your machine of the same name but different font manufacturers than the ones used in the file.

TEXT RECOMPOSING WHILE OPENING AN OLDER QUARK DOC?

It's pretty easy to convert a Quark document from versions as far back as XPress 3.1—use the Open command. If you just want to make a few changes, you don't need to do anything special. By default, text doesn't recompose and line breaks stay the same. But if you're overhauling the file, you can use the improved hyphenation introduced in Quark 4. You get better-looking text with the more recent Expanded hyphenation method when text is reflowed. Quark re-hyphenates words based on its own dictionary and makes up hyphenation if needed. Though not perfect, expanded hyphenation is the best bet. Apply expanded hyphenation to an older file by going to the Open dialog box and pressing Option or Alt when clicking Open. If the file is already open, you can apply the expanded option by opening Preferences (Cmd-Option-Shift-Y or Ctrl-Alt-Shift-Y) and choosing Expanded for Hyphenation Method (Paragraph preference).

BLEEDS—GOING OVER THE EDGE

In print design, when a color extends to the edge of the paper, it's called a *bleed*—an effective way to bring drama to a page. It seems like the artwork—picture, type, colored box, or line—would extend right to the trim edge of the page. But imagine the printer trying to cut the paper right on that colored edge. Forget it, nothing in printing is that exact. Artwork must extend beyond the edge, usually ⅛" or 9pt. Then when the cut is made, it doesn't matter if it's a little off. To bleed an item off the top *or* bottom, simply add +.125" or +p9 to the Height value in the Measurements palette—that's .25" or 1p6 for top *and* bottom bleeds. To bleed off the outside left or right trim edges, add the same number to the item's Width. Make sure the picture or type goes that far. For top and left page bleeds, subtract the same number from the Y (top bleed) or from the X (left bleed).

  ## SPREAD GUIDES MAKE ALIGNMENTS EASY

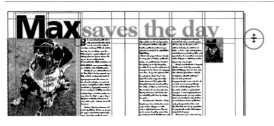

Most left or right alignments are handled by column guides. But when aligning items by their top or bottom edges across facing pages of a spread, you need help. Compared to the Space/Align box or the Measurements palette, a *spread* guide is fast and intuitive—just drag down a guide and snap everything to it. Start as if you're just bringing down a ruler guide from the top ruler. But when you release it, the cursor needs to be on the pasteboard around the page, *not on the page*. Easiest, one-step method—bring your mouse down to the right or left pasteboard, going far enough down so that the guide aligns where you want. When you let go, with cursor on the pasteboard, it's a spread guide! Now just drag each item to the guide and it snaps right in. Check 'em by the numbers—you'll find no mistakes.

   ## ALIGN ITEMS FROM THEIR CENTERS

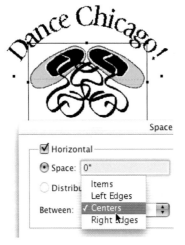

Sometimes you just have to do those odd-ball alignments for items of various sizes and shapes—from the vertical centers of side-by-side items or from the horizontal centers of top-to-bottom items. And in Quark, there's only one good way, but it's a tricky pass with the Space/Align dialog. Select your items using Shift-and-click or marquee them with the Item or Content tool. Then press Cmd-comma or Ctrl-comma to open Item> Space/Align. There are two quagmires. First, is it Horizontal or Vertical alignment? Once you make the wrong move *and choose Apply*, there's nothing you can do except cancel and start over. Think of the axis on which each item must move to align—side-by-side items use Vertical and top-to-bottom items use Horizontal. Second pitfall, Between: Items *isn't* what you want, typically—that's only for butting items. But for this tip, you want Centers anyway. The rest is a piece of cake.

SPACING ITEMS—ALL THINGS BEING EQUAL

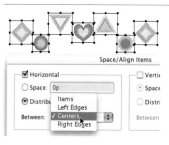

How do you get a set of three or more items equally spaced? This calls for the dreaded Space/Align dialog box. Why so feared? You can easily waste your time and have to start over (see previous tip). With your items selected, press Cmd-comma or Ctrl-comma to open Item> Space/Align. As above, think of the axis on which each item must move to align—to equally space side-by-side items, use Horizontal alignment and with top-to-bottom items, use Vertical. The key is choosing Distribute Evenly, rather than the Space option. If items are identical, it won't matter which option you choose from the Between menu. If items aren't the same, experiment with the Between choices and see what works.

Settings in the Space/Align Dialog

Item Arrangement	Align	Space Equally
Side-by-side	Vertical	Horizontal
Top-to-Bottom	Horizontal	Vertical

STEP AND REPEAT *AND* SUPER STEP AND REPEAT

Use Step and Repeat to duplicate one or more selected items with or without offsets as many times as you want. Press Cmd-Option-D or Ctrl-Alt-D to start. To duplicate right on top—great for aligning—set Offsets to 0, click OK, then Shift-drag the item to keep it aligned. The command is also good for making multiple copies of anything, like a set of lines down the page. Super Step and Repeat is a fascinating way to work with a single selected item, and optionally its content, that can be cumulatively scaled and rotated. Go to Item> Super Step and Repeat. Choose number of copies, offsets, angle, and a series of attributes for the end state—ending line weight or frame width, box shade, item scale and skew. Pick from nine points of origin for the rotation and scaling. The XTension of the same name must be loaded and active—check Utilities> XTensions Manager.

IDENTICAL BOXES THAT PERFECTLY FIT A GIVEN SPACE

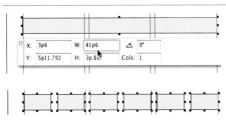

My friend Clint Funk gave me this great tip. Want to fit a bunch of identical boxes into a given space so it looks perfect? Say you want 6 identical boxes, equally spaced apart by 1p6 (.25"), fitting perfectly across the space from left-to-right margins. Draw a box that goes the full width of that space, at the desired height. Now, in the Measurements palette, subtract from the Width the total width of the gutters. With six boxes, that's five gutters (one less than the number of boxes), each gutter 1p6 wide. Total gutter is five times one gutter or 5*1p6 or 5*.25". Don't try to do the math, type it in and let Quark do it.

With total width of the space at 41p6 (6.917"), it looks like this: 41p6-5*1p6 (6.917"–5*.25"). Press Return or Enter. Now divide that width by the number of boxes to get the width of one box: 34p/6 = 5p8 (5.667"/6 = .944").

Copy that number W and open Step and Repeat. Repeat Count 5 (you already have one). Vertical offset is 0. For Horizontal offset, paste in your number—plus one gutter width: 5p8+1p6 (.944"+.25"). Click OK and your boxes should be perfectly fitting that space!

   ## DON'T ALWAYS WANT YOUR TEXT AT THE TOP OF A BOX?

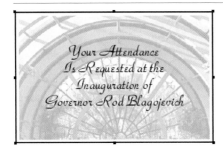

When you color a text box, you usually don't want the type hugging the top edge. For that fancy headline in a blended box or a simple headline with a colored frame width to set it off, vertically centered is usually better. Or for something like an invitation, you want the title vertically centered *on the page*. All easy matters for the Text tab of the Modify box. With your text box selected, go to Modify (Cmd-M or Ctrl-M). Click the Text tab, and check out the Vertical Alignment popup menu with options for Centered, Bottom, Justified, and the default Top. To vertically center text to the page, first extend the top and bottom box handles to the top and bottom page edges. Or just enter the page height as the box Height in the Measurements palette. Then set the Y to 0. Finally, vertically center the text.

MULTIPLE PICTURES WITH EXACT POSITIONING

X: 5p+26p6   W: 26p6   △ 0°   X%: 87.7%   X+ 0p
Y: 20p1.946 H: 18p.16   ⤢ 0p   Y%: 87.7%   Y+ p.

X: 31p6+1p   W: 14p10.075 △ 0°   X%: 50.3%   X+ 0p
Y: 20p1.94   H: 10p3.161   ⤢ 0p   Y%: 50.3%   Y+ 0p

Positioning pictures in a row or column gives them strength. Using the Measurements palette to calculate, you can butt pictures edge-to-edge or separate them by an equal space. With pictures A and B in a row, select A, copy its Width (double-click the number to highlight)—26p6 — and add that to its X location: 5p+26p6, press Return or Enter. Copy that number X, then Undo (click on the page first), which puts A back where it was. Select box B, and paste that number into its X, which puts box B butted to A. If you want it one pica out, add one pica to the X: (current X)+1p, press Return or Enter. If pictures are stacked vertically, substitute Height for Width, and substitute Y for X. Another method, though less exact, is easier. After A is positioned, drag out the zero point from the intersection of the rulers and align the vertical axis along the right edge of A. Then B's X coordinate is simply the distance out you want—1p, and so on.

WITH COLORED BOXES, TRY UNEQUAL TEXT INSETS

Text Inset	
☑ Multiple Insets	
Top:	48 pt
Left:	0 pt
Bottom:	36 pt
Right:	0 pt

Use asymmetrical color borders for a text box to get a more unusual effect with a sidebar or pull quote. Think of insets as the text box margins. With your box selected, press Cmd-M or Ctrl-M to go to Item> Modify and click on the Text tab. Under Text Inset, check Multiple Insets, then enter values for all four sides. Consider a large inset at the top, half of that at the bottom, and none on the sides. Then add a large initial cap and justify the body. Or how about a big left inset with an image overlapped onto that area. Another idea—with a top or large bottom inset, overlap a picture box of the same width so that there's about a quarter-inch of color extending above or below the picture. The sidebar now has the text and picture in one neat package.

GOING ALL THE WAY…AROUND

There are occasions when wrapping text all the way around four sides of a box is the look you're after. But if you plunk a picture into the middle of a text box, you'll find that the text only wraps on three sides—top, bottom, and either the left or right side, depending on which side is wider. But you can have your cake and eat it too using the Run Text Around All Sides option in Item > Modify. There is a trick, however. You're used to setting the runaround for the picture box so it seems natural to do the same for this feature, *but* this time it's the text box underneath the picture that has the "run all around" option. Go to Modify by double-clicking on the text box with the Item tool to set this four-way wrap. Click on the Text tab, then check Run Text Around All Sides.

BOSS SAYS, "KEEP THOSE PICTURES LOCKED TO THE TEXT!"

When pictures need to stay at a particular point in the text, use anchored boxes. Then, when text is edited, pictures "travel" with the text. To anchor a picture box into text, copy or cut it using the Item tool. Then, with the Content tool, make an insertion point in the text and paste. To put the picture in its own space, add a blank line before pasting. Set the leading of that line to Auto so the vertical space automatically fits the picture height. Position it horizontally with paragraph alignments. If the picture is on the same line as text, click on the picture to see handles, then use the two buttons on the left end of the Measurements palette to Align with Text Ascent or with Text Baseline. The former drops the picture down to roughly top align with the text. The latter sits the picture bottom on the first line text baseline. Anchored boxes are best for a one-column book layout or for small drop-in icons.

RUN, RUN, RUNAROUND, I GET AROUND—IRREGULARITY

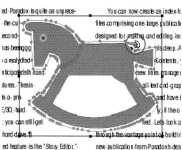

Hear the Beach Boys playing?—a tip for sunny Californians and everyone else! You've got an irregular shaped EPS graphic or a cutout photo, outlined with a clipping path to drop out the background, done in Photoshop or in Quark. How do you control the runaround for that irregular-shaped picture? Select the picture box and do Cmd-T or Ctrl-T to open Item> Runaround. For an easy way out, select Type: Auto Image, and enter a number for Outset to control the distance from the text to the picture edges. This may be enough. However, if you want to edit the outset boundary, then there are two steps. Step one, change runaround Type to Non-White Areas. Click OK. Step two, press Option-F4 or Ctrl-F10 to turn on (or off) Item> Edit Runaround. Zoom in, and edit the magenta path by moving points, control handles, and path segments. Option-click or Ctrl-click on a point to remove it. Dragging from between boundary points goes faster than dragging a point.

DOESN'T LOOK LIKE A RUNAROUND UNLESS…

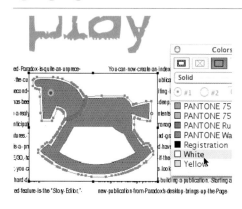

Here's one I stumbled over, and it really caught me off-guard. You know how the default color of a picture box is white? Well, if you leave it white and then try to make an irregular text wrap around the picture, it will look like nothing's working. The white box background is covering up the text that's wrapping around, underneath the box! If you're zoomed in close enough to read the text, you'll probably notice what's happening. But from any kind of distance, you'll think you're doing something wrong. So get in the habit of setting the box color to None *before* you make an irregular runaround so you won't be thrown for a loop <ha ha>.

TYPE MASKS IMAGE—TEXT TO BOX

Turn text into a picture box shaped the same as those letters—then fill with a picture! First, style a headline with a very bold font, such as Futura Extra Bold or Gill Sans Ultra Bold, probably with tracking. Put the headline on top of the image you plan to use, and size the type to match. Then highlight the first line of the text—you can only do one line at a time. Convert the text with Style> Text To Box. Keep the original text, still there, on the pasteboard for possible changes. With picture box background color set to None, you can see the image through the text. If your picture is dark, temporarily add a light-colored frame width. Move the picture-text until it lines up with the image the way you want. Repeat for any additional lines. Now, use Get Picture for each picture box. With the Content tool, move the image within the box so it lines up with the big picture behind. Then delete that big picture box.

  GETTING TEXT INTO A TABLE

You can type right into a table if you've got text cells, not picture cells—choose Link Cells in the Table Properties dialog when you drag out the Table tool. To go to the next cell, press Enter on the *keypad*. You can change picture cells to text cells—highlight with the Content tool, then choose Item> Content> Text. But there's no direct way to import a text file so that it flows into all the cells of your table. You've got an extra step—import the table text into a simple text box, then convert it to a table. First, make sure the fields are separated with tabs, spaces, or commas, and the lines of text are separated with returns. The rest is easy. Highlight the text, then choose Item> Convert Text to Table. In the Convert Text to Table dialog, the default row and column numbers reflect what's in your text. Click OK.

   FORMATTING THE TEXT OF AN ENTIRE TABLE

ProCorp, Inc.					
Projected Sales					
In millions					
	2003	2004	2006	2006	2010
Corporate	198	395	791	1,977	3,954
Commercial	94	188	376	939	1,878
Chicago	59	119	238	594	1,189
Region	42	85	169	423	846
State-wide	32	64	128	321	641
National	12	24	48	121	242
International	30	6	12	24	60

Because you use Cmd-A or Ctrl-A to select *all* the text in a story, you might think that would work fine to highlight all the text in the table, after clicking in one cell. Wrong. It should work that way. Instead, it highlights all the text in one cell—anyone ever put a novel in a cell? But the answer is easy. Just take your Content tool, and drag from the top-left cell down to the bottom right cell so all cells are highlighted. Or, same tool, from just outside the selected table, drag across or down along any table edge to highlight column by column or row by row. Then style from the Style menu, not the Measurements palette! If you're using style sheets, highlighting across cells is necessary for both character and paragraph styles. Click on one cell of table text and apply a paragraph style sheet—you get the text in one cell styled!

   INSERT ROWS AND COLUMNS USING EXISTING FORMATTING

Number of Rows: 1

◉ Insert Above Selection

◯ Insert Below Selection

☑ Keep Attributes

You know that scene—you've got that table all done, it took hours to get everything to fit and be formatted and now they need another row or column! (See next tip.) It could be worse. Now in Quark 6 you can add a row or column, and pick up existing formatting. With the Content tool, click in a cell or highlight cells that you want to match in your new row or column. Go to Item> Table> Insert Rows, or > Insert Columns. I prefer getting the same commands from the Context menu (control-click/Mac or right-click/Win). Choose where to insert, either above or below (rows), or left or right (columns) in relation to where you clicked or highlighted cells. Then, the key step, click Keep Attributes, which copies type specifications, including style sheets, local formatting, picture attributes (angle, skew, offset), and settings in the Text and Cell tabs of Modify dialog.

IF YOU *HATE* MATH, BUT NEED MORE ROWS AND COLUMNS

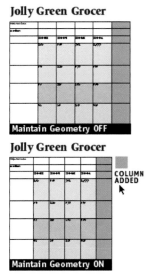

I'm just teasing. You don't have to love math to like this feature called MAINTAIN GEOMETRY (accompany with trumpet fanfare). With this option on, when you add or delete rows or columns to or from your table, the outside dimensions of the table stay the same size—very useful if you don't have room on your page to enlarge. If you add a column, your cell widths get smaller. If you delete a row, your cell height increases. To turn on Maintain Geometry (it's off by default), do Cmd-M or Ctrl-M (Item> Modify), click on the Table tab, and check Maintain Geometry. Or easier—use the Context menu (Control-click/Mac or right-click/Win), then choose Table> Maintain Geometry. But if you like your current cell width or height, and want to add on ("Honey, let's add a second bedroom"), then go direct to Item> Table> Insert Rows, or > Insert Columns—even better, use the Context menu again.

COMBINING TEXT AND PICTURES IN A TABLE

Because tables condense a lot of information, use pictures to make tables easier to understand. Pictures are the visual anchors for the text on each line. How do you get the pictures? If you don't have a blank column or row to use, insert one. If you've only got text cells, convert them to picture cells. Drag across to highlight those cells with the Content tool, then choose Item> Content> Picture or use the Context menu (Control-click/Mac or right-click/Win). Finally, put your insertion point in a cell and do Get Picture. For fast sizing, use Cmd-Option-Shift-> or -</Mac

or Ctrl-Alt-Shift-> or -</Win to size the picture larger or smaller in 5% increments. For in-between sizes, use the X% and Y% fields in the Measurements palette. Extra perk—you can use or make a clipping path to silhouette an image inside your table!

See also "Insert Rows and Columns Using Existing Formatting?" (this chapter).

GRIDLESS AND SEE-THROUGH TABLES

Make tables transparent! Then why use the table tool? Can't you just apply styles to the text (or use the Tab ruler) to get the same effect? Yes, *but* not with text that wraps around within a cell. Using tabs just doesn't cut it. Another related idea—use horizontal gridlines or no lines and no table color background to see a picture underneath! To remove gridlines, select your table with the *Item* tool, go to the Grid tab of Modify (Cmd-M or Ctrl-M). On the right, choose from the default Select All (gridlines), as well as Select Horizontal or Select Vertical. For just horizontal lines, click Select Vertical, then set Width to 0. To see the full effect on your page, use Hide Guides (F7). Now put that table over an image. Select the table with the Item tool and set table background color to None in Colors palette (F12). Then drag across all cells with the *Content* tool and again choose None for box color. Yes, doing it twice with Item and Content is what's called for!

   ### MISCELLANEOUS, BUT CRUCIAL, TABLE TIPS

Here are a handful of tips you won't want to miss.

Combine cells. To combine two or more adjacent cells, across or down, highlight the cells with the Content tool, then choose Item> Table> Combine Cells (or Context menu). Content in all but the top-left cell is deleted.

Scale a table—and its cells—*non*-proportionally by simply dragging any handle. Type and pictures stay the same size, but text may re-wrap and pictures may get cropped.

Scale a table—and its contents—proportionally. Drag a handle while pressing Cmd-Option-Shift or Ctrl-Alt-Shift.

Convert a table back to text. Choose Item> Table> Convert Table to Text (or Context menu).

Make a series of identical tables and skip that dialog when you drag out to make a table. Go to Preferences—double-click on the Table tool in the toolbox. Click the Modify button, then the Creation tab. Choose table attributes (number of rows and columns, and the like), and uncheck Show Creation Dialog.

SNAZZ UP THAT TABLE WITH COLOR

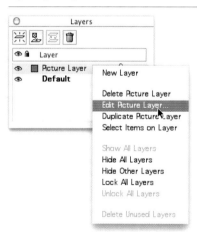

The Content tool is King of table styling. Drag across or down, just outside the selected table, using the black arrow cursor. From the Colors palette, apply a box background color as you would for any box. Apply a blend to the whole table. For Linear and Mid-Linear blends, try reversing the blend direction for every other column or row. Shift-click from outside the table edge to select. Then change the blend degree to 90°, –90°, or 180°. Or be more conventional with alternating color rows, using a color and a tint. Color the type of highlighted cells also. Change the gridline attributes, color, weight, style, and so on by directly selecting the lines on the page using Shift-click. Or click with the Item or Content tool to bring up the Context menu, with commands Gridlines> Select Horizontal/Vertical/Borders/All. Color them, or if changing other attributes, go to Modify, Cmd-M or Ctrl-M, then click the Grid tab.

LAYER PALETTE TRICKS

There's more to the Layers palette than meets the eye. There are "hidden" commands in the Context menu for Duplicate Layer, Hide Other Layers, Hide All Layers (why?), Lock All Layers, and more. And there are always shortcuts. Instead of moving an item to a new layer by clicking a button (top of palette) to open a dialog box, use that small dotted-line square that appears next to the layer name, when an item is selected. Drag it up or down to move the item to another layer. Using that same item icon, you can copy the item to a new layer by dragging it while pressing Control or Ctrl. If you want to rearrange the layer order, just drag the layer to a new position— no key needed in Quark 6.

TURN OFF THOSE LAYER MARKERS

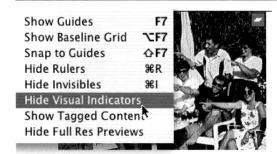

Show Guides	F7
Show Baseline Grid	⌥F7
Snap to Guides	⇧F7
Hide Rulers	⌘R
Hide Invisibles	⌘I
Hide Visual Indicators	
Show Tagged Content	
Hide Full Res Previews	

Quark calls them Visual Indicators— those colored boxes with white centers that appear in the upper-right corner of any item on a layer other than the Default layer. The color of the marker tells you which layer an item is on, corresponding to the color assigned to each layer in the palette. They're kind of big and clunky, but useful, especially if you're often moving between layers, hiding and showing layers to get to what you want. And, there's always a *but*…when you're going to be working on one layer for a while, you might find it less distracting to hide all those colored markers on your page. Easy to do. Just go to the View menu and choose Hide Visual Indicators. Turn them on again with another trip back to the menu.

SELECT ITEMS ON LAYER

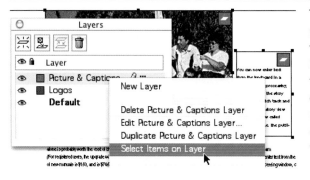

The Context menu gets more powerful in Quark with each new version. In Quark 6 there's a very handy command that's only on the Context menu—select Items on Layer. Access the Context menu by Control-clicking/Mac or right-clicking/Win on the layer whose items you want to select. Doesn't matter if another layer is highlighted or not. Selecting all items on a layer can be useful for changing attributes for all your layer items in one fell swoop— from Modify, there are attributes in the Group and Frame tabs, as well as Picture tab and Text tab. And there are a host of other commands in the Item menu that you can choose for multiple selected items. Using Select Items on Layer is also good to see what's on a given layer, without having to turn on the Visual Indicators (View menu).

THE LAYERED LOOK—VERSIONING

To create versions for different audiences and markets, use layers. Put all the base elements, art, text, rules, and such on the Default layer. Now, transfer the versioned content to a new layer. Open the Layers palette (Window menu). Click the New Layer button, top left, and double-click the layer name to rename it. Select the text and picture boxes that have custom content. A selected item is indicated by the dotted square on the right of the corresponding layer name. Drag the dotted square to the new layer, leaving a blank spot below, on the Default layer of the page. The custom content is now on the second layer. For each new version, Duplicate the second layer with the Context menu, Control-click/Mac or right-click/Win the layer name. Then replace the text and picture contents as necessary. Quark prints the visible layers only, so tell your service provider how to print each layer.

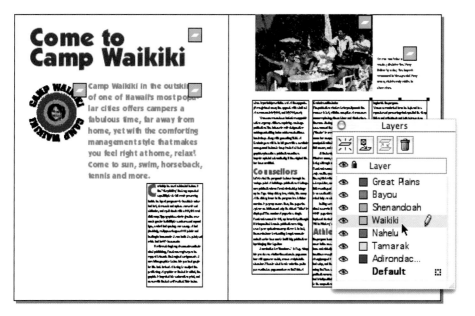

SPEED PERFORMANCE—HIDE PICTURES GLOBALLY

If you want to edit text, scroll faster, and print pages without those pictures dragging you down, put them on a hidden layer. Or, if you're doing a product catalog and want to have multiple versions specific to different markets and readers, put all the pictures of one version on a single layer. Those pictures no doubt have runarounds to keep the text wrapping around. And if those picture boxes were on the page and you deleted or moved them, the text would fill in those spots in a second. Right? So what happens when you use a layer for your pictures and then hide the layer, will your text totally recompose? (The mice will play while the cat's away?) No way! And that's because of the default layer attribute Keep Runaround—even when those boxes are hidden. But to turn it off, double-click the layer name to open Layer Attributes.

TEXT BOXES WITH VERSIONS

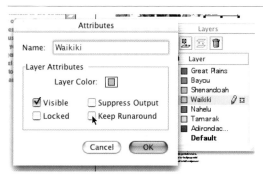

Product catalogs and foreign language versions typically have text variations in boxes *identically* positioned on the page, stacked on multiple layers. One problem—try editing that custom text on any layer but the top one. You turn off all the above layers—and that's easy to do by clicking the eyeball to the left of the layer name. But the text is gone! *What*? Yes, the default layer runaround is the culprit, *if your text boxes have a runaround.* A text box at the same page position, on any higher layer, causes your text to look invisible—even if you zoom in. You can remove the runarounds for those higher layers by double-clicking on each layer name and unchecking Keep Runaround. Better, when you make that second layer, your first custom version, turn the layer runaround off *before* you duplicate the layer.

   ## PRINTING LAYERS

In Quark 5 you couldn't control which layers to print from the Print dialog. You'd have to open Layer Attributes for each layer of the Layers palette to see if the Suppress Output option was checked. Now make those choices in the Print box instead. (And, in Quark 6, you can just look at the Layers palette and tell which layers are suppressed—the layer names are displayed in italic.) Back to the story. Go to the Layers tab of Print (Cmd-P or Ctrl-P), where all your layers are listed. Just check or uncheck each layer to turn it off or on for printing. And if you check Apply to Layout, then turn off a layer and print, Suppress Layout is now chosen for that layer in the Layers palette. If a layer is hidden, then printing and applying to layout means it's now showing and not suppressed.

Time for a Paint Job

KILLER COLOR

Color is one of the Crown Princes of Page Design. Color calls out to the reader in song, makes the page enticing and fun. It celebrates the message being

Time for a Paint Job
killer color tips

communicated. Of course, how you use color is the subject for another book! This chapter contains tips on almost all other aspects—how to set up different kinds of colors, such as spot colors, tints, multi-inks, spot colors converted to CMYK, rich blacks, and spot varnish. There's more. Applying color fast and easy by doing trial runs, using style sheets, as well as changing colors mid-stream, and avoiding applying the wrong "black." Have you played with Quark blends? Blends are one of the most fun capabilities in Quark for on the spot gradients. Finally, a few words on managing color in imported EPS graphics, spot colors in CMYK jobs, printing separations and CMS, Quark's color management system. By the time you're done, you'll whiz through setting up colors, applying and modifying them, blending them, and managing them. Not bad for a few pages!

FAST-TRACK TO COLORS DIALOG BOX

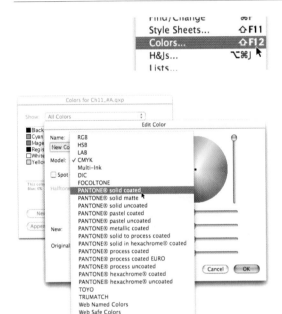

F12 is the magic key for color in Quark. It opens and closes the Colors palette (Window> Show Colors), and Shift-F12 opens the Colors dialog (Edit> Colors). First, if you're doing print work, delete colors you'll never use—Red, Green, and Blue are RGB. The most popular color libraries for selecting colors (Model popup menu) are Pantone spot colors (solid coated and uncoated) for 1- 2- or 3-color jobs, and Pantone process colors (coated and uncoated) for full color process printing, with photographs. A Pantone color is referred to by its PMS (Pantone Matching System) number, such as PMS 135 or 1355. (Don't change the color name, when you choose a color!) And don't choose a color based on how it looks on screen. Check it out in printed sample books you can buy from Pantone and other color manufacturers, such as Trumatch. Quick shortcut to get back to Colors—Cmd-click or Ctrl-click on the color name in the Colors palette.

TINTING A BOX BACKGROUND

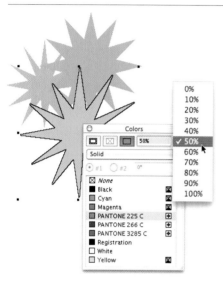

Tints are often used in spot color jobs that typically have just a few colors. You can get the illusion of more color by making and using tints or percentages of a color. In Quark, you can set them up in advance or make them on the fly, using the Colors palette (F12 to open). Choose the button at the top of the palette to specify where the color will be applied, then click in the color list to apply it. When it looks like too much color, however, cut it back by using the Tint % field at the top right of the Colors palette. Type in a number or choose from the popup. Note that a 10% tint may be too light to really see when output to high resolution. Your best bet, if you use lots of spot color, is to get the Pantone Tint Specifier to see tints in 10% increments for each PMS number.

See also "Don't Keep Choosing the Same Tint" (this chapter).

BE A DARE-DEVIL—MIX TWO SPOT COLORS

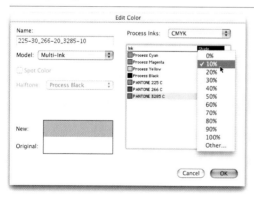

Combine tints of two (or more) spot or process colors to make some unusual color combos. Avoid making color decisions based on what looks good on-screen, however. Try to look at the individual colors in a printed selector book to get a rough idea. Press Shift-F12 to open Colors (Style menu), and set up your colors first. Click New, then Multi-Ink from the Model popup menu. Click on a color in the list, then choose a tint value in the Shade popup menu at the top or use Other to enter another number. You can mix more than two colors, but the combined color gets duller. Enter an appropriate name, such as "326-10%_977-30%." Each color in the mix outputs to a different separation. Be sure to talk this over with your printer so you set up appropriate screen angles and avoid printing errors.

DON'T KEEP CHOOSING THE SAME TINT

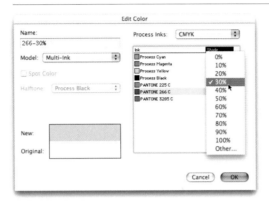

This tip is a variation on the previous one so please read that one first. When you repeatedly create different tints on the fly, it's not only tedious but there's a good chance you'll make mistakes. Why not set them up with the Multi-Ink option so they're ready to use in your Colors palette? Press Shift-F12, click New, and in the Edit Color dialog, choose Multi-Ink from the Model popup menu. Then simply choose your color in the list (from the ones you've already set up).

Choose a tint percent from the Shade popup at the top of the list. Select Other to enter a percent not listed. Before you click OK, type a good name, such as "PMS 360-35%" or just "360-35%." Repeat the process for each tint you want to use.

  BUDGET SAYS *NO* TO A SPOT COLOR IN YOUR CMYK JOB?

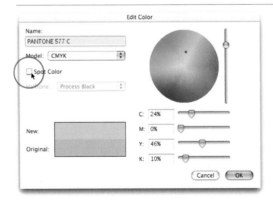

Ever have to include in a full color job some logo or other that demands a spot color? No doubt, it was the corporate color. This inexpensive work-around gets you pretty close to what you need and saves you an additional color on the printing. Go to Colors with Shift-F12 (Edit> Colors). Click New, then from the Model popup menu, select the spot color library you'd choose, if money were no object—Pantone or another standard color library. Pick your color from the list, then *uncheck* Spot Color, right below the Model menu. Last, move your mouse up to the Model popup and choose CMYK. You've got the closest possible color in CMYK to the original spot color after conversion, and the CMYK values are shown in the dialog. Finish up the job by renaming your color for its CMYK values—0C/44M/100Y/7K or drop the letters to make it 0/44/100/7. Fast and cheap!

"RICH BLACK" ADDS, WELL, RICHNESS

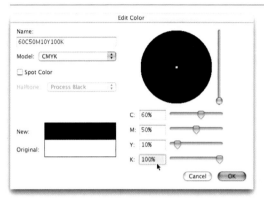

Rich black is an old printing industry trick for CMYK jobs that makes large areas of black color look royal. Flat black just isn't that great, looking thin or even cheap. But when you add in other colors, it comes to life. You're already paying for cyan, magenta, and yellow inks, throw tints of those colors into the mix for rich black. Be sure to talk to your printer. Typically, rich black can consist of 60C-50M-10Y-100K, *or* 40% for CMY with 100% black. Maybe you want a "cool" black, just add cyan to 100% black. For a "warm" black, add magenta. Create a color for black in Colors (Shift-F12), building a CMYK black based on your printer's recommendations. Name it with percents for each color: 40C40M40Y100K. Rich black solves trapping issues for overlapping or butting colors when it contains all four colors. Avoid small serif type reversing out of the black—too hard to register.

  ## SPOT VARNISH PERKS UP THOSE PICTURES—BIG TIME

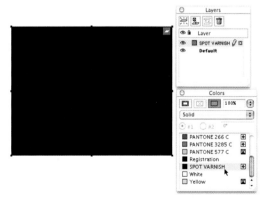

Spot varnish is a very classy printing effect that enhances images and headlines (it looks "wow" on a heavy-weight, coated paper stock). Gloss or matte varnish, applied to printed photos and graphics, makes those pictures pop. Go to Colors (Shift-F12) to make a spot varnish color. Duplicate Black, but name it Spot Varnish. Check the Spot Color option. Then choose Show Layers (Window menu) to put the spot varnish onto your pages. Click the top left button on the palette to make a new red layer. Double-click it to rename it Spot Varnish. Duplicate the picture using Step and Repeat (Cmd-Option-D or Ctrl-Alt-D) with offsets set to zero. Move the duplicate to the varnish layer by dragging up the dotted square icon on the right. Then delete the image, and apply the Spot Varnish color to the box background. Do this to all your pictures, then hide the Spot Varnish layer until the job goes to print. Discuss your varnish plans with your printer up front.

TRY ON A COLOR BEFORE YOU APPLY IT

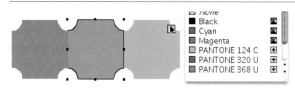

Drag and drop color is a fun way to see how color looks on a line, box background, or frame—but not text. Open the Colors palette (F12) and select something on the page. If you want to see how color looks on a box frame, make sure you give the box a frame weight first (Cmd-B or Ctrl-B). Start by dragging a color from the palette to a selected something on the page. Notice that as you drag your mouse over other things that aren't selected, they temporarily turn color! If you decide not to apply the color, just bring your cursor back to the Colors palette before you let go. Easier—let go of your dragged color over any blank area of the page to cancel drag and drop. Nothing's changed.

APPLY COLOR TO TYPE AND PARAGRAPH RULES AUTOMATICALLY

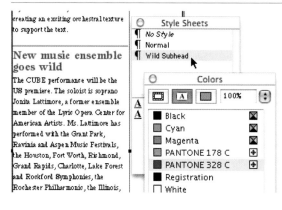

For multi-page layouts, you're working efficiently if you're applying color manually to text only when making initial design decisions. After that, set up your style sheets to automatically apply color to text using a paragraph or character style. Create a style by first making some sample text that's formatted the way you want your style to look. This way you can see whether your color and type choices look right on the page before you go further. When it looks good, click in the text. Press Shift-F11 (Edit> Style Sheets) and click New…Character or Paragraph. Enter a name, click OK, and Save. To apply a paragraph style to a headline or subhead, click in the paragraph, or, if a character style, highlight the text. Then click on the style name in the Styles palette (F11 to open). Now it's colored and styled with two clicks!

NEED TO CHANGE THAT COLOR YOU'VE GENEROUSLY APPLIED?

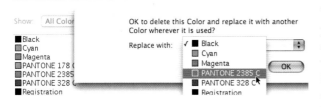

This problem can be agony if you don't know this tip. You've applied a color to a bunch of things—type, boxes and maybe lines. Now they tell you, gotta change the color! It's actually a breeze, and Quark's going to take care of the whole thing for you! After you set up the new color in Edit> Colors (Shift-F12), don't close the dialog. In the Colors list, select that color you were going to use, then click the Delete button. Up pops a dialog asking you to choose a replacement color for the one you're deleting. Select the new color in the popup menu provided, click OK, then click Save to close the Colors dialog. Now, all the places where the old color was used are replaced with the new color. Thank you Quark!

REGISTRATION COLOR IS NOT BLACK!

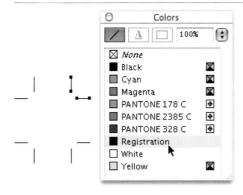

Using Registration color instead of black is an easy mistake to make, especially when you're on deadline. You need black, you see black, and you apply it. It happens more often when you've got lots of colors and only the lower half of your scrollable color palette is showing. You see the Registration color at the bottom, but not the black at the top. What's wrong with using Registration color? It sure looks black. *But*, it prints out to *all* color-separated films, and printing plates, instead of just the black film or plate—that thing will print in every color! Apply Registration color to things like hand-drawn crop marks for a 10-up-on-a-page business card. Those marks can be used to register printing plates because they're on every color plate. But when you want black, don't settle for anything else.

OPTICAL EFFECTS WITH BLENDS IN BOX BACKGROUNDS

Combine linear blends that go in opposite directions. Wicked. Draw any size text box (no more banding problems using Postscript level 3 output). From the Colors palette (F12), apply a box background color. Select Linear Blend from the popup menu that says Solid. Click #2 button, choose the second color. Light-dark color contrasts are dramatic. From the Measurements palette, copy the box W or H value, whichever is smaller. Then do Step and Repeat (Cmd-Option-D or Ctrl-Alt-D) and paste into the appropriate offset. If you copied H, then paste into the Vertical offset, and vice versa. The other offset is zero. Click OK and you've got a duplicate butting the original. Switch the blend colors of the duplicate fast using a 180° rotation in the Colors palette, where it now says 0°. Select both boxes, then again Step and Repeat and enter "*2" in the Offset field after the number previously pasted. Repeat Count: How many pairs do you want? Click OK. It's blazing!

See also "Type with Gradients" (Chapter 8).

PUT BLENDS INTO LINES

This amazing tip lets you put a gradient-blend into a line! Of course, if you want a gradient in a straight line, just draw a box and specify its line "width" in the W or H field of the Measurements palette (F9), then apply a blend. But how about all those other lines you can draw with the Bezier and Freehand Line tools (*see Chapter 4*)? Give some weight to that line width so you'll see the gradient—use the W field in the Measurements palette. With the line selected, go to Item> Shape> and select the Bezier shape. ↻ Now you have a box shaped the same as the line you just had. So naturally, you can apply a blend in the Colors palette by choosing a blend type from the popup at the top, then select your colors using color #1 and #2 buttons.

NO WORK-AROUNDS NEEDED FOR IMPORTED PMS COLORS

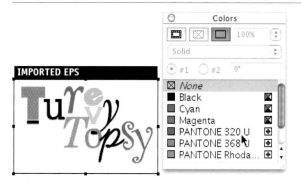

Why would a PMS color specified in an EPS graphic have a different name than the same PMS color specified in Quark? No good reason. But it's been that way since PMS colors first appeared in Quark. So then you needed a tip telling you how to synch up those colors so that the different names for the same color don't output to different films and plates. Well the miracle is, now you don't need a tip! Or, the tip is, starting with Quark 6, a PMS color specified in an imported graphic looks, acts, tastes, *and is* the same color in Quark. No duplication! In fact, even if you try to set up a spot color in Quark, after importing an EPS that uses that color, you can't. It says you have to choose another name because the default color name is taken. Good news.

SPOT-COLOR EPS GOING INTO CMYK QUARK JOB

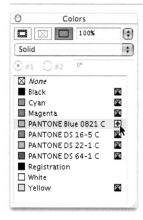

The EPS graphic you just imported into your full-color Quark job uses spot colors instead of process. Oops! Another reason why printing out separations from Quark can save you time and money down the line. If this color-mismatch goes unnoticed, your monster print bill will include charges for printing 5, 6, 7, or more colors! (In Illustrator, define your colors in CMYK, then, when you save as EPS, make sure you check the CMYK Postscript option in the EPS Format Options dialog.) In Quark, there's a real easy way you can keep track of your colors. When you import an EPS graphic, first open up your Colors palette (F12). After you choose Get Picture, if you see new colors added to the Colors list, they are spot colors. CMYK-defined colors are not added. Also, a spot color has a colorless square icon opposite the color name.

See also "Budget Says No to a Spot Color in Your CMYK Job?" (this chapter).

COLOR MANAGEMENT IN QUARK

Color management in Quark helps you control how printed color looks on-screen, how it outputs to high-resolution and to your color comp—that hardcopy you show your boss or client who says thumbs up or down to your design. Turn on Quark CMS (Color Management System) in Preferences and choose settings (that's Cmd-Option-Shift-Y or Ctrl-Alt-Shift-Y). But color management ain't perfect—first, it slows down your performance as you import images into Quark because QuarkCMS is translating the CMYK content of that image to an RGB display device, your monitor, to generate the display correctly. When you print, color management translates the color back from the RGB device to your CMYK printer. That conversion time is overhead. Second, Quark can't color manage EPS graphics. So while you can get better control printing the color you set up in Quark and the imported color in TIF images, there's nothing you can do about matching the printed colors used in EPS graphics and those same colors in Quark items and text.

PRINT SEPARATIONS TO CHECK COLOR BREAKS

Applying colors to shapes and type seems easy enough but that doesn't mean you never make mistakes. Little errors are easily overlooked. Ever apply red to type or a box instead of using a PMS or CMYK color? Did you happen to graze by that subhead that should have been PMS 710? Use different tint percents by mistake? A surefire way to catch all kinds of color mistakes is to print out separations to your desktop printer. Check Separations in the Layout panel of the Print box. Then see if all the items and text on each separation are supposed to be there. Tints of varying percentages output to the same separation but you can see differences in *printed* tints more easily than on screen. So give those seps a good look over, and you just might spot at least one to fix.

Detailing Makes the Difference

Sometimes it seems like nothing is more important than printing your layout. Remember the last time you lavished attention on a layout and didn't

Detailing Makes the Difference
printing & preflight tips

print for hours? Just when you thought you had every detail in place, you made your first proof and…Oh! So many wrong calls. Easy to do. The Quark environment is a visually noisy one—toolbox, palettes, margin and column guides, and more. No wonder your type and pictures are too big. That dingbat you thought was so "kewl" turns out to be "klunky." As we say in Chicago, print early and often—oops, that's another game! This chapter takes you through the bells and whistles of printing, exporting to PDF, making an EPS, trapping, and job assembly, including some dynamite preflight and packaging checklists. Be amazed, for instance, by what Quark doesn't include when it makes a package of your Quark layout, fonts, and linked pictures. Speed your printing time, not only through all those settings in the tabs of the Print dialog, but lowering your print time also. Thinking about trapping your file? Read on to learn the secrets of printing and file prep.

DON'T KEEP CHOOSING THOSE SAME PRINT BOX SETTINGS

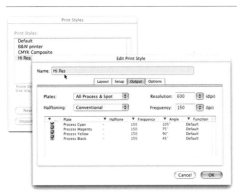

Quark remembers your choices in the Print dialog and saves them with the file. So who needs Capture Settings or Print Styles? Sometimes you choose print options on multiple panels (Cmd-P or Ctrl-P), then realize you're not ready to print. Click Capture Settings to remember those settings, while closing the dialog. Next time you're a step ahead. Print Styles, on the other hand, is perfect if you print to different printers or need different print settings at various times—such as when switching from a black-and-white to a color printer. Though Quark can remember one set of choices, you need Print Styles (Edit menu) to switch between sets. Click New, name your style, then choose your settings. Next time you're printing, grab your Print Style at the top of the Print dialog, enter your page numbers, and you're done!

  GOT A BIG PAGE TO PRINT?—TILING!

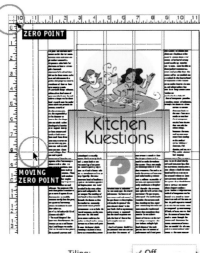

Tiling:

When your Quark page is bigger than the paper in your printer, use Tiling. In the Print dialog's Layout tab (Cmd-P or Ctrl-P), select Tiling> Manual to print using fewer sheets and overlaps. The current location of the zero point on the rulers marks the upper-left corner of the page area that's printed. For your first print, though, don't worry about the zero point, unless you've moved it. To reset, click in that small box at the intersection of the rulers. If your layout is tabloid and you're printing to a standard sheet for a range of pages, choose Landscape in the Setup tab to print the entire top half of each tabloid page. Before making the second print, move the zero point down. Drag from the intersection of the rulers in the upper-left corner of the layout window. With your mouse down, X on the Measurements palette is 0, Y is 51p (8.5"). Now print again for the bottom half of your pages.

TURNING ON REGISTRATION MARKS

Choosing Centered or Off Center for Registration (in the Print dialog's Layout tab) puts printing marks and document information on your printed page. Why bother? With registration on, Quark puts the date and time of printing, which helps you find the latest proofs and track your changes on any job. If you're printing from multiple files of a book or magazine, the filename on each proof keeps your mind clear. If you're printing a "comp" for your client and your layout page is smaller than your printing sheet, Quark places crop marks at the trim edges. And when checking separations on a black-and-white printer, the option prints the color name on each proof. Here's the catch—all marks are placed *outside* the trim edges. So, if your printing sheet matches your layout page, you've got to have a printer that handles tabloid or oversized pages—or reduce the output percent in the Setup tab.

WANT TO CHECK BLEEDS, SEE REGISTRATION MARKS?

The Fit in Print Area option in the Setup tab of the Print dialog (Cmd-P or Ctrl-P) is somewhat buried but eminently handy for checking bleeds (for extension beyond the trim edge, ⅛ inch) and to see registration marks. As for bleed pictures, type or colored items—anything that's on the page and extends off of it—is imaged to your desktop printer and to a high-resolution imagesetter. Most of the time you don't see the bleed because all desktop printers have that non-printing border and the page and sheet sizes are usually 8.5×11 inches (A4 is standard in Europe). Clicking Fit in Print Area is also a great way to get a quick look at an oversized page, without having to paste pages together—with *glue*—if you don't have an 11×17-inch or larger printer. You can also use the Reduce or Enlarge field to enter a specific percent.

DOING A COMP AND WANT SPREADS?

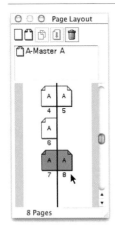

When you're printing a composite proof to show your boss or a client, it's a lot nicer to have two facing pages on one sheet of paper. It's easy to do *if* your printer can handle paper that big or you're willing to settle for reduced prints of your pages (see the Setup tab of the Print box). Click the Spreads option in the Layout tab of the Print dialog (Cmd-P or Ctrl-P), and enter your page numbers using a hyphen, as in "2-3." (If you type "2,3" you won't get spreads.) Printing spreads is a natural for a facing pages document. But you can also choose Spreads for a single-sided document if you've arranged side-by-side pages in the Page Layout palette. And even when you've got *three* or more pages across—facing or not, like a brochure with three 8.5×11-inch panels on a side—you can also print spreads, typing "2-4 in" Pages.

See also "Use Margins to Clarify Your Content" (Chapter 13).

BETTER RESULTS WITH BLACK-AND-WHITE PRINTERS

Print Colors: Grayscale	Resolution: 600 (dpi)
Halftoning: Conventional	Frequency: 120 (lpi)

Even if you have a color printer, chances are you use a black and white printer for most proofing. So it pays to get the most from your fast printer. Go to the Output tab of the Print dialog (Cmd-P or Ctrl-P). If you're initialized to a Postscript printer, you can change the Frequency setting, above the color list. By default the Frequency setting is set by your PPD (Postscript Printer Description), typically to 60 lines per inch (lpi). Frequency controls the fineness of the halftone screen used to print tints in colored items, type, and pictures. If you increase the lines per inch, you get more dots and a finer line screen when printing— especially good for light colors. Although you can go up to 400lpi, don't go there. With greater frequency, you get fewer gray values in tints and halftones. Best bet is to choose what's offered—the lpi values specific to your printer.

GOTTA CHANGE THOSE SPOT COLORS TO CMYK?

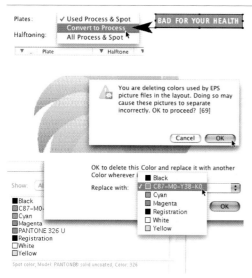

Your job was going to be real classy with full-color photos *and* spot colors for the logo and flat color areas. Then someone yells, "Hold the budget! No spots with that CMYK." Dare I mention that Quark has this printing feature, Convert to Process? Look for the Plates option, in the Output tab of the Print dialog (Cmd-P or Ctrl-P), but only when you click Separations in the Layout tab. But *buyer beware*—I only mention this to warn you *not* to use it! Output settings routinely get changed at your printer or service bureau, and so can this check mark. Instead, set up a new process color for each of your spot colors in Edit> Colors (Shift-F12). Then delete your original spot color, and Quark prompts you to choose a replacement color from the list. Every instance of that original color is now replaced by the new color. (Well, okay, not in imported EPS files!)

See also "Budget Says No to a Spot Color in Your CMYK Job?" (Chapter 11).

PREVENT TYPE RECOMPOSING AT HI-RES OUTPUT (*WIN ONLY*)

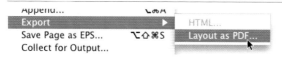

A long-standing Windows output problem—type on your page can recompose when the Quark file is printed from a *different* printer for high-resolution output. Happily, the solution has improved. The answer used to be saving the file as Postscript. But outputting Postscript, one huge text file, is unstoppable. Once the job is set in motion, there's nothing that can be done if a problem arises. The job runs until it's done. With long files, that can be costly. Instead, export your file to PDF (see the next tip). *But* also send along the original Quark file so that corrections can be made, if needed. And send along or fax a complete set of black-and-white laser prints so that they can compare their output to your proofs to make sure you're both on the "same page."

PDF IS THE WAY TO GO FOR HI-RES OUTPUT

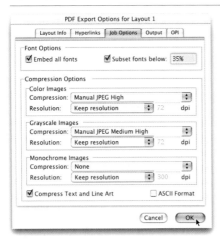

Saving your file to PDF got a lot easier in Quark 5, and now in Quark 6, you don't even need Adobe Acrobat Distiller because Quark has developed its own "Adobe-free" Postscript—but you do need a Postscript printer. Why bother with PDF? Any problems that would occur when the job is output at high-resolution happen instead when *you* make the PDF, which optimizes the Postscript. You control the show now, with lower costs in the end. Choose File> Export> Layout as PDF. Name your file, select the pages, if not all. Click the Options button in the lower right to open a second dialog with settings on five tabs. In Job Options, you can embed fonts or a subset, as well as set compression and resolution for color, grayscale and monochrome images. In Output, choose composite or separations, and CMYK or other color modes, with options for OPI, registration and bleed. Lots of control and it's almost a breeze!

MAKING A PDF FROM WINDOWS

Making a PDF has a few extra steps on Windows. The basic recipe is that you have to have a Postscript printer. Then you need to "print the file to disk." Go to your Control Panels, from the Start menu. In XP, double-click on Printers and Faxes, which opens another window. Right-click on the name of your Postscript printer, then in the Context menu, go down to Properties. In the Properties dialog, click the Ports tab. In the list of possible ports, at the bottom, is the FILE: Print to File check box. Check that box, then click OK. Go back to Quark, and choose File> Export> Layout as PDF. See the above tip for information about export options available from the Options button in the dialog. Don't forget to go back to the Ports dialog from Printer Properties and reselect your default printer port, likely LPT1!

SAVE PAGE AS EPS SAVES THE DAY

| Save Page as EPS | Bleed | OPI |

Page: 1   Format: Color
Scale: 100%   Space: CMYK
    Preview: TIFF
☐ Spread   Data: Binary
☑ Transparent Page   OPI: Include Images
Size: 66p x 102p

Ever need to scale a group of objects *together*? The ad you designed is now going in another paper at a smaller size. If you group the items first, you can scale them together by dragging a handle pressing Cmd-Option-Shift or Ctrl-Alt-Shift. *But*, group scaling isn't a perfect solution— box frame widths and line weights don't scale. Here's when to use Save Page as EPS (Cmd-Option-Shift-S or Ctrl-Alt-Shift-S). Enter a filename, and below, in a tab of the same name, specify which page, Scale %, Color Format, and the rest. Don't forget the options in the lower left for Spread and Transparent Page. The latter is what happens when you save an EPS in a drawing program and the white page becomes transparent. Now make a picture box and choose Get Picture (Cmd-E or Ctrl-E) to have all those items as one graphic that you can size—including widths and weights!

See also "Size Items Together" (Chapter 5).

WHAT'S WORTH TRAPPING IN QUARK, AND WHAT'S NOT

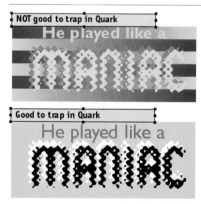

Trapping in Quark is like a can of worms, with a few good crumbs. Trapping is the solution to slivers of white space occurring between butting or overlapping colors when color registration on press isn't perfect (rarely is). By extending color, light over dark, to create a buffer zone, mis-registration is handled. Most designers let their printer or service provider make the traps. Bottom line: If you make trapping mistakes in your Quark file and the printed job is a botch, it's your problem (gulp). If your printer or service provider makes mistakes, it's *their* problem. Trapping is fine in Quark for a headline in a colored box or overlapping colored boxes. But when any item or picture has multiple colors at the edge, Quark's solution is too basic—one trap fits all. In high-end trapping, the trap changes pixel by pixel, to spread or choke depending on how the colors change.

  ### SPEED PRINTING—TURN OFF TRAPPING

If you have a color Postscript printer, this tip will reduce your printing time for every Quark job. The more pages printed, the more time saved. Whether or not the job needs trapping when it's finally output, the fact is, you're not printing separations until one of your last steps. And even then, you're probably just checking how your colors break, not trapping. By default, with Quark's Absolute Trapping Method, trap information is automatically passed to the printer, whether it's needed or not. So go ahead and turn off that processing time. Go to Preferences (Cmd-Option-Shift-Y or Ctrl-Alt-Shift-Y), click Trapping under Print Layout, and, for Trapping Method, click Knockout All. Watch your print times go down. Oh yes, want to do this for *all* new files? Close all your open Quark docs, and then go to Preferences.

   ### COLLECT FOR OUTPUT—LET QUARK PACKAGE IT FOR YOU

Collect for Output (File menu) is very handy for gathering *almost all* the files you need for hi-res output or offset printing. (What doesn't Quark include? See the next tip.) Quark assembles your layout, linked pictures and fonts, color profiles, and more. But first, make a folder to locate all the files in one place. In the dialog, at the bottom, Layout and Linked Pictures are already checked. Check Fonts also (Screen and Printer Fonts for Mac users). Click Save, then click OK to a warning about copying fonts. If you have missing pictures, click List Pictures in a second alert box to go to Picture Usage (Utilities> Usage). To skip a missing or modified picture, click Show to see it, then if you're sure, uncheck it in the Print column. If you have fonts missing, go to Font Usage to resolve the problem. Continue with a Save or two to process the collecting and generate a handy report. Everything's now in one folder!

See also "Generate a Complete Report About Your Layout Anytime" (this chapter).

"BATTERIES NOT INCLUDED"—PICTURE AND FONT USAGE

IMPORTED EPS WITH "LIVE" FONTS & PHOTO

Font Usage and Picture Usage (Option-F13 or Shift-F2/Win) keep track of the fonts you use and the pictures you import onto your pages—TIF, EPS, and the rest. And when you get ready to assemble that final package for output or offset printing, you'll need all those linked pictures with the Quark file and often some or all of the fonts. But there's *one hitch*. If any of your imported EPS pictures have editable text with fonts that are different from those in your Quark document or they have bitmap images embedded in them—well, Quark just doesn't see them (it's only a passing glance). So be sure to include those fonts and picture files in the package you send out the door—*or else*! (Tip within a tip—in your drawing program, convert your editable text into path outlines for the final version, then no fonts are needed.)

See also "Collect for Output—Let Quark Package it for You" (previous tip).

GENERATE A COMPLETE REPORT ABOUT YOUR LAYOUT *ANYTIME*

To get a ton of information about your Quark layout, go to File> Collect for Output. If you're preparing your package for final output, the report is generated automatically. But you can just click Report Only. The default filename is useful—your document name with "report" at the end. Click Save. Then use Get Text (check Include Stylesheets) to import the report on your page and see a clutter of information about your file—path name, last modified, file size, version number, number of pages, dimensions, fonts, style sheets, and much more. Even better, open Quark's Output Request Template (Quark's application folder> Templates> English> template file). Fill out the top part with contact and job handling information. Then use Get Text and import the report into the empty text box at the bottom of that page. *Again be sure Include Style Sheets is on* to see that same report fully formatted and a pleasure to read!

USE LAYERS TO COMMUNICATE WITH YOUR PRINTER

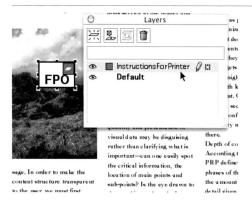

To communicate with your printer, some things are best handled right on your Quark layout, rather than in a separate Read Me file, such as those FPO labels (For Position Only) or any last minute details. Put the instructions on a layer (Window> Show Layers), clicking the top left button in the palette to make a new layer. Double-click the layer name to type a name like "Instructions for Printer," then click OK. With this layer name highlighted, the text boxes you draw now for your written instructions go on this layer. Until the file is ready to go, hide the layer by clicking in the palette on the eyeball. When you want to add another message or the file is ready for output, show the layer again by clicking that same spot—and then highlight the layer by clicking the layer name to add more items.

FASTER OUTPUT, LESS HASSLE (AND LESS MONEY?)

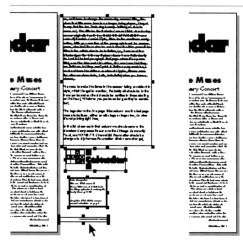

This tip is easy to do, makes your file size smaller, and ensures the file will output faster (which could mean fewer dollars). When the job is done (is it ever done until it's out the door?), do a Save As (Cmd-Option-S or Ctrl-Alt-S) to create a new file to send, giving it a different name. Try not to beg the question by naming it FINAL.qxp! Then, in that duplicate file, delete all the items on the pasteboard, that area around each page or spread where you might be storing logo's, boilerplate text, boxed text, and such. Those things can make your email attachments larger and longer to send, as well as eat up processing time on output. You might also want to delete all colors that aren't being used in Edit> Colors (Shift-F12). Now your file is cleaner, meaner, and a screamer, besides.

ON A MAC WITH A WINDOWS CLIENT? (*MAC ONLY*)

This is a fast one. When you hand off your finished project to a Windows client or boss, you've got to do something that's not required on a Mac—add an extension to the end of the filename. For any Quark 6 file, it's .qxp (which stands for Quark–XPress-Project). For earlier versions, it's the .qxd extension. Otherwise, the file will have a generic icon and Windows won't recognize it. Second, don't give clients your Mac fonts, unless they're Adobe OpenType fonts, which work on both platforms. They'll have to get their own.

   MASTER CHECKLIST #1—GET READY (FINAL FILE CLEANUP)

Use this form to help yourself through all the necessary steps to getting your job ready for high-resolution output at the service bureau, prepress house, or offset printer. As they say, so many things to think about, so little time.

Check the File(s)

- ❏ Searches—Find/Change (Cmd-F or Ctrl-F):
  - ❏ True fonts, not bold and italic style.[1]
  - ❏ Spell checking—One last time.[2]
  - ❏ Remove double spaces, double returns, stray characters.[3]
  - ❏ Change underlines to italic (fonts, not styles)[4] especially if you've gotten new copy since you last did these passes.
- ❏ Typographic proofing—do from *printed* proofs:
  - ❏ Look for bad line breaks, widows and orphans, justified text with too much space between words and letters.[5]
- ❏ Bleeds: Items extend off the page $^1\!/_8$ inch (.125")?[6]
- ❏ Marks that print outside the trim edges of the page, including *manually drawn* crop marks, fold lines, perforation lines, die-cut lines, registration marks:
  - ❏ Correctly drawn to dimensions of your job?
  - ❏ Registration color applied?[7]
- ❏ Pasteboard—remove everything, items fatten file size and eat up processing time.[8]
- ❏ Red "X" in text boxes—Overset text?
- ❏ Colors:
  - ❏ All valid colors, CMYK or spot color, as needed.[9]
  - ❏ No Registration color applied to layout items.[10]
  - ❏ No RGB colors: Red, Green, Blue.[11]
- ❏ Hairline rules:
  - ❏ Not Quark's Hairline but specified as .25pt.[12]
  - ❏ No accidental variations in line weight—.25, .5 and 1pt (all look the same at 100% view or less).[13]
- ❏ Picture Usage—Check for missing or modified pictures.[14]
- ❏ FPO: If submitting photographs for the printer to scan, does each for-position-only image on the page have an obvious label, "FPO," right on top of the image?[15]
- ❏ Print dialog (optional):
  - ❏ Registration: Centered—to turn on all registration marks (Layout tab).[16]
  - ❏ Reduce or Enlarge: 100% (Setup tab).
  - ❏ Separations checked.

1   See also "Use True Fonts, Not Bold and Italic Type Styles" (Chapter 8).
2   See also "Spell Checking from the Keyboard"(Chapter 7).
3   See also "Make Text Look like Typesetting Without Anyone Noticing," (Chapter 7).
4   See also "Replace Unsightly <u>Underlines</u> with Italic"(Chapter 7).
5   See also "Hyphens: Getting Too Many or Not Enough?" (Chapter 8).
    See also "On the Spot Fixes: Discretionary Hyphens" (Chapter 8).
    See also "Styles for Widow and Orphan Control" (Chapter 9).
6   See also "Want to Check Bleeds, See Registration Marks?" (this chapter).
7   See also "Turning on Registration Marks" (this chapter).
    See also "Crop Marks for Business Card Art" (Chapter 13).
8   See also "Faster Output, Less Hassle (and Less Money?)" (this chapter).
9   See also "Budget Says No to a Spot Color in Your CMYK job?" (Chapter 11).
    See also "Gotta Change Those Spot Colors to CMYK?" (this chapter).
10 See also "Registration Color Is Not Black!" (Chapter 11).
11 See also "Delete Bogus Colors for All Time" (Chapter 1).
12 See also "Five Ways to Change a Line 'Width' or Weight"(Chapter 4).
13 See also "Get Identically Styled Lines Every Time," (Chapter 4).
14 See also "'Batteries Not Included'—Picture and Font Usage" (this chapter).
15 See also "Use Layers to Communicate with Your Printer" (this chapter).
16 See also "Turning on Registration Marks" (this chapter).
    See also "Want to Check Bleeds, See Registration Marks?" (this chapter).

   ## MASTER CHECKLIST #2—GO (PACK IT ALL UP)

Delivery

❏ Include a job description sheet (see just below) whether emailed, faxed, or couriered.

❏ If sending the job via courier, such as FedEx, include a complete set of laser prints.

❏ If job is going to a printer, also include a complete mock-up of the piece. (Cut, folded, and trimmed, made from final proofs; and if possible, the PMS color chips for the colors used in job.)

❏ If emailing as attachment or FTP, BBS: Fax a complete set of laser prints.

Job Description That Goes with the Job (*and Also Helps You Assemble All the Pieces*)

❏ Quark supplies an excellent form Output Request Template.qxt in: QuarkXPress application folder> Templates folder> English folder.[1]

❏ Quark's Report that comes with the Collect for Output command—you can use this although it includes lots of nonrelevant info.[2]

I Prefer to Make My Own Job Description

❏ Job handling.

❏ Your name, company, address, contact info: Email, cell, day and night phone numbers, fax.

❏ Bill to info.

❏ Delivery info: pickup date/time and turnaround time to delivery.

❏ Due dates: color proofs, hi-res output and/or printed job.

❏ Items you're submitting (check list for you but also *include list* with job):

    ❏ Files:

        ❏ Mac/Windows.

        ❏ Type of files: Quark 5.0-6.0/PDF/Postscript.

        ❏ Filenames.

        ❏ Font names and manufacturers: for Mac OS 9—screen *and* printer fonts. (Check with your provider for which fonts you need to send.)

            ❏ Use Collect for Output to assemble Quark file with its fonts and pictures.[3]

            ❏ Imported EPS graphics: manually include all "live" fonts and embedded images used.[4]

        ❏ Picture files: EPS, TIF, etc.—list filenames and total number.

    ❏ Films: if sending films to printer, include lpi (lines per inch) that films were output at.

- ❏ Photos for scanning at hi-res:
    - ❏ Yes/No.
    - ❏ Number of photos/scans.
    - ❏ Color or black-and-white.
    - ❏ Scan at 100% or other percents (optional: record on laser proofs percent used for each picture on Quark page).
- ❏ Color proofs:
    - ❏ Yes/No.
    - ❏ Type: digital proof (Iris, Rainbow, Kodak Approval, Epson, etc.), Blueline, Matchprint, etc.
    - ❏ Type of service: overnight, same day, etc.
- ❏ Service bureau or prepress house:
    - ❏ Type of output:
        - ❏ CMYK jobs: you don't have to say, they are always output to film.
        - ❏ Spot color jobs: film or paper; paper (cheaper) is okay if no halftones (photos) or tinted items are used.
    - ❏ LPI (lines per inch, line screen) for outputting job: typically 133, 150lpi, check with your printer.
    - ❏ Emulsion side down (or up).
    - ❏ Type of service: overnight, same day, etc.
- ❏ Document description for service bureau or pre-press house, *add*:
    - ❏ Page numbers if not outputting all pages.
    - ❏ Trapping: indicate if traps need to be added.
- ❏ Document description for printer, *add*:
    - ❏ Description of the piece to be printed (flyer, brochure, annual report, etc.).
    - ❏ Page numbers if not outputting all pages.
    - ❏ Trapping: indicate if traps need to be added.
    - ❏ Quantity.
    - ❏ Colors: CMYK and/or spot colors (number and names).
    - ❏ Paper stock: cover and inside—name of stock, finish, color, weight, and manufacturer.
    - ❏ Printed dimensions of job (trim size).
    - ❏ Number of pages.
    - ❏ Finishing and Bindery: die-cuts, emboss, score, perforate, type of binding (saddle stitch, perfect, etc.).
    - ❏ Special instructions.

---

1 See also "Generate a Complete Report about Your Layout Anytime" (this chapter).
2 See also "'Batteries Not Included'—Picture and Font Usage" (this chapter).
3 See also "Collect for Output:—Let QUARK Package It for You" (this chapter).
4 See also "'Batteries Not Included'—Picture and Font Usage" (this chapter).

The Winner's Circle

MASTER DESIGN

Usually a software tip book like this doesn't have "design" tips, so why include them? Good question. The answer is that people who write books geared

The Winner's Circle

way cool design tips

to design are usually writing to a market of people who use different page layout programs. So they present each idea with lots of cool pictures, but then let you the reader try to figure out how to do that particular thing in the software you use. So here is a mixed breed, if you will. Here are some solid tips that are driven purely by design and production concerns. But they include the back end too— all the details you need for implementing these techniques in Quark. Here you've got tips for making brochures, newsletters, magazines, manuals, and long documents, as well as business cards. Of course, this chapter could easily have become a whole book (they wouldn't let me!), so of course these tips are just a smattering of some of the more useful and classic situations you encounter with a variety of projects. Use these tips to blast off into flights of creative design that are also production-worthy!

USE MARGINS TO CLARIFY YOUR CONTENT

Travels of a Costa Rican Technologist

COSTA RICA RAIN FORESTS

Raratonga Rocks

In your brochure, will Wigit A content be on a left page and Wigit B on the right? Or will each Wigit fill a complete spread? Use margins to visually clarify your intentions to the reader. If a product fills two facing pages, you can enhance that message by unifying the *spread*, making it look like one big space. Use small inside margins, such as 3p (.5"), and big outside margins, such as 7p6 (1.25").* But if there are two products or categories on a spread, then emphasize *that* message with the *individual page* as the module. Use the same set of unequal margins for each page, such as wide margins on the left, narrow on the right. How? Quark 6 has it! Start your document as single-sided (uncheck Facing Pages). Add your pages using the Page Layout palette or Page> Insert. Then choose Layout menu> Layout Properties, and check Facing Pages. Instantly, you have facing pages spreads with identical margins, left and right!

* When printing, click the Spreads option in Print> Layout tab to print both pages to one large sheet.

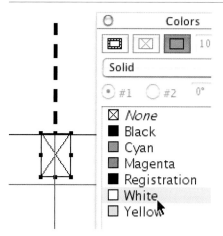

INDICATING FOLD LINES FOR THE PRINTER

For any folds within a Quark page, you need small lines to indicate folds to the printer. When folds are vertical, use vertical ruler guides to mark them. Later, draw right on the guide a vertical orthogonal line of .25pt line width and dotted line style, starting near the top of the page, extending off the page about 2p (.33"). About p9 ($\frac{1}{8}$") stays *on the page* so that the line gets imaged when output. But cover up the part that's on the page with a small white-filled box, the default fill color. The top of that box should be at the top page edge. Now group the line and the white patch (Cmd-G or Ctrl-G). In Step and Repeat, set the Offsets to 0 and Repeat Count 1, then click OK. Shift-drag the group across the page, snapping the line to the next vertical guide. Duplicate the last line-patch group at the top, using Cmd-D or Ctrl-D. Shift-drag it down to the bottom of the page so that the bottom edge of the patch is on the bottom page edge. Without ungrouping, use the Content tool and Shift-drag the line down so that it extends off the bottom edge about .33". Duplicate the group again to set the remaining bottom fold-lines.

P.S. If you have color or an image bleeding to a fold line, extend the box so it snaps to the vertical guide. *And*, be sure to discuss this with your printer as this is a challenging problem for them to fold on that edge *exactly*!

THE "THREE-FOLD" BROCHURE

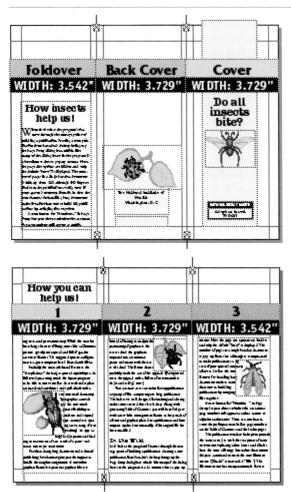

Hey, it's not a "three-fold," it's a "two-fold"—that #10 brochure that fits into a business envelope. Three *panels* on a side, *two* folds. Use a standard page with Landscape orientation, one column, 2p6 (.417") margins left and right. No Facing Pages or Auto Text Box. Using equal panels is the dumbed-down version. The foldover panel is narrower, so the panel won't go crunch when it's folded in. On page one, the cover is on the right, back panel in the middle and the *short* foldover panel is on the left. Equal panels would be 3.667" wide. Take $\frac{1}{8}$" from the short and add $\frac{1}{16}$ to each of the other panels. Draw a box for the short panel, set W to 3.542" on the Measurements palette and X to 0. Duplicate that selected box in Step and Repeat with Offsets set to 0, Repeat Count 1, click OK. Move that box over with X at 3.542" (copy W and paste into X). Then set Width to 3.729". Now duplicate that box for the cover (Cmd-D or Ctrl-D). Copy W and add it to X: 3.542 + 3.729". Press Return or Enter. Now three boxes are on your page marking the two folds. Drag out vertical ruler guides to mark those exact positions (zoom way in, if needed). Then drag out two more guides *for each fold* to set the gutters, each 1p6 (.25") from the fold guide, 3p (.5") apart. On page two, the short panel is on the *right!*

ROLL-FOLD BROCHURE—MORE THAN THREE PANELS PER SIDE

A brochure with four or more panels is dramatic and mysterious because it keeps unfolding and uncovering more—a bit like toilet paper! If you followed the previous tip, this one just takes it farther. But do the math first so you know the dimensions. Three panels take 11". Now add on to that the fourth panel which is $\frac{1}{16}$" less than the short panel: 3.542" – .0625" = 3.4795". For a fifth panel, deduct another $\frac{1}{16}$" from 3.4795", which is 3.417. With six panels, the smallest inside panel is 3.3545". Now to get the page width, add up 11" plus the widths of each additional panel beyond three. For four panels, the page width is 14.4795"—Quark calls it 14.479". For five, it's 17.8965" or 17.896". And six, 21.251". Give your offset printer this weird specification—it's okay, I've done it—but make sure their presses can handle it. Keep the same gutters of 3p (.5") between panels.

   ## ARTWORK SPANNING FRONT AND BACK COVERS

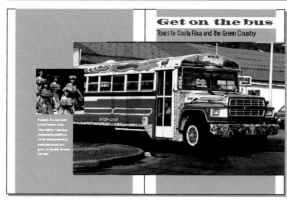

Get on the bus
Tours to Costa Rica and the Green Country

There are several ways to produce a spread of covers with shared art or type. Here's an easy solution. Put the cover and back cover spreads at the *end* of your Quark layout. Page one is your first *numbered* page, not your cover. For offset printing, your last numbered page is even, such as page 12, and, with the two cover spreads, that's a 16-page layout. In the Page Layout palette, page 12 has no right page, but below it are the two cover spreads as facing pages 13-14 and 15-16. In the Page Layout palette, page 6 has no right page, but below it are the two covers as facing pages 7 and 8. You can also make the covers an entirely separate file. Checking with your printer is always good, though. Don't worry about artwork, headlines, or pictures that go across the spread. Imposition software that turns your reader spreads into printer spreads is sophisticated enough today to handle it. Use the Spreads option (Print box, Layout tab) to print your covers to one large sheet.

GATE-FOLD BROCHURE

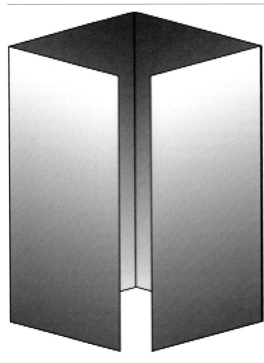

Gatefolds are like grand-opening performances. Capture attention on those two facing foldover panels, which open out to reveal center stage, four panels total. Page size is larger: 15.25"×8.5". The front and back covers are the inside panels, $3\frac{7}{8}$" wide. The two outside panels are $3\frac{3}{4}$". Use landscape orientation with left-right margins 2p3 (.375"), one column, two pages. Start with a big box from left to right trim edges. X is 0, W is 15.25" on the Measurements palette. Divide the width in half— 15.25/2. Press Return or Enter. W is now 7.625". Drag out a ruler guide to that location, watching the palette as you go. Set W to the short panel width 3.75". Put another guide there. Now drag the left center handle across and snap to the center guide. This is the inside panel width, 3.875". Change the box's X to 7.625", then put the third guide at 11.5". As in the above two tips, drag out two guides for each fold to mark the gutters.

The specs for this gatefold come from a wonderfully creative, longtime, now-defunct publication called ThePage, published in Chicago and mostly written by designer extraordinaire David Doty.

SHORT PANEL COVER OR REPLY-TEAR-OFF PANEL

Short-panel covers arouse interest—they look different. Take the one pictured as an example, starting with a portrait orientation file in Quark. To get the Height dimension, start with the *folded* size, say 5.5"×8.5" (based on a U.S. standard page). For the cover, subtract the amount you're lopping off from two times the folded height, here 1" from the 5.5"×2. Page height for this short-cover file is then 10". On page one, the short 4.5" cover panel is on the bottom, the 5.5" back cover panel at the top. Drag out a horizontal guide to 5.5", checking its location in the Measurements palette. For page two, the inside view, the short panel is at the top. If your finished piece will be vertical, use Landscape orientation, Width 10", Height 8.5". On page one, the short 4.5" cover panel is on the right and the wider 5.5" back cover is on the left. (Be sure to include fold lines, see "Indicating Fold Lines for the Printer," earlier in this chapter.) A short panel can also be used for a tear-off registration or coupon panel inside. For a 3" tear-off panel on the inside of a portrait 8.5×11" brochure (folded size), use 11.5" for the Width of your Quark file, 11" Height. Position the tear-off panel on the left for page one and, for page two, the inside view, on the right. Put a dotted line right on the fold and consider having your printer add a perforation there, extra charge. (Again, be sure to include fold lines.)

GREAT-LOOKING PAGES WITH LOTS OF COLUMNS

Sometimes people think that grids are limiting. Hogwash! Grids don't make the layout unless you just fill up every column with text. Much more is possible. Consider working with four, five, or six columns on a standard page. With more than four columns, the body copy is not confined to the single-column width, too small. Instead use text boxes the width of two columns. With a five-column grid, you'll have an extra column. Small pictures can go in that single column or extend into the body area, occupying two or more column widths. With this approach, you get a lot of contrast in size between small pictures in a single column and large pictures going the full width, and all the widths in-between. This kind of layout is more labor intensive, but you get lots of layout choices and a dynamic, exciting look.

THE FLUSH-BOTTOM LAYOUT

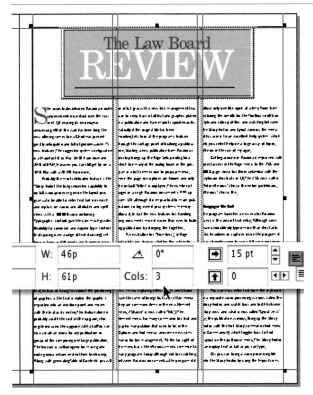

Middle managers, no offense, love this flush-bottom look, especially when the body is justified (across). I call it the "blocky" look but there are many standard formats that call for it, such as newspapers, magazines, books, and the like. Hey, you can't fight city hall! One of the easiest ways to get everything going down to the bottom of the page is to use the multi-column text box, a text box that's subdivided into columns. You can use the Auto Text Box when you start a new file, or you can draw your own boxes and subdivide them using the Measurements palette or the Modify dialog. With one big box on the page, your flush-bottom is assured. Newspapers use these types of boxes for each story, instead of having to keep multiple boxes of the story together. Then the spacing between stories, as well as the size of the pictures, can be used to achieve that trimmed-off bottom look.

GET CONSISTENT VERTICAL SPACING BETWEEN ITEMS

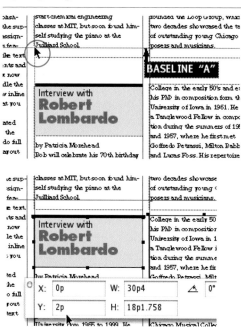

Getting consistent vertical spaces between items helps deliver your message without the distraction of varying white spaces. It's easy to do with typesetting, using paragraph spacing before and after, but how about when it comes to items? The space between a two-column headline and the two body-copy text boxes of that story is controlled by the runaround of the headline box. The top edges of the body-copy text boxes coincide with the top edge of the headline box. In the stacking order, the headline box is on top, so its runaround determines the space to the story below. Be sure the headline box is trimmed up to the bottom of the highlighted headline text and not a single pixel deeper. But what about the space between the baseline of the lowest line of that story (call it A) and, *below* that, the top of the uppercase letters of the headline farther down? First, re-set the zero point to A. From the upper-left corner of the document window, where the rulers intersect, drag out a floating X-Y axis and, in the same action, align the horizontal to A. Then select your headline box, and perhaps also the body copy boxes for that story. On the measurements palette, set Y to 2p (.33"), or whatever interval you want to use.

PULL-QUOTES ARE EYE CANDY

The corporations that lend the World Games throug direct contributions are i sustain an effort that highlights t accomplishments of young peopl world. These companies will in t association wit tic energy and to make a succ today's world . The World Ga rare opportuni worldwide aud ously through broadcast med of intense new advertisers and unusually long

❝ *Corporations that lend their support to the World Games are in a position to sustain an effort that highlights the positive accomplishments of young people throughout the world.* **❞**

to plan display ad placement and A survey of the 1986 World C servative estimates of increased v. participation in the 1990 Game!

With lots of dreary text and no pictures to break up the page, throw in a pull-quote. Feature an important statement taken directly from the text on that page or spread. Draw the reader in by enticing them with a stimulating thought, creatively styled and as graphic as possible. Use a very bold or decorative font that contrasts well with the body copy. The point size can be larger—perhaps 14 to 18 pts, maybe italic. Try exaggerated quote marks that stand out—hang them outside the text box so that the left-aligned text makes a nice vertical alignment. To do this, add a word space in front of the open quote mark, then kern back the space between the quotes and the word space until you can't see the quotes. But when you print, they're there. Kern with Cmd-Option-Shift-[or Ctrl-Alt-Shift-[. Add paragraph rules for extra emphasis (Cmd-Shift-N or Ctrl-Shift-N).

NEWSLETTERS LOOK GREAT WITH VERTICAL RULES

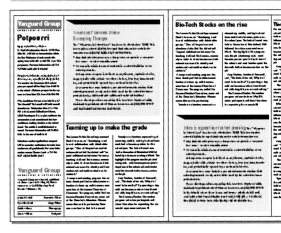

Vertical rules, or lines, can make an attractive and crisp look for a newsletter or journal. But…production with rules is more time-consuming and detail-oriented. You must be dedicated! First, your gutters should be 6 points wider, such as 1p6 (.25"). Draw rules with the Orthogonal Line tool and, on the Measurements palette, set their W to .25 pt, not "Hairline." Rules are exactly centered to the gutter width and are top and bottom aligned to the type, using ruler guides. At the top, align to the cap height or top of lowercase letters. At the bottom, align by the baseline of the longest line. But it gets worse. In a layout where you've got one story above another on the page, one rule per gutter won't work. Rules must start and stop, repeatedly and as needed, to make way for multi-column headlines that extend across the gutters.

JUMP LINES—AUTO-UPDATE CONTINUED ON AND FROM

there
.at was
nal use
ever he
ounded
iently
a more
ney had
ever, he
y soon!"

It was most unfortunate that it
leaked to the press," she said.

Security in sight?

"The reason for the delay was
unknown, but the spokesperson
for HomeLand Security said that
while they *hoped* that everything
would be locked down and in
secure order for the event, there

(continued on page <None>)

there
.at was
nal use
ever he
ounded
iently
a more
ney had
ever, he
y soon!"

It was most unfortunate that it
leaked to the press," she said.

Security in sight?

"The reason for the delay was
unknown, but the spokesperson
for HomeLand Security said that
while they *hoped* that everything
would be locked down and in

(continued on page 7)

Very few magazines run a story continuously. They throw a bunch of things at you up front and let you go chasing the details as the story jumps. Quark has a cool feature that *automatically* updates "continued on" and "continued from" page numbers, when a pagination change affects either the jump-from or jump-to page numbers. Create a small text box the width of the body copy and with no runaround. Type inside, "(continued on page" then type Cmd-4 or Ctrl-4, followed by a close parenthesis. Overlap the jump line slightly at the bottom of the body-copy text box. The jump line's baseline should fall at the next body-copy leading line, so first pull the body text box down a line, briefly, and mark it's baseline with a ruler guide. Then close it back up and line up the jump line to that line. If you've already linked to another page, the code you entered is replaced by the jump-to page number. Do a similar number at the top for the continued *from* page, with Cmd-2 or Ctrl-2. The text box must overlap the top of the body text.

DECKS FOR MAGAZINES—GIVE THE READER A PEEK

Decks are introductory copy that visually steps down in size from the headline to the body copy and gives the reader an inkling of what the story is about. In short, a kind of teaser. Get 'em interested. Typically the deck appears above the body copy, several point sizes larger and often in italic with generous leading. It can be in a contrasting font to the body and set to a wider width. It should look distinct but not steal the show from the headline. Consider it another design element on the page to work with for adding style and flair to the layout. And of course, you'll want to turn your first deck into a style sheet so that you have it for all the other stories. Then just click on the deck and click on the deck style name and it's handled.

BREAK UP A LARGE DOCUMENT INTO MULTIPLE FILES

There are two reasons to break up a document into multiple files. One—you and others are doing team production and, obviously, you can't all work on the same file. Two—it's a long document, say over 24 pages, with pictures, and your Quark file is more likely to crash and burn when it's large—not to mention performance slows down. Break up the file where there's some absolute page break, like the story ends. Chapter or section breaks are naturals. But, as text is edited, you don't want to be copying and pasting same-story text from one file to another! Save your file, then do a Save As and delete the second half.

Reopen the full version and resave after deleting the first half. Or be more systematic, set up a template that has all the master pages set up, style sheets, standing items, and defaults in place. Base your files on that.

See also "Quark's Template Versus the Real Thing" (Chapter 2).

IF YOU'RE DOING MULTIPLE FILES, YOU NEED THIS TIP

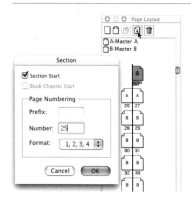

You've broken up your files, then ask, "How do you get the second file to start with the correct page number?" Sections! Go to page one or the page that starts your new section. Click the Section Start button at the top of the Page Layout palette (or Page> Section). If your first file is 24 pages, enter "25" here. Choose a numbering scheme in Format—iii, 3, III, C, or c—then click OK. Add a Prefix, a four-letter maximum section indicator that appears with auto-page numbering. Because you can restart your page numbering to one, *within* a document, you can use sections to combine the front and back matter—a preface, table of contents or index—with the body of your document by using i, ii, iii, then 1, 2, 3. Don't forget to add auto-page numbers on the master pages. Also, with multiple files for the same document, put the start page number in each filename to help you locate your content.

See also "Automatic Page Numbers Instantly Aligned" (Chapter 2).

GREAT LAYOUT FOR TEXT-HEAVY DOCS

This easy layout is based on a three-column grid, standard page, but only has a single one-column text box per page. Start a layout, using three columns and the Auto Text Box. Go to the master pages, select each Auto Text box, and set number of columns to 1 in the Measurements palette. In this layout, the body copy's left indent is equal to the width of the left column. Easiest way to figure that is to draw a box the width of the first column, but extend it right to cover the gutter. W on the Measurements palette equals the left indent for body copy. Major heads have no indent and start at the left margin. Secondary heads, like subheads, have the same indent as the body. Pictures can be a single column, on the left, or extend into the body the width of two or three columns, lots of choices. Use style sheets to make this layout a breeze.

See also "Controlling the Layout with Special Characters" (Chapter 10).

PARAGRAPH RULES—CLARIFYING WHAT'S IMPORTANT

Using rules to emphasize headers and subheads is a great way to go. Paragraph rules can be part of a style, move with the text as it's edited and retain a fixed position in relation to the paragraph. In the layout described in the previous tip, you can use two weights of paragraph rules to express the header and subhead levels. For both, the paragraph rule is set to Indents—go there with Cmd-Shift-N or Ctrl-Shift-N (Style> Rules). Choose a rule Width for the header that's heavy but doesn't drown your text. Try an offset in points equal to the point size (disregard the % symbol, but enter using the form: "18pt" or "p18"). For the subhead that falls in the body copy width, set its Length to Indents. Choose a much lighter contrasting weight so its lower hierarchical level is apparent.

ANCHORED HEADLINES STAY WITH BODY

This tip goes a step farther than the one two tips up—that layout with one big text box per page and an indented body. But those major headers that start at the left margin? Instead of letting them run on into the two right columns, wrap each in its own text box, the width of the single column, alongside the body. But when the body copy is edited, don't be chasing after those header boxes to realign them. Instead make anchored text boxes, so the header box travels with the body! The first paragraph of body copy after the header has a Hanging Indent style. Make the first line indent equal to the left indent and make it negative, –15p4 (–2.556"). Draw the header text box across the first column. Select it with the Item tool, and cut. With the Content tool, click before the first character on the first body copy line, then paste. Press Tab to push the first word of the body over to properly align. Then click on the anchored text box and, from the Measurements palette, far left, click the top button (Align by Ascent, not Baseline). When text is added or deleted above, the anchored text box travels with the body!

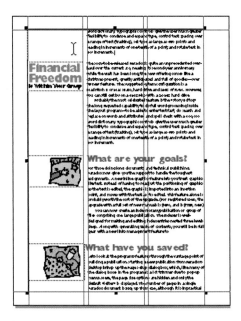

TABLE OF CONTENTS USING LISTS

Use lists to make a dynamic table of contents (TOC), based on your style sheets. Set up and apply styles for the heading levels you want to include, such as Headline and Subhead. In Edit> Lists, click New, name your list, then select the style names you want, clicking the right arrow. Set formatting options from the header popups. Use the Numbering popup to set the location of the page number, before or after the listing. Text Only is good for headings. OK, Save. Open the Lists palette, Option-F11 or Ctrl-F11. The Lists palette previews the paragraphs in your TOC. Use the palette to navigate your document by double-clicking on a paragraph to go there. To make a TOC, select an empty text box, then click Build in the palette. Style the TOC, then make TOC style sheets to match each level. Edit your list by applying these styles in the Format As popup so your TOC updates retain the current formatting. For changes, click Update in the palette, then Build again, after selecting the same or a new text box.

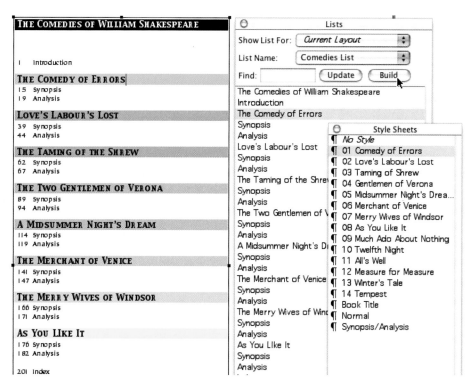

"10-UP" LAYOUT

Because business cards are quite small, art work is usually produced in multiples—though check with your printer first. Get the card completely designed, then duplicate it out to ten on a standard page. Select all the items for one card, including the 3.5" × 2" rectangular box that frames it but has no frame Width. Group them (Cmd-G or Ctrl-G), and go to Step and Repeat (Cmd-Option-D or Ctrl-Alt-D). Use Repeat Count 1 with Horizontal Offset set to 3.5", Vertical Offset set to 0. Click OK. Now you have two cards, butted side by side. Select the two, and return to Step and Repeat. Repeat Count is 4, Horizontal Offset is 0, Vertical Offset is 2". Click OK and now you have all ten cards butted together on one sheet so that when they cut the sheet into cards, there's only nine cuts per ten cards. If the card is vertical, rotate it 90° after grouping, then follow the above steps. *See next tip for crucial second step.*

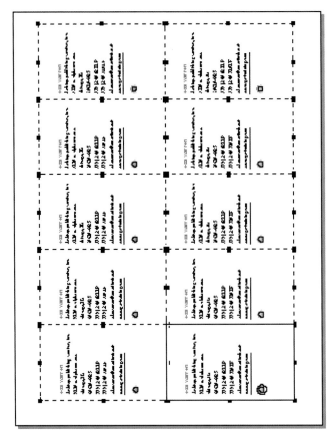

CROP MARKS FOR BUSINESS CARD ART

Add crop marks to your 10-up card layout (*see above tip*) to indicate the trim size of each card, so the sheet can be cut once the job is printed. About ⅛ inch to the outside of the top-left card, drag out a short horizontal line with the Orthogonal Line tool. In the Measurements palette, enter .25pt for W. If your job is two or more colors, apply Registration color to the line so it outputs to all color films. Select the top box, and copy its Y from the palette. Reselect the line and paste that number into Y. Make sure the Line Modes popup isn't set for Endpoints. Duplicate the line using Step and Repeat (Cmd-Option-D or Ctrl-Alt-D). Use Repeat Count 1 with both Offsets set to 0. Click OK. Now Shift-drag the line across the top right card, about ⅛ inch to the outside. (Mouse down, add Shift, then drag.) Now select the two lines, click, then Shift-click. In Step and Repeat, use Repeat Count 5, Horizontal Offset 0 and Vertical 2". Click OK. You also need three sets of vertical crop marks top and bottom to mark the center line and outside edges. Use the left box's X for positioning the first one. Offset is 3.5".

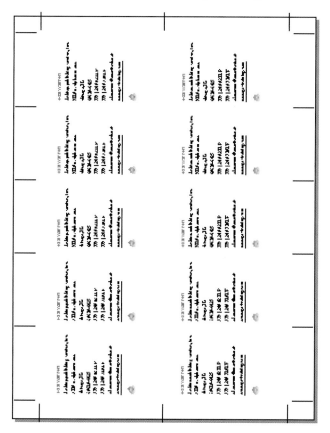

INDEX

SYMBOLS

10-up layout, business cards, 226

A

accessing
Item tool, 13, 39
tools
fly-out tools, 40
without toolbox, 40

adding
color
to tables, 175
to type and paragraph rules automatically, 186
master pages, 27
pages, 91
type to pictures, 79

adjusting type vertically with baseline shift, 117

alerts for picture changes, 86

aligning
by X and Y, 65
items from their centers, 164
numbers when some are in parentheses, 132
page numbers, master pages, 22
rules to other items (Orthogonal Line tool), 65
spread guides, 164
text
with Baseline Grid, 160
with subheads, 159

Alt key, 13

anchored headlines in long documents, 224

anchoring picture boxes in text, 169

angled type, 119

angles, resizing lines, 48

Application preferences, 4
Auto Backup, 6
Auto Save, 6
Live Scroll, 4

application settings, 2-7

applying
styles, 143
type styles, 113

arranging pages, 163-168

arrow keys, moving insertion point, 96

art, crop marks for business card art, 227

assembly, 200-207

Auto Backup, 6

Auto Save, 6

Auto Text Box, 20

automatic ligatures with Character Preferences, 125

automatic page numbers, master pages, 22

automating hyphenation with styles, 137

Auxiliary Dictionary, 98

avoiding
bad resolution, 79
long font lists, 110

B

background colors, picture boxes, 95

backgrounds, box backgrounds
blends, 188
tinting, 183

backing up
files, Auto Backup, 6
preferences file, 5

based-on styles, 145

Baseline Grid, aligning text, 160

baseline shift, adjusting type vertically, 117

Bezier Drawing tools, 54-57
drawing shortcuts, 54
editing shortcuts, 55
editing points, 56
flipping images, 55
heart-shaped or scalloped curves, drawing, 54
Merge commands, 57
moving shapes, 56

bitmap images, 78

bitmaps versus vectors, 78-79

black, rich black, 185

black-and-white printers, 196

bleeds, 163
checking, 195

blends, 181, 188
box backgrounds, 188
putting into lines, 188

box backgrounds
blends, 188
tinting, 183

boxes, 51-53
circles, 52
colored boxes, text insets, 168
colors, 52
drawing more than one, 51
identical boxes that perfectly fit a given space, 166
matching line lengths to box widths, 49
of text, linking, 90
picture boxes, anchoring text in, 169
placing text lower in the box, 166
reshaping, 53
shaped boxes, wrapping text, 123
shapes, 53
sizing with contents proportionally, 66

skewing pictures within, 83
squares, 52
transforming, 68

breaking up long documents into multiple files, 222

brochures, 210-215
fold lines, 211
gate-fold brochures, 214
margins, 210
reply-tear-off panels, 215
roll-fold brochures, 213
short panel covers, 215
three-fold brochures, 212

budgets, spot colors, 184

bullets, 105

buried items, selecting, 60

business cards, 226-227
10-up layout, 226
crop marks for art, 227

C

calculating with Measurements palette, 64

capitalization
drop caps, 120-121
small caps, 118

Capture Settings, 194

Center Picture command, 77

centering
page numbers, master
pages, 22
pictures, 77

centers, aligning items from, 164

changes to pictures, alerts for, 86

changing
colors, 187
columns, 21
to different pages, 37
margins, 21

master items, 25
master pages, 25
print layout settings, 21
stacking order, 61
styles, 144
with Find/Change, 104
weights of lines, 49

character attributes, 110-117

Character Preferences, automatic ligatures, 125

character styles, 142

characters
removing strange characters
from text, 102
special characters, searching
for, 106

charts, paragraph rules, 133

checking
bleeds, 195
what you did by deselecting
text, 93

checklists, preflight, 204-207

circles, 52

**cleaning up text. *See also*
searching**
removing strange
characters, 102
replacing underlines with
italic, 100
searching for double
spaces, 100
that was pasted into an
email, 101

clipping paths, 83-84

Cmd key, 13

**CMS (Color Management
System), 190**

CMYK, spot colors, 184
EPS graphics, 189

Collect for Output, 200

**color breaks, printing
separations, 191**

color conversion, 75

color management, 190

**Color Management System
(CMS), 190**

colors
adding to tables, 175
applying to type and paragraph
rules automatically, 186-187
background colors, picture
boxes, 95
black, rich black, 185
blends, 181, 188
putting into lines, 188
boxes, 52
changing colors you've already
applied, 187
Colors palette, 182
deleting, 9
dragging and dropping, 186
duotones, faux duotones,
81-82
managing, 189-191
mixing spot colors, 183
modifying, 186-187
Multi-Ink option, 184
Pantone, 182
PMS color, 189
printing separations to check
color breaks, 191
Registration color, 187
setup, 182-185
spot colors, 197
budgets, 184
EPS graphics, 189
mixing, 183
spot varnish, 185
testing, 186
tints, 183
trapping, 199
type, Text to Box, 121

Colors palette, 182

columns, 18
  changing, 21
  inserting into tables with existing formatting, 172
  in newsletters and magazines, 216

Combine, 57

combining text and pictures in tables, 173

combo shortcuts, 13

commands
  Center Picture, 77
  Fit Box To Picture, 77
  image editing commands, accessing (Mac only), 80
  Merge, 57
  Redo, 38, 102
  Select All, 93
  Undo, 38, 102

communicating with printers through layers, 202

comparing style sheets, 146

composite proofs, printing, 196

constraining moves without deselecting, 62

Content tool, 39
  deleting items, 70

context menu, 12

Continuous Apply, 135

controlling layout with special characters, 159

correcting mistakes, Undo, 102

crop marks for art, business cards, 227

cropping pictures, 76

Ctrl key, 13

curves, drawing heart-shaped or scalloped curves, 54

D

dashes, 127
  hyphens, 136
    automating with Styles, 137
    discretionary hyphens, 138
    exceptions to, 139
    No Hyphens, 135

Dashes & Stripes, 50-51

decks in magazines, 221

default line styles, setting, 50

Default Print Layout preferences, changing to picas, 9

default type specifications, editing, 110

defaults, global word spacing, 131

Delete Changes, 25

deleting, 70-71
  colors, 9
  guides, 43
  items, 71
    for faster output, 202
    with Content tool, 70
  locked items, 70
  spot colors, 197
  text, shortcuts for, 96

deselecting
  items, all items, 60
  text, 93

design tips
  for brochures
    fold lines, 211
    gate-fold brochures, 214
    margins, 210
    reply-tear-off panels, 215
    roll-fold brochures, 213
    short panel covers, 215
    three-fold brochures, 212
  for business cards
    10-up layout, 226
    crop marks for art, 227

for manuals and long documents
  anchored headlines, 224
  breaking up into multiple files, 222
  layout for text-heavy documents, 223
  paragraph rules, 223
  table of contents using lists, 225
for newsletters and magazines
  columns, 216
  decks, 221
  flush-bottom layout, 217
  jump lines, 220
  pull-quotes, 219
  vertical rules, 219
  vertical spacing, 218

Designer Frames, 51

dialog boxes, indenting, 134

discretionary hyphens, 138

Document preferences. *See* Print Layout preferences

documents
  anchored headlines, 224
  breaking up long documents into multiple files, 222
  layout for text-heavy documents, 223
  paragraph rules, 223
  table of contents using lists, 225

Doty, David, 214

double spaces, searching for, 100

Drag and Drop Text, 95

dragging and dropping
  color, 186
  pictures from your desktop (Windows only), 74

drawing
Bezier Drawing tools, shortcuts, 54
boxes, multiple boxes, 51
heart-shaped or scalloped curves, 54
straight lines, 48

drop caps, 120-121

duotones, faux duotones, 81-82

duplicate master pages, 26

duplicating items, 165

E

editing
default type specifications, 110
points, Bezier Drawing tools, 56
shortcuts, Bezier Drawing tools, 55
text
by dragging and dropping, 95
moving insertion point with arrow keys, 96
over pictures, 95
spell checking from the keyboard, 99

editorial style tags, searching for and replacing with style sheets, 103

Em dashes, 127

emails, cleaning up text that was pasted into emails, 101

En dashes, 127

Endcap styles, 50

Environment dialog, 7

EPS graphics, 189

Exclusive Or, 57

exporting files, 75

extensions
to filenames for Windows clients, 203
.s$v, 6

eye candy, pull-quotes, 219

F

faking right-aligned tabs, 134

faux duotones, 81-82

filenames, extensions for Windows clients, 203

file sizes of pictures, managing, 86

files
exporting, 75
preferences file, backing up, 5

file setup, 16-20

Find/Change. *See also* searching
bullets, creating, 105
changing styles, 104
correcting mistakes, 102
searching
for numbered lists, 107
for special characters, 106
text on master pages, 106

Fit Box To Picture, 77

Fit in Windows, 35
Greeking, 8

Fit Picture To Box, 76

fitting,
pictures to boxes, 76
text to layouts, 158

fixing
mistakes, Undo, 102
short lines with tracking, 115

flipping images with Bezier Drawing tools, 55

flush-bottom layout in newsletters and magazines, 217

fly-out tools, accessing, 40

fold lines for brochures, 211
gate-fold brochures, 214
roll-fold brochures, 213
three-fold brochures, 212

folioing, 222

Font Usage, 201

fonts. *See also* type
avoiding long lists of fonts, 110
default type specifications, editing, 110
Font Usage, 201
point size, 111
true fonts, 111
for styles, 145
type styles, applying, 113

foot marks, 97

formatting text
as it's importing, 147
as you type, 148
of entire tables, 172

FPO (For Position Only), 202

fractions, type, 125

full resolution preview, 85

fun-house mirrors, 80

Funk, Clint, 166

G

gate-fold brochures, 214

generating reports, 201

Get Picture dialog, 75

get text with styles, 147-148

global word spacing, 131

Grabber Hand, scrolling, 35

gradients, type, 122

graphic effects, 80-83

graphics. *See also* pictures
creating from boring pictures, 82
EPS graphics, 189
skewing within a box, 83

Greek Text Below option, 8

gridless tables, 174

grids, 18

grouping items, 62
  sizing, 63

groups, scaling, 199

grunge type, 123

Guide Manager, 45

guides, 41-45
  deleting, 43
  Guide Manager, 45
  hiding, 41
  limiting, 44
  master pages, 42
  positioning numerically, 43
  Snap-to-Guides, 42

gutters, 20

H

hanging indents, 133

hanging punctuation, 119

headlines
  anchored headlines in long
    documents, 224
  tracking, 149

heart-shaped curves,
drawing, 54

hidden commands, 61

hiding
  guides, 41
  pictures, 178

high-resolution output
  PDF, 198
  recomposing type, 197

highlighting text, 93-94

hyphens, 127, 135-139
  automating with Styles, 137
  discretionary hyphens, 138
  exceptions to, 139
  No Hyphens, 135

I

image editing commands,
accessing (Mac only), 80

image effects, 80-83

images. See also pictures

importing PDFs, 75

importing pictures, 74-75

importing text, 90-92

inch marks, 97

Include Style Sheets, 147

indenting
  with dialog boxes, 134
  paragraphs, 153
  styles, 149

indents
  hanging indents, 133
  specifying in points, 130

inserting rows and columns
with existing formatting into
tables, 172

insertion points, moving with
arrow keys, 96

insets, text insets, 168

italic, replacing underlines, 100

Item tool
  accessing, 13, 39
  getting pictures, 38

items
  aligning from their centers, 164
  deleting, 71
    with Content tool, 70
  deselecting all items, 60
  duplicating, 165
  grouping, 62
  locating from the bottom of the
    page, 66
  locked items, deleting, 70
  master items
    changing, 25
    locking, 24
  moving

in groups, 63
one point in any
  direction, 61
rotating, 69
selecting
  buried items, 60
  on layers, 176
sizing in groups, 63
ungrouping, 62

J

job assembly, 200-207

job descriptions, 206

jump lines in newsletters and
magazines, 220

K

Keep Changes, 25

Keep Project Settings, 162

kerning, 114
  Kerning Table Edit, 116
  manual kerning, removing, 116
  pair kerning editor, 116

Kerning Table Edit, 116

keyboard shortcuts
  Alt, 13
  Cmd, 13
  combo shortcuts, 13
  Ctrl, 13
  deleting text, 96
  Item tool, 13
  Option key, 13
  Shift, 13
  Zoom tool, 33
  zooming, 33

keyboards, spell checking
text, 99

L

launching Quark, 14
  XTensions, 15

layer markers, turning off, 176

Layer palette, 175

layers, 175-179
communicating with
printers, 202
printing, 179
selecting items, 176
versions, 177

layout
aligning
*items from their
centers, 164*
text with Baseline Grid, 160
Auto Text Box, 20
bleeds, 163
changing print layout
settings, 21
colored boxes, text insets, 168
columns, 18
controlling with special
characters, 159
different versions and page
sizes, 156
documents, text-heavy
documents, 223
duplicating items, 165
fitting text to, 158
flush-bottom layout, 217
gutters, 20
identical boxes that perfectly fit
a given space, 166
margins, 19
naming, 156
positioning pictures, 167
removing pages, 162
synchronizing text, 157
tables. *See* tables
text
move down the box, 166
vertically justifying, 161

layout and pagination, 156-163

**layout pages, moving to master
pages, 37**

**Layout Properties dialog
box, 21**

leading, 129

libraries, 29

**ligatures, automatic ligatures
with Character Preferences, 125**

limiting guides, 44

lines, 48-50
default line styles, setting, 50
Designer Frames, 51
Endcap styles, 50
matching lengths to box
widths, 49
putting blends into, 188
resizing at same angles, 48
straight lines, 48
weights, changing, 49

lines of text, selecting, 94

lining up tabs, 132

Link tool, 90

linking, 20
boxes of text, 90
text, 90-92

**lists, font lists (avoiding long
font lists), 110**

Live Scroll, 4, 36

**locating items from the bottom
of the page, 66**

Lock to Baseline Grid, 160

locked items, deleting, 70

locking master items, 24

M
....

Mac users
accessing image editing
commands, 80
automatic ligatures with
Character Preferences, 125
Zapf Dingbats, 97
Zoom tool shortcut, 33

magazines
columns, 216
decks, 221

flush-bottom layout, 217
jump lines, 220
pull-quotes, 219
vertical rules, 219
vertical spacing, 218

Maintain Geometry, 173

managing
color, 190
pictures, 85-87

manual kerning, removing, 116

manuals, 222-225
anchored headlines, 224
breaking up into multiple
files, 222
layout for text-heavy
documents, 223
paragraph rules, 223
table of contents using
lists, 225

margins, 19
for brochures, 210
changing, 21

master items, changing, 25

master pages, 20-27
adding pages, 27
changing, 25
changing master items, 25
duplicate master pages, 26
guides, 42
locking master items, 24
moving to layout pages, 37
multiple master pages, 26
naming, 26
page numbers, automatic page
numbers, 22
picture boxes, 24
running headers and
footers, 23
searching text, 106
text boxes, 23

**matching line lengths to box
widths, 49**

**measurements, positioning
guides numerically, 43**

Measurements palette, 64
    aligning by X and Y, 65
    calculating moving and
      sizing, 64
    line weights, changing, 49

menus
    context menu, 12
    Undo History, 38

Merge commands, 57

merging shapes, 57

minus leading, 123

mistakes, Undo command, 102

mixing spot colors, 183

Modify box, Text tab, 166

modifying. *See* changing

moving
    between layout pages and
      master pages, 37
    calculating with
      Measurements palette, 64
    insertion point with arrow
      keys, 96
    items, 61-63
    shapes, Bezier Drawing
      tools, 56

moving and stacking, 61-69

Multi-Ink option, 184

N

naming
    layouts, 156
    master pages, 26

negative images, pairing with
positive images, 81

newsletters, 216-221
    columns, 216
    flush-bottom layout, 217
    jump lines, 220
    pull-quotes, 219
    vertical rules, 219
    vertical spacing, 218

Next Style, 148

No Hyphens setting, 135

non-breaking spaces, 128

nudging items one point in any
direction, 61

numbered lists, searching
for, 107

numbers, aligning when some
are in parentheses, 132

O

objects, scaling groups, 199

on-the-fly color conversion, 75

on-the-fly full-resolution
preview, 85

opening
    Preferences dialog, 4
    Tools preferences, 10

Option key, 13

orphans, 151

Orthogonal Line tool, 48, 65

output, speeding up, 202

P

Page Layout palette, 25

page numbers
    adding to multiple
      documents, 222
    master pages, centering, 22

pages, 36-37
    adding, 91
    changing pages, 37
    layout pages, moving to
      master pages, 37
    master pages, moving to
      layout pages, 37
    moving between layout pages
      and master pages, 37
    rearranging in Thumbnails
      view, 161
    removing, 162
    seeing both pages in
      spreads, 36

pagination and layout, 156-163

pair kerning editor, 116

pairing positive and negative
images, 81

palettes
    Colors palette, 182
    Layer palette, 175
    Measurements, 64
    Measurements palette
      aligning by X and Y, 65
      calculating moving and
        sizing, 64
    Page Layout palette, 25

panel covers for brochures, 215

Pantone process colors, 182

Pantone spot colors, 182

paragraph attributes, 129-131

paragraph rules
    adding color, 186
    charts, 133
    in long documents, 223

paragraph spacing, 130

paragraphs
    indents, 153
    rules, 151
    selecting, 94
    spacing, 150
    subheads, 152

parentheses, aligning
numbers, 132

paths
    clipping paths, 83-84
    type, 122

PDFs
    creating in Windows, 198
    importing, 75
    printing, 198

performance, hiding
pictures, 178

picas, 9

Picture Box tool, 11

picture boxes
anchoring in text, 169
master pages, 24

Picture Usage, 201

pictures. *See also* **graphics**
alerts for changes to, 86
as fun-house mirrors, 80
centering, 77
clipping paths, 83-84
color conversion, 75
combining with text in
tables, 173
cropping, 76
dragging and dropping
from your desktop
(Windows only), 74
duotones, faux duotones,
81-82
editing text over, 95
file size, managing, 86
fitting to box, 76
flipping with Bezier Drawing
tools, 55
getting with Item tool, 38
hiding, 178
pairing positive and negative
images, 81
PDFs, importing, 75
positioning, 167
resolution, 78
avoiding bad resolution, 79
full-resolution preview, 85
scanning, 79
sizing, 77-78
incrementally, 67
skewing within a box, 83
turning into graphics, 82
type, 79, 169-171
updating, 87

placing
favorite settings in every
file, 10
text in tables, 171

PMS color, 189

point size, 9
of fonts, 111

points
editing with Bezier Drawing
tools, 56
paragraph spacing and
indents, 130

positioning
guides, numerically, 43
pictures, 167

**positive images, pairing with
negative images, 81**

Posterize button, 82

PPD Manager, 14

**PPDs (Postscript Printer
Description files), 14**

preferences
Application preferences. *See*
Application preferences
Default Print Layout prefer-
ences, changing to picas, 9
Print Layout preferences. *See*
Print Layout preferences
Tools preferences, 10-11

Preferences dialog, opening, 4

preferences file, backing up, 5

preflight, checklists, 204-207

preventing
copy from wandering when
linking text, 92
type from recomposing at
high-resolution output, 197

prices, type, 125

Print box, 7
shortening time in, 14

printing and exporting, 194-199

Print Layout preferences, 8
colors, deleting, 9
Greek Text Below option, 8
placing favorite settings in
every file, 10

print layout settings, 8-9
changing, 21

Print Styles, 194

printers
black-and-white printers, 196
communicating through
layers, 202

printing
black-and-white printers, 196
Capture Settings, 194
checking bleeds, 195
Collect for Output, 200
composite proofs, 196
fonts, 201
layers, 179
PDFs, 198
preventing type from
recomposing at high-
resolution output, 197
Print Styles, 194
registration marks, 195
Save Page as EPS, 199
separations to check color
breaks, 191
speeding up, 200
spot colors, 197
spreads, 196
Tiling, 194
trapping, 199-200

proofing text, 98

**pull-quotes in newsletters and
magazines, 219**

**punctuation, hanging
punctuation, 119**

Q

Quark, launching, 14
XTensions, 15

**Quark CMS (Color Management
System), 190**

Quark XTensions, 12-15

R

rag-bottom, 23

rearranging pages in Thumbnails view, 161

recomposing text
when opening older Quark documents, 163
when opening someone else's file, 162

Redo commands, 38, 102

Registration color, 187

registration marks, printing, 195

removing
kerning, manual kerning, 116
pages, 162
PPDs, 14
strange characters, 102
styles from style sheets, 148

replacing underlines with italic, 100

reply-tear-off panels for brochures, 215

Report Only, 201

reports, generating, 201

repurposing, 156

reshaping boxes, 53

resizing lines at same angles, 48

resolution, 78
avoiding bad resolution, 79
full-resolution preview, 85

reverse type, 117

roll-fold brochures, 213

rotating items, 69

rows, inserting into tables with existing formatting, 172

rules
Orthogonal Line tool, aligning to top of other items, 65

paragraph rules in long documents, 223
paragraphs, 151
vertical rules, 219

runarounds, 11
master pages, 24

running footers, 23

running headers, 23

S

Save Page as EPS, 199

saving Auto Save, 6

scaling groups, 199

scalloped curves, drawing, 54

scanning images, 79

scrollbars, Live Scroll, 4

scrolling, 35-36
Grabber Hand, 35
Live Scroll, 36

Scrolling slider, 4

searching, 102-107. *See also* cleaning up; Find/Change
for double spaces, 100
for editorial style tags and replacing with style sheets, 103
text, 99
for numbered lists, 107
for special characters, 106
on master pages, 106

see-through tables, 174

Select All command, 93

selecting, 60. *See also* deselecting
items
buried items, 60
on layers, 176
lines of text, 94
paragraphs, 94
text, 94
words, 94

separations, printing color breaks to check separations, 191

shadow text, 124

shaped boxes, wrapping text, 123

shapes, 53
merging, 57
moving with Bezier Drawing tools, 56

shaping boxes, 53

Shift, 13

Shift key, constraining items, 62

shortcuts
Alt, 13
Cmd, 13
combo shortcuts, 13
Ctrl, 13
deleting text, 96
drawing, Bezier Drawing tools, 54
editing, Bezier Drawing tools, 55
Item tool, 13
Option key, 13
Shift, 13
Zoom tool, 33
Zooming, 33

shortening time in Print box, 14

size of pictures, managing file size, 86

sizing
boxes with contents proportionally, 66
calculating with Measurements palette, 64
items in groups, 63
pictures, 76-78
incrementally, 67
type, 111-112
incrementally, 67

skewing pictures within a box, 83

small caps, 118

Smart Quotes Interactive preference, 97

Snap-to-Guides, 42

soft returns, 126

spaces, non-breaking spaces, 128

spacing
default global word spacing, 131
paragraphs, 130, 150
vertical spacing, 218

special characters
controlling layout, 159
searching for, 106

special returns, dashes, and word spaces, 126-128

Speed Scroll, 4

speeding up
output, 202
printing, trapping, 200

spell checking, Auxiliary Dictionary, 98

spot colors
budgets, 184
deleting, 197
EPS graphics, 189
mixing, 183
printing, 197

spot varnish, 185

spreads
guides, alignments, 164
printing, 196
seeing both pages, 36

squares, 52

stacking order, changing, 61

Step and Repeat, 62, 165

straight lines, 48

strange type effects, 124

style sheets, 142. *See also*

styles
basics, 142-146
character styles, 142
comparing, 146
formatting text as it's importing, 147
including, 147
Next Style, 148
removing styles, 148
replacing editorial style tags, 103

styles. *See also* style sheets
applying, 143
based-on styles, 145
changing, 144
with Find/Change, 104
headlines, tracking, 149
indenting, 149
orphans, 151
paragraph rules, 151-153
paragraphs
indenting, 153
spacing, 150
removing from style sheets, 148
subheads, 152
tabs, 150
true fonts, 145
type styles, applying, 113
widows, 151
workflow for, 145

subheads
aligning text, 159
paragraph rule style, 152

Subscript, 114

Super Step and Repeat, 165

Superior, 114

Superscript, 114

synchronizing text, 157

T

table of contents, using lists, 225

tables, 171-175
adding color, 175
combining text and pictures, 173
formatting text in an entire table, 172
gridless tables, 174
inserting rows and columns with existing formatting, 172
placing text in, 171
see-through tables, 174
tips for, 174

tabs, 131-135, 150
faking right-aligned tabs, 134
lining up, 132
setting, 131

templates, 28-29

testing colors, 186

text. *See also* type
aligning
with Baseline Grid, 160
with subheads, 159
anchoring picture boxes in, 169
cleaning up, 99-102
removing strange characters, 102
replacing underlines with italic, 100
searching for double spaces, 100
text that was pasted into an email, 101
combining with pictures in tables, 173
deleting shortcuts for, 96
deselecting, 93
double spaces, searching for, 100

editing, 94-99
   by dragging and dropping, 95
   moving insertion point with arrow keys, 96
   over pictures, 95
   spell checking from the keyboard, 99
fitting to layouts, 158
formatting
   as it's importing, 147
   as you type, 148
   entire tables, 172
highlighting, 93
inch and foot marks, typing, 97
insets, 168
justifying vertically, 161
linking, 90-92
   adding pages, 91
   preventing copy from wandering, 92
linking boxes, 90
placing in tables, 171
placing lower in a box, 166
proofing, 98
recomposing
   when opening older Quark documents, 163
   when opening someone else's file, 162
searching, 99
   for numbered lists, 107
   for special characters, 106
   on master pages, 106
selecting, 94
shadow text, 124
spell checking
   Auxiliary Dictionary, 98
   from the keyboard, 99
synchronizing, 157
turning into picture boxes shaped like letters, 171
unlinking, 92
wrapping
   all the way around, 168
   around irregular objects, 170
   in shaped boxes, 123
   Zapf Dingbats, 97

text boxes
   master pages, 23
   typing in angles, 119
   versions, 179
Text tab, Modify box, 166
Text to Box, 121
***ThePage*, 214**
three-fold brochures, 212
Thumbnails view, rearranging pages, 161
Tiling, 194
tinting box backgrounds, 183
tints, 183
toggling between views, 34
Tool preferences, 10-11
   opening, 10
   runarounds, 11
tools, 38-41
   accessing without toolbox, 40
   Bezier Drawing tools. *See Bezier Drawing tools*
   Content, 39
      deleting items, 70
   fly-out tools, accessing, 40
   Item, 13
      getting pictures, 38
   Item tool, accessing, 39
   keeping tools, 41
   Link, 90
   Orthogonal Line, 48, 65
   Picture Box tool, 11
   Zoom, 32
      keyboard shortcuts, 33
tracking, 114, 149
   to fix short lines, 115
   Tracking Edit, 115
   type for open spaces, 118

Tracking Edit, 115
transforming boxes, 68
trapping, 199-200
troubleshooting style sheets, 143
true fonts, 111
   styles, 145
turning text into picture boxes shaped like letters, 171
turning off layer markers, 176
turning on registration marks, 195
type. *See also* fonts; text
   adding to pictures, 79
   adjusting vertically with baseline shift, 117
   aligning numbers when some are in parentheses, 132
   changing angle of text, 119
   charts, paragraph rules, 133
   with colors, Text to Box, 121
   Continuous Apply, 135
   dashes, 127
      hyphens, 136
      No Hyphens, 135
   default global word spacing, 131
   drop caps, 120-121
   Em dashes, 127
   En dashes, 127
   fractions, 125
   gradients, 122
   grunge type, 123
   hanging punctuation, 119
   hyphens, 127, 136
      discretionary hyphens, 138
      exceptions to, 139
      No Hyphens, 135
   indents
      creating with dialog boxes, 134
      hanging indents, 133
      specifying in points, 130

kerning, 114
   air kerning editor, 116
   Kerning Table Edit, 116
leading, 129
non-breaking spaces, 128
paragraph spacing, 130
paths, 122
pictures, 169-171
preventing from recomposing
  at high-resolution output, 197
prices, 125
reverse type, 117
shadow text, 124
sizing, 111-112
   incrementally, 67
small caps, 118
soft returns, 126
spaces, 128
spacing, paragraph
  spacing, 130
strange type effects, 124
Subscript, 114
Superior, 114
Superscript, 114
tabs
   faking right-aligned
   tabs, 134
   lining up, 132
   setting, 131
tracking, 114
   for open spaces, 118
   Tracking Edit, 115
vertically overlapping type, 123
wrapping text inside shaped
  boxes, 123

type effects, 117-123

type masks image, 171

type rules, adding color, 186

type styles, applying, 113

**typesetting, automating,
149-151**

typing inch and foot marks, 97

U

**underlines, replacing with
italic, 100**

Undo commands, 38, 102

Undo History popup menu, 38

ungrouping items, 62

Union, 57

unlinking text, 91-92

updating pictures, 87

V

varnish, spot varnish, 185

vectors, 78

versions
  layers, 177
  text boxes, 179

**vertical rules in newsletters
and magazines, 219**

**vertical spacing in newsletters
and magazines, 218**

vertically justifying text, 161

**vertically adjusting type with
baseline shift, 117**

vertically overlapping type, 123

view percent field, zooming, 32

**view thresholds, limiting
guides, 44**

**views, toggling between 100%
and 200%, 34**

Visual Indicators, 176

visually sizing type, 112

W

weight of lines, changing, 49

white space, 19

widows, 151

widths of lines, changing, 49

Windows
  extensions to filenames, 203
  PDF, 198
  pictures, dragging and drop-
    ping from your desktop, 74

**word spacing, default global
word spacing, 131**

words, selecting, 94

workflow for styles, 145

working fast, 12-14

wrapping text
  all the way around, 168
  around irregular objects, 170
  inside shaped boxes, 123

X

X and Y, aligning by, 65

**XTensions, sets for different
clients and projects, 15**

XTensions Manager, 15, 75

Y-Z

Zallman, Toby, 145

Zapf Dingbats, 97

Zoom tool, 32
  keyboard shortcuts, 33

zooming, 32-35
  Fit in Window, 35
  keyboard shortcuts, 33
  view percent field, 32
  Zoom tool, 32

Photoshop® 7 with a Wacom® Tablet

Photoshop's behind-the-scenes photo editing power...

1. Dynamically change tool size

A Wacom pen tablet gives you the power to change the size of any of Photoshop's 20 pressure-sensitive tools with pen pressure. Press softly to get a thin stroke–press harder to get a thicker stroke. Here's the Clone Stamp set up to be pressure-sensitive for size–try out the other pressure-sensitive tools for fun! *(Visit our web site for a list of all 20 pressure-sensitive Photoshop tools.)*

2. Change tool opacity on the fly

Set the Paintbrush for Opacity, and you have Photoshop's most powerful tool for great layer masks! Paint lightly for a semi-transparent look, press harder for a clean knock-out. And when you're done with your Layer Mask, give the Art History brush a try–press lightly with your pen for transparent strokes, press harder for more opaque strokes.

3. Blend colors with your Paintbrush

Being able to change color during a brush stroke can give you some great effects. Set the Photoshop 7 Paintbrush to be color-sensitive in the Color Dynamics sub-palette, and try it out. We've set the Paintbrush to be color-sensitive for an "organic" look as we colorize the black & white photo below with two different shades of peach.

4. Try a little tilt

Select the Shape Dynamics sub-palette, and you can set the Angle to be affected by Pen Tilt. Modify a round brush to be an angular calligraphy brush, tilt the pen to the left or right, and you'll get beautiful calligraphic brushstrokes. *(By the way, almost all of the pressure-sensitive tools are tilt-sensitive too!)*

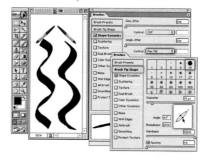

5. A finger on the Wacom Airbrush

Wacom's Airbrush Pen now offers you a new method of control in Photoshop 7–the Fingerwheel. Grab the Wacom Airbrush, select the Photoshop Paintbrush, and you can set size, opacity, scatter, color, and more to respond to the roll of the fingerwheel.

6. The comfort you need

The Intuos2 Grip Pen is built for comfort. It has a cushioned, contoured grip area and features Wacom's patented cordless, battery-free technology for a natural feel and superior performance.

7. Put it all together

Now imagine editing photographs with some of your favorite Photoshop techniques and the Wacom tablet. Control size and opacity with pressure to create accurate layer masks, burn and dodge quickly, and make subtle color corrections exactly where you want them.

National Association of
Photoshop Professionals

The only tool you need to master Adobe® Photoshop®

If you use Photoshop, you know that it's never been more important to stay up to date with your Photoshop skills as it is today. That's what the National Association of Photoshop Professionals (NAPP) is all about, as we're the world's leading resource for Photoshop training, education, and news. If you're into Photoshop, you're invited to join our worldwide community of Photoshop users from 106 different countries around the world who share their ideas, solutions, and cutting-edge techniques. Join NAPP today—it's the right tool for the job.

informIT

www.informit.com

YOUR GUIDE TO IT REFERENCE

New Riders has partnered with **InformIT.com** to bring technical information to your desktop. Drawing from New Riders authors and reviewers to provide additional information on topics of interest to you, **InformIT.com** provides free, in-depth information you won't find anywhere else.

Articles

Keep your edge with thousands of free articles, in-depth features, interviews, and IT reference recommendations— all written by experts you know and trust.

Online Books

Answers in an instant from **InformIT Online Books'** 600+ fully searchable online books.

POWERED BY

Catalog

Review online sample chapters, author biographies, and customer rankings, and choose exactly the right book from a selection of over 5,000 titles.

VISIT OUR WEB SITE

WWW.NEWRIDERS.COM

On our Web site you'll find information about our other books, authors, tables of contents, indexes, and book errata. You will also find information about book registration and how to purchase our books.

EMAIL US

Contact us at this address: **nrfeedback@newriders.com**

- If you have comments or questions about this book
- To report errors that you have found in this book
- If you have a book proposal to submit or are interested in writing for New Riders
- If you would like to have an author kit sent to you
- If you are an expert in a computer topic or technology and are interested in being a technical editor who reviews manuscripts for technical accuracy

- To find a distributor in your area, please contact our international department at this address: **nrmedia@newriders.com**

- For instructors from educational institutions who want to preview New Riders books for classroom use. Email should include your name, title, school, department, address, phone number, office days/hours, text in use, and enrollment, along with your request for desk/examination copies and/or additional information.
- For members of the media who are interested in reviewing copies of New Riders books. Send your name, mailing address, and email address, along with the name of the publication or Web site you work for.

BULK PURCHASES/CORPORATE SALES

The publisher offers discounts on this book when ordered in quantity for bulk purchases and special sales. For sales within the U.S., please contact: Corporate and Government Sales (800) 382-3419 or **corpsales@pearsontechgroup.com**. Outside of the U.S., please contact: International Sales (317) 428-3341 or **international@pearsontechgroup.com**.

WRITE TO US

New Riders Publishing
800 East 96th Street, Suite 200
Indianapolis, IN 46240

CALL US

Toll-free (800) 571-5840. Ask for New Riders.
If outside U.S. (317) 428-3000. Ask for New Riders.

FAX US

(317) 428-3280

New Riders

VOICES THAT MATTER

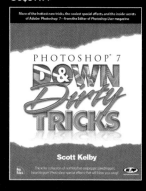
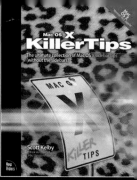
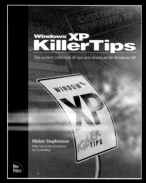

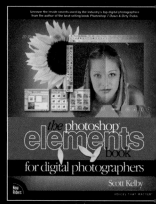